Crime in an Insecure World

CRIME IN AN INSECURE WORLD

Richard Ericson

polity

Copyright © Richard Ericson 2007

The right of Richard Ericson to be identified as Author of this Work
has been asserted in accordance with the UK Copyright, Designs and
Patents Act 1988.

First published in 2007 by Polity Press

Polity Press
65 Bridge Street
Cambridge CB2 1UR, UK

Polity Press
350 Main Street
Malden, MA 02148, USA

ISBN-10: 0-7456-3828-7
ISBN-13: 978-07456-3828-7
ISBN-10: 0-7456-3829-5 (pb)
ISBN-13: 978-07456-3829-4 (pb)

A catalogue record for this book is available from the British Library.

Typeset in 11 on 13pt Berling Roman
by Servis Filmsetting, Ltd, Manchester
Printed and bound in Malaysia by
Alden Press Ltd.

The publisher has used its best endeavors to ensure that the URLs for
external websites referred to in this book are correct and active at the
time of going to press. However, the publisher has no responsibility
for the websites and can make no guarantee that a site will remain
live or that the content is or will remain appropriate.

Every effort has been made to trace all copyright holders, but if any
have been inadvertently overlooked the publishers will be pleased to
include any necessary credits in any subsequent reprint or edition.

For further information on Polity, visit our website: www.polity.co.uk

Contents

Illustrations and Figures

Illustrations

Figures

Acknowledgments

This book emerged through a series of invited lectures, including the 2005 John Edwards Memorial Lecture co-sponsored by the Centre of Criminology, Woodsworth College, and Faculty of Law, University of Toronto; a keynote lecture to the 2005 British Criminology Conference held at the University of Leeds; the keynote lecture to the Toronto Regional Conference of Justices of the Ontario Court of Justice; and a lecture and workshop to the International Graduate Course, Crime and Security in the Post-Wall Era, Department of Criminology, University of Stockholm. I thank William Bateman, David Cole, Ian Cowan, Adam Crawford, Rita Donelan, Janne Flyghed, Magnus Hornqvist, Mariel O'Neill-Karch, Lorne Sossin, and David Wall for their respective parts in organizing these lectures, and all those present who asked challenging questions and made critical interventions.

Citations in this book testify to the influence of a large number of exceptional scholars, most of whom have also taught me through correspondence, meetings, and conversations. At risk of omitting some, for which I apologize in advance, I would like to thank Andrew Ashworth, Tom Baker, Zohreh Bayatrizi, Aaron Doyle, François Ewald, Liz Fisher, Ian Hacking, Kevin Haggerty, Joe Hermer, Bridget Hutter, Pat

O'Malley, Michael Power, Nikolas Rose, Violaine Roussel, Cecilia Wells, Reg Whitaker, and Lucia Zedner.

I am grateful to the following people and organizations for permission to reproduce the following figures:

- Illustration 1.1 The Leviathan – Tommy Castillo
- Illustration 1.2 The Leviathan Frontispiece – Frontispiece to 'Leviathan or the Matter, Forme and Power of a Common Wealth Ecclesiasticall and Civil', 1651, by Thomas Hobbe by English School (17th century)/Private Collection/ Bridgeman Art Library
- Figure 2:1 Citizen Guidance on the Homeland Security System – Federal Emergency Measures Administration and the American Red Cross
- Illustration 2.1 Advertisement: But Do You Have a Whistle? – Allison Phinney, Verified Identity Pass, Inc.
- Figure 5.1 Pyramid of Responsibility for Domestic Security – Federal Emergency Measures Administration and the American Red Cross

I am fortunate to have this book published by Polity. John Thompson, Emma Hutchinson, and all of their staff have been most professional and helpful in the publication process. Michael Welch and a second, anonymous, reader for Polity provided useful criticisms and sources which have improved the book.

Finally, and most importantly, I thank Matthew and Diana Ericson for their unfailing support. Their tolerance of my academic obsessions and itinerant nature is truly remarkable and can only be grounded in love.

1

Crime in an Insecure World

Introduction

This book investigates the alarming trend across Western countries of treating every imaginable source of harm as a crime. I argue that this urge to criminalize is rooted in neoliberal political cultures that are obsessed with uncertainty. We live in uncertain times, with issues of national security (threats of terrorism), social security (benefits system integrity), corporate security (liabilities for harm), and domestic security (crime and disorder) at the top of the political agenda. This politics of uncertainty leads to enormous expenditures on risk assessment and management that ironically reveal the limits of risk-based reasoning and intensify uncertainty. Catastrophic imaginations are fueled, precautionary logics become pervasive, and extreme security measures are invoked in frantic efforts to preempt imagined sources of harm.

The intensification of security measures occurs through legal transformations. New laws are enacted to criminalize not only those who actually cause harm, but also those merely suspected of being harmful, as well as authorities who are deemed responsible for security failures. There is not only an expansion and transformation of criminal law, but also new uses of civil and administrative law in processes of criminalization. Traditional principles, standards, and procedures of criminal law are eroded or eliminated altogether, and these other forms of law become more salient. These legal transformations within the politics of uncertainty reflect Ashworth's (2003: 55) view that "The main determinants of criminalization continue to be political opportunism and power, both linked to the prevailing political culture of the country. The contours of criminal law are not given but politically contingent. Seemingly objective criteria such as harm and offence tend to melt into the political ideologies of the time."

The intensification of security measures also occurs through innovative surveillance technologies and networks. Closed-circuit television (CCTV), smart cards, data matching, data mining, private policing, and environmental designs all facilitate criminalization of the merely suspicious and of security failures. This "surveillant assemblage" (Haggerty and Ericson 2000, 2006) is enabled through new laws that are part of the legal transformations noted above. At the same time, a great deal of its use in processes of criminalization occurs beyond the law.

The vast majority of crimes are defined and responded to through the internal mechanisms of institutions other than criminal justice. Each institution – for example, the family, community associations, schools, healthcare, welfare, business enterprise, and insurance – has a distinctive approach to criminalization based on its own private justice system and mobilization of the surveillant assemblage. Most crimes are not reported to the police or other legal authorities. Moreover, the majority of crimes officially recorded are not investigated, and most of those investigated remain unsolved, so that remedies are sought through the institution in which the crimes occurred. Even when culprits are identified, most are diverted back into other institutions to be dealt with more directly. These other institutions also have the primary role in crime prevention, which they effect through the surveillant assemblage. The use of the surveillant assemblage by other institutions must be analyzed, in conjunction with the legal institution and criminal justice system, in any effort to understand criminalization as a response to uncertainty.

In this chapter I initially describe key features of the politics of uncertainty. I then indicate how the contemporary politics of uncertainty and criminalization play out in four fields of security: national security with respect to terrorism (chapter 2), social security with respect to the integrity of disability and welfare benefits systems (chapter 3), corporate security with respect to liabilities for harm created by the activities of corporate entities (chapter 4), and domestic security with respect to crime and disorder in everyday life (chapter 5). These analyses reveal ironies of security within the politics of uncertainty. These ironies are used in the concluding chapter (chapter 6) to highlight the insecurity that characterizes Western societies in the 21st century.

Politics, Risk and Uncertainty

Charles Taylor (2004) has recently analyzed modern, Western, liberal "social imaginaries." Social imaginaries are shared understandings among a people about their existence, relations with one another, expectations, and normative commitments. Social imaginaries provide a capacity to act and a sense of legitimacy of actions taken. Just as social imaginaries make actions possible, so actions carry social imaginaries and reproduce them.

The starting point for liberal social imaginaries is individuals served by political society through "an ethic of freedom and mutual benefit" (ibid.: 21). This ethic focuses on life and the means to support it. From Hobbes to Rawls, *the* organizing principle of liberalism is life as an original position from which the moral, legal, political, and economic frameworks of society are envisaged (Seery 1996; Bayatrizi 2005).

The most important benefit is security, defined as anything that provides or assures freedom from harm to life and its potential. Security enables freedom in the form of uncensored action taken by a rationally calculating individual seeking a prosperous future. Security as both safety and a capacity for taking action to secure a better future requires law, especially law in defense of individual rights and equality. In liberal social imaginaries:

> Our primary service to each other . . . [is] the provision of collective security, to render our lives and property safe under law. But we also serve each other in practicing economic exchange. These two main ends, security and prosperity, are now the principal goals of organized society, which itself can come to be seen as something in the nature of a profitable exchange among its constituent members. The ideal social order is one in which our purposes mesh, and each in furthering himself helps others. (Taylor 2004: 13–14)

Liberal social imaginaries promise that governmental mechanisms of security will enable freedom in the form of the smooth flow of market relations, entrepreneurial risk-taking, creative enterprise, self-governance, prosperity, and well-being. But this is very much an *imaginary* because security and freedom are more within us as a yearning than outside us as facts. Mechanisms of security and freedom are imaginary because they require knowledge of the future in order to govern the future. But the future is in many ways unknowable, and uncertainty is "the basic condition of human knowledge" (Douglas 1985: 42). This creates a paradox for liberal politics: how to provide security and freedom through knowledge of the future in the face of uncertainty as the basic condition of human knowledge.

In struggling to configure the future consequences of their actions, individuals require knowledge of risk and engage in risk assessment. Risk assessment is rarely based on perfect knowledge, and typically frays into uncertainty. Uncertainty can lead individuals to hunker down, engage in risk avoidance, and limit the freedom of others in the name of security. Paradoxically, uncertainty is also a source of freedom. It creates room for the imaginative production of better and more useful knowledge of risk, and ultimately for more rational and responsible decisions. Uncertainty is also a source of creative enterprise, a feature that is dear to the liberal emphasis on wealth creation and attendant promotion of market uncertainty as a kind of freedom. Thus liberalism imagines the indeterminate future through uncertainty as well as knowledge of risk. There is perpetual tension between the modernist desire for greater certainty through scientific knowledge of risk and the entrepreneurial desire for uncertainty as an engine of enterprise. A connected paradox, articulated most brilliantly by Isaiah Berlin (1969), is that liberalism must curtail freedom through security measures in order to promote conditions in which freedom can flourish. Liberal social imaginaries not only juggle risk and uncertainty for freedom, but also freedom and restriction for security.

As Pat O'Malley (2004) demonstrates, the imaginaries of classical liberalism, social liberalism, and neo-liberalism each give different emphases to risk and uncertainty. The contemporary neo-liberal emphasis on uncertainty, especially on the uncertain world of market-based competition, is much stronger than under classical liberalism. In the era of classical liberalism only members of the business elite were given license to be free-wheeling entrepreneurs who profited from uncertainty, but now everyone is to seek freedom through "the enterprising self" (Rose 1999). Even liberalism itself is "enterprised," that is, used to constitute a world in which every activity is seen as risk-taking in an environment of competitive uncertainty. In the extreme, writers such as Peter Bernstein (1998) popularize the view that people thrive on chaos, and the only threat derives from those who see uncertainty as a threat rather than as an opportunity for pleasure and profit. Similarly, neo-liberal political gurus such as Anthony Giddens (1998, 1999) proclaim that the greater the uncertainty, the greater the opportunity for innovation and profit.

This neo-liberal imaginary is juxtaposed to social liberalism, which is said to emphasize too much security. Neo-liberalism seeks to transform risk from being a technique of social security provision to a responsibility to be assumed by individuals and other self-governing entities. In this transformation, the state is to serve first and foremost as a facilitator and enabler of entrepreneurial risk-taking. At the level of the individual, the emphasis is no longer on the classical liberal imaginary of prudence and self-discipline, nor on the social liberal imaginary of a "national minimum" of security provision, but rather self-fulfillment through enterprise and consumption. Self-esteem through designing a personal "lifestyle" is promoted, and with it new duties, including a duty to be well – a fit and able liberal subject – and a duty to choose among a bewildering array of consumption alternatives. At the same time there is an emphasis upon *responsible* risk-taking, which requires individuals to choose among products that will yield personal security and prosperity. In this respect at least, there is a new prudentialism as well as new adventurism in the neo-liberal imaginary. However, this new prudentialism is seen as conducive to enterprise, and in sharp contrast to the docile bodies envisaged by the prudence and discipline of classical liberalism, or the national standards of well-being envisaged by the risk-spreading practices of social liberalism.

Science, Risk, and Uncertainty

Douglas and Wildavsky (1983: 1) ask, "Can we know the risks we face, now or in the future?" and they answer, "No, we cannot: but yes, we must act as if we do." One way in which we act as if the future is knowable and governable is through scientific assessments of risk. While probabilistic reasoning and scientific assessments of risk have long been an integral component of liberal social imaginaries and practices (Hacking 1990), the recent salience of risk is unprecedented. The word 'risk' hardly appeared at all in political or even scientific vocabularies 30 years ago, but it has become *the* word of the 21st century (Garland 2003). Risk is "the single point upon which contemporary societies question themselves, analyse themselves, seek their values and perhaps recognize their limits" (Ewald 2000: 366). Risk is the term through which we imagine and act as if we know the future and can do something about it.

It is no coincidence that the rise of risk discourse and practice has been coterminous with the rise of neo-liberal social imaginaries. People need, above all, knowledge and technologies of risk in order to function as neo-liberal subjects. This need is paramount in a regime that stresses uncertainty, a stress that can only be coped with through knowledge of risk and its promise of competitive advantage in risk-taking, prosperity, security, and freedom. Thus we witness an explosion of scientific knowledge of risk, diffused through the mass media, Internet, educational establishments, clinical settings, and expert services. There is also a rapid expansion of databases on populations to manage security, not only in government contexts of health, education, welfare, and policing, but also in private industry contexts such as the insurance industry, other financial institutions, and consumer profiling for market segmentation and credit ratings (Haggerty and Ericson 2006). Furthermore, there is a proliferation of risk-based technologies – ranging from pharmaceutical products to electronic surveillance devices – marketed to neo-liberal subjects as consumers of approaches to personal security and prosperity. Neo-liberal subjects imagine, think, and act under scientific descriptions of risk.

The sciences of risk involve three interconnected languages for governing the future: a language of probability, a language of management, and a forensic language. *Risk as a scientific language of probability* involves a calculus of the frequency of harmful occurrence and the severity of harm caused. This calculus is applied to cost–benefit analyses of two types. First, whether an action should be undertaken in spite of the chance of harm of an estimated magnitude. Second, whether there should be investment in new security measures that might reduce harm and create more certainty.

Risk as a scientific language of probability is also a language of uncertainty. Scientists themselves express uncertainty in their methodological, epistemological, and ontological debates over how to assess harm. When statements of probability are produced, they are of course only statements of chances and thus degrees of certainty and uncertainty, knowledge and ignorance. As Adams (2003: 90) observes, "Risk is a close relation to uncertainty. Where we cannot be certain about the relation between cause and effect we clutch at the straw of probability . . . Estimates of the probability of particular harms are quantified expressions of ignorance." When knowledge of risk is applied in open-ended natural and human systems, indeterminacy is the rule and uncertainty magnifies.

There are also virtual risks: risks that are easy to imagine but impossible to perceive, even with scientific expertise and technology, at least until catastrophe strikes (Adams 1995, 2003). The story of asbestos is an interesting case in point. Asbestos was introduced in building construction as a fire-resistant technology that would greatly reduce risks to property and persons. It was celebrated by the scientists who created it, innovative building engineers, and grateful customers. It was also promoted by insurance risk experts, who are always eager to introduce new technologies of loss reduction. But asbestosis, for a long time a virtual risk, was eventually observed, and it became a health risk that trumped fire risk. At the last count, in the United States alone, the insurance industry was $65 billion out of pocket in claims for a liability it did not even know existed at the time of underwriting. Dozens of commercial enterprises also went out of business because they could not bear their share of the liabilities (Ericson and Doyle 2004a).

There are many similar examples in the scientific and technological chronicles of risk and uncertainty. We have reached the point where the methodological, epistemological, and ontological uncertainties debated in the process of doing science are now also debated in political culture. As Ewald (2002) observes, in many contemporary controversies about how to govern the future, the language of scientific risk has given way to the language of scientific uncertainty. "The new paradigm of security calls forth a new economy of rights and duties. While the language of risk, against a background of scientific expertise, used to be sufficient to describe all types of insecurity, the new paradigm sees uncertainty reappear in the light of even newer science. It bears witness to a deeply disturbed relationship with a science that is consulted less for the knowledge it offers than the doubt it insinuates" (ibid. 274).

In this context of scientific uncertainty, there is recognition that decisions about potential harms and security provision must be based on non-scientific forms of knowledge that are intuitive, emotional, aesthetic, moral, and speculative. There is also appreciation that these forms of knowledge are embedded in scientific risk assessment itself. As Douglas (1990: 10) points out, "risk is not only the probability of an event but also the probable magnitude of its outcome, and everything depends on the value that is set on the outcome. The evaluation is a political, aesthetic and moral matter." Similarly, cost–benefit analyses regarding risk-taking and risk management are based on values over which there are sharp moral and political differences (Sunstein 2002, 2005). It is highly doubtful that people simply calculate risks and then choose among alternative risk–return possibilities. Rather, decisions are made on the basis of values, intuition, emotion, aesthetics, morals, speculation, context, timelines, accessible information, reputation of information sources, attention capacity, and so on. In other words, cost–benefit analyses of risk are made in the context of local cultures and contingencies of uncertainty.

> Even the concept of probability, an apparently fundamental input into any technical risk calculus, involves the framing of uncertainty for a specific purpose and with a specific legitimizing function. Actual organizational decision-making may operate at best in an informal "probabilistic climate" where characterizations of likelihood are often crude. Indeed, "possible outcomes with very low probabilities seem to be ignored, regardless of their potential significance" (March and Shapiro 1987: 1411), suggesting that the specter of the high-impact, low-probability event, so important to the operational risk debate (Power 2005a), is just a matter of framing ignorance or non-decidability

in an acceptable way. However, low-probability, high-impact events also characterize a "space of fear" which can induce hyper-precautionary attention to risk and security. From this point of view rogue traders, fraudulent chief executive officers (CEOs), and terrorists are "demonic" functional equivalents. (Hutter and Power 2005: 8)

These insights are mirrored in statements of political authorities charged with making hard decisions in conditions of uncertainty. For example, in a now famous statement about how he experiences decision-making regarding terrorism and other national security issues, Donald Rumsfeld, the United States Secretary of Defense, said, "we pull all this information together, and we say well that's basically what we see as the situation, that is really only the known knowns and the known unknowns. And each year we discover a few more of these unknown unknowns. It sounds like a riddle. It isn't a riddle. It is a very serious, important matter" (cited by Rasmussen 2004: 381). Addressing another serious and important matter, BSE (bovine spongiform encephalopathy), Lord Phillips had this to say about governmental decision-making in the politics of uncertainty:

> How does government set about addressing risk in a situation of scientific uncertainty? Is government to be expected to share all that it learns, and to do so before it is in a position to answer the questions that the public is bound to ask when the knowledge is disclosed? How can the public have confidence in the accuracy and adequacy of the information that is given? Who should have the task of assessing the risk and advising on the appropriate response to the risk? To what extent should government refer to scientists the task of considering the policy decisions that have to be taken in confronting risk? How does government ensure that the scientific advice that is given is, and is seen to be, independent? (BSE Inquiry Oral Transcript, 17 December 1999: 4–5)

Risk as a scientific language of management is intended to answer such questions. In all corporate institutions, both state and non-state, there is a new "risk commonwealth" in which "risk has become *the* language of rational discourse. The proper assessment and management of risk is now the common weal that the state and its citizens should seek to promote and defend" (Fisher 2003: 11). In this common-wealth all management processes are constituted through risk (Ericson and Haggerty 1997). As such, risk is the way organizations make sense of their environment and act upon it. External sources of harm are converted into organizational risks through technologies such as early warning systems, risk profiling, and red flag indicators. Internal sources of harm are converted into operational risks through technologies such as inspections, audits, reporting procedures, and electronic sur-veillance. Risk management has become engrained in the social imaginary of organizations. Much broader than a prob-ability concept, it is "increasingly used to frame the processes by which organizations deal with many different kinds of uncertainty" (Hutter and Power 2005: 10). This corporate view of risk management filters down to the neo-liberal citizen, both because she is constituted in such terms by the risk management systems of state and non-state corporate entities, and because she herself must assess and manage risk as a citizen of the risk commonwealth (Fisher 2003: 462).

The politics of uncertainty is played out through risk man-agement. Efforts at risk management are fallible and there-fore entail a perpetual political discourse of failure, reform, and improvement. Just as it is a paradox of the sciences and technologies of risk that the advances they make in improv-ing the human condition also generate new risks (Beck 1992, 1999), so it is a paradox of risk management efforts by orga-nizations that they both advance the ability to govern uncer-tainty and at the same time produce new uncertainties. "Organizations are both centres for processing and handling risk as well as potential producers and exporters of risk . . . [T]here is now widespread recognition that disasters and accidents are in a very important sense *organized* . . . 'organi-zational encounters with risk' are as much about how orga-nizations – such as corporations and states – experience the nature and limits of their own capacity to organize as they are about the external shocks and disturbances in the environment" (Hutter and Power 2005: 1–2).

As Vaughan (1999) has shown, risk management systems are characterized by "routine non-conformity": unanticipated outcomes that deviate from the best science, the best technologies, and the best management efforts. There may be technological failure in operating a monitoring system. There may be human failure as signs of risk are misread, absent, inadequate, contradictory, or ignored. In particular, the fact that risk is reactive and subject to compensation – changing in the very instant of human actions to interpret and manage it – means that it is extremely difficult to keep knowledge for risk management up to date and applicable to the situation facing decision-makers. As Adams (1995: 30) expresses it, "[R]isk perception is risk acted upon. It changes in the twinkling of an eye and as the eye lights upon it." When failures in science and technology interact with human failures to assess risk, "normal accidents" (Perrow 1984) result. Normal accidents are risk management system accidents, a result of system characteristics of interactive complexity and tight coupling of system components aimed at efficient operations. "The odd term *normal accident* is meant to signal that, given the system characteristics, multiple and unexpected interactions of failures are inevitable" (ibid.: 5). The term normal accident also signals normal uncertainty.

The routine failure of risk management systems leads to further efforts at risk management, based on a belief that more will work where less has not. The reform and refinement of organizational risk management systems are relentless, to the point where we are now witnessing "the risk management of everything" (Power 2004). The risk management of everything is characterized by an intensifying regime of internal procedures – inspections, audits, regulations, surveillance – that become the primary focus of organizational members. As Power (2004: 40) states, the increasing "demand for governance of the unknowable requires organizational proceduralization." Internal control systems, focused on operational risks, collect data on anything that is possible, regardless of its relevance to the real risks the organization is supposed to be addressing. Regulations similarly proliferate to cover any imagined eventuality. Data collection and rules burgeon because they are what risk managers need to demonstrate that they are indeed managing some risk, even if it is not the risk that actually poses harm to the organization. The radical uncertainty of harms such as contaminated products, rogue traders on financial markets, and terrorist activity are translated into petty internal controls that are at least "describable, and in aspiration, manageable. Killer events and sources of fear become translated into routines, regulations and data collection processes; anxiety, as the secondary risk of attempting to mange the unmanageable, is 'tamed' by a kind of naming" (ibid.: 31).

These processes result in an organizational culture of "defensible compliance" and "responsibility adversity" whereby actors are rewarded for being able to demonstrate that they followed procedures when things go wrong and thereby avoid blame. Expert judgment is diminished as actors try to avoid hard decisions and expressions of honest opinion for fear they might be liable; and as thinking, acting, and communicating transpire within the four square corners of the risk management formats for internal control. "This trend is resulting in a dangerous flight from judgment and a culture of defensiveness that create their own risks for organizations in preparing for, and responding to, a future they cannot know" (ibid.: 14–15). Defensive compliance and responsibility adversity not only lead to tunnel vision, but also incubate failures in risk management that produce more normal accidents. Relevant risk signals might not be accessed because the risk management system is more of a procedural spotlight than a sensitive searchlight. In cases such as the Challenger and Columbia space launch decisions (Vaughan 1996, 2005), the terrorist activity of 9/11 (Kean and Hamilton 2004), and financial institution failures (McQueen 1996), "crises and catastrophes do not just happen suddenly; they are in an important sense 'organized' and have their origins in failures of management and intelligence processes over a long period of time" (Power 2004: 44).

The politics of uncertainty transpires not only at this micro-level of the risk management of everything in organizational life, but also at the level of political culture where there is a need to dramatize control over what may be unknowable and ungovernable. At both levels, but in particular at the level of political culture, risk management is a rhetoric of reassurance. In this capacity, it meets "a functional and political need to maintain myths of control and manageability . . . organises what cannot be organised . . . holds out the promise of manageability in new areas . . . [and] implies a new way of allocating responsibility for decisions which must be made in potentially undecideable situations" (ibid.: 10).

Risk as a forensic language is exemplified in this use of risk management as a rhetoric of reassurance and responsibility. Risk is a "forensic resource" (Douglas 1990, 1992), a rhetorical device deployed in arguments about what harms should be given priority, how they should be dealt with, and who is blameworthy and therefore responsible for addressing them. As Douglas observes, the scientized language of risk provides an apparently neutral vocabulary for bridging facts and values: the facts of an uncertain existence and who should be held socially responsible for dealing with uncertainty. However, risk language is not neutral. The identification of risks that require attention involves a political process of selection in which some harms are given special attention while others are relatively unattended or ignored. Moreover, the harms selected are coded as threats to the security and prosperity at the heart of the liberal social imaginary, and this code legitimates intensified control including criminalization (ibid.; Hacking 2003).

Risk as a forensic resource is used in political culture to address the big issue uncertainties of the 21st century, for example the new terrorism, the integrity of health and welfare systems, corporate integrity, and public order. It is also used at the level of organizations and individuals to make decisions and attribute responsibility for them. "[R]isk language functions as part of a web of normative framing practices in organizations in which risk management can be conceived as a moral technology for the attribution of responsibility (see also Baker and Simon 2002; Ericson and Doyle 2003)" (Hutter and Power 2005: 9–10). Indeed, the forensic uses of risk in political culture are meant to articulate with the forensic practices of risk management in organizational cultures.

All decision-makers in organizations must be selective in their attention to risks – what they take into their risk portfolio and what they exclude – and bear responsibility for their selection when things go wrong. The selection may be based on best evidence, but it stretches beyond the sciences of risk and risk management to situational decisions about what should and should not be left to uncertainty. Consider the following statement by a senior executive of a reinsurance company, addressing the fact that his company paid out several billion dollars in claims for losses suffered from the terrorist activity of 9/11 as a result of not paying particular attention to this potential source of catastrophe prior to 9/11:

> An international reinsurer is supposed to have a certain experience with catastrophes. But the question is . . . given the diversity of liability scenarios, how can we meaningfully process such experience? This is scarcely possible using actuarial methods alone. It calls for professional methods that are probably more akin to those of a social historian than those of an actuarial scientist or a legal expert . . . So the problem is not know or not to know, the problem is . . . what you should consider . . . This is a sophisticated game, obviously, but this sophisticated game is based on the selection of four, five, six catastrophes out of twenty, thirty, forty, fifty. And this selection is absolutely dependent on, I don't know what, *casual* developments. And so the whole basis of this sophisticated and rational game is not so sophisticated. (cited in Ericson and Doyle 2004a: 217)

Even the most vehement advocates of scientific reason in risk management appreciate that risk is a forensic resource used to select particular harms for attention while ignoring others, and that judgments are based on social influences, economic benefits, cultural values, and political processes of blame and responsibility. For example, Sunstein (2002) develops a sustained argument for scientific approaches to risk and cost–benefit analysis, and decries non-scientific "ordinary thinking" among both risk management organizations, such as the Environmental Protection Agency in the United States, and individuals. At the same time – in spite of his "celebration of science" and cost–benefit analysis in risk selection and management, and derision of "ordinary thinking" about risk – Sunstein valorizes non-scientific reasoning if it can be used to induce more "rational" responses to risk. "If government is seeking a method to ensure that people will take a more rational approach to risk, it might well appeal to their emotions" (ibid.: 46). For example, Sunstein uses research on the effects of social advertising for harm reduction, such as anti-smoking campaigns, to indicate how appeals to people's emotions, values, identities, and subjectivities might make them take a more "rational" approach to risk.

Law, Risk and Uncertainty

Law is another institution and technology through which we act as if the future is knowable and governable. As O'Malley (2004: 77) observes, "Common law is one of a number of sources of inventing and assembling the technologies and discourses of uncertainty that have become central to liberal governance." In this capacity law engages the three interconnected languages of risk considered in the previous section: a language of probability, a language of management, and a forensic language. In making hard decisions about risk assessment, risk management, and allocation of responsibility for risk, legal authorities place law at the center of the politics of uncertainty.

Law takes into account scientific knowledge of risk as a tool for decision-making and setting standards about acceptable levels of harm. However, risk assessment in the legal arena is not simply a matter of frequency and severity probability statements or narrow cost–benefit analyses. Rather, legal decisions require broader consideration of "how individuals wish to conduct their lives and what limits it is perceived the state should place on that conduct" (Fisher 2000: 113). Administrators and courts thus define risk with respect to public perceptions of harm and socio-political contexts beyond scientific knowledge of risk (ibid.: 114–15). This task inevitably draws the law into the politics of uncertainty because there is no consensus or legitimate meta-rationality for addressing risk and establishing standards for risk management. "[A]t any one time there will be a number of different images of legitimacy in operation. It is thus not surprising that law has become the great battleground for standard setting" (Fisher 2004: 55–6). Hard decisions must be made, and these decisions inevitably privilege the proponents of one perspective on risk at the expense of others.

Hard legal decisions must also be made in the face of scientific uncertainty about risks. Legal agents step in to express authoritative certainty about risks where scientific authority is too equivocal. Law must decide what risk-taking activity should be allowed: who is entitled to place wagers on activity that may cause harm? Law must decide what risk-taking activity should be curtailed: when should one invoke the precautionary principle that scientific uncertainty over possible harms should not be used as the reason for not taking action to prevent those harms? A world of uncertainty is also a world of necessary decision (Ewald 2002: 292), and law is at the apex of the inter-institutional system of necessary decision. Louis Jaffe, the leading American administrative lawyer, observed that these hard decisions involve "the active principle of choosing or preferring" and as such have "the inherent power to hurt, to awaken resentment, to stir the sense of injustice" (quoted by Fisher 2003: 470).

Law also intersects with regimes of risk management, creating a public role for the state in the management of private organizations. Law makes risks and controversies about them public and visible. It articulates cost–benefit tradeoffs in risk-taking and risk management. It develops and oversees standards about acceptable levels of risk. It allocates and reviews discretion and responsibility for dealing with risk. As Power (2004: 25) observes, "far from being a private organizational matter, the effectiveness of internal control has come to play a very significant external *public* role; organizations . . . are being turned 'inside out' in its name, and this more than anything else drives a risk management explosion which demands the externalization and justification of organizational control arrangements." This new public role of internal risk management systems "is part of a macro- and micro-level politics of responding to crises by creating new accountability structures supporting claims of public and private reassurance" (ibid.: 27). Administrative rules become part of the defensive risk management of everything.

Law is also integral to risk as a forensic resource. Law is at the apex of inter-institutional processes for naming, blaming, and holding responsible for harm. In making risks visible, articulating cost–benefit tradeoffs, establishing standards, allocating discretion and responsibility, and holding parties responsible for failures in risk management, law is a forensic resource used to make hard decisions and express authoritative certainty in doing so.

Beyond the languages of risk, law functions more generally as an institution and technology for addressing uncertainty and governing the future across different legal forms.

Contract law provides a framework for governing uncertainty by making parties to the contract anticipate possible harms and by assigning obligations for both preventing these harms and compensating loss. As O'Malley (2004) documents, the law of contract emerged as a central institution of liberalism and remains so. Contract law did not embrace the statistical project of risk calculation with its focus on the distributional norm, but rather the classical liberal project of articulating moral norms as criteria of individual competence in dealing with uncertainty. Contract law sought "rules derived from an imaginary of entrepreneurial calculation that is pragmatic, rather than abstract or quantifiable" (ibid.: 92). The focus became "reasonable foresight," which requires figurative reasoning, or reasoning by analogy, based on experience. Liberal government in this form entails perpetual articulation of rules for the moral conduct of transactions in conditions of uncertainty. These rules alter subjectivity because they assume and sanction specific forms of reasoning about the uncertain future. The liberal subject of contract law is more a subject of uncertainty than of risk, governed through a regime of moral conduct about how to negotiate and manage the future.

Tort law provides a framework for governing uncertainty by shifting the cost of loss to those with the deepest pockets – for example, manufacturers and insurers in product liability cases – which in turn ideally fosters greater attention to risk management and harm prevention by those entities. Tort law is also thoroughly liberal in that it allocates responsibility for harm to the entities involved in risky activity. Since manufacturers and their insurers are in the business of profiting from uncertainty, they are to be held to account for uncertain outcomes. This includes compensating losses that arise from the unanticipated consequences or normal accidents of their entrepreneurial activities. It also includes their responsibility for internal risk management systems that address everything that can be anticipated about what might cause harm to others.

Administrative law provides a framework for governing uncertainty by allocating discretion to the administrative branch of government on the view that each problem posed by uncertainty is fact and context specific, requires expertise, and is best resolved by negotiating compliance with the regulated entity. Standards regarding acceptable levels of risk and requirements for risk management are usually not written into primary legislation on the view that the legislature has neither the expertise nor the institutional capacity to do so. Legislative powers are delegated to the executive branch of government. For example, in the UK powers are delegated to the Secretary of State to set standards and pass enforceable regulations. There is also increasing delegation to government departments and agencies that produce policy guidance and technical notes, the status and legitimacy of which are debated in public law (Fisher 2000: 119). Similar to the legislature, the courts have traditionally deferred to the law as constituted by the administrative branch of government because they themselves lack the expertise and institutional capacity to assess risk and seek compliance. "The courts state that they cannot review questions of fact and tend to defer to decision-makers in matters of a complex and technical nature, particularly where delegated legislation is being passed" (ibid.: 120). The rise of the administrative or regulatory state in the era of the risk management of everything is troubling for liberal social imaginaries (Levi-Faur and Gilad 2004). Executive legal authority over private entities and subjects rests uneasily with liberal conceptions of popular sovereignty, democracy, freedom, and security.

Criminal law provides a framework for governing uncertainty by identifying harms and devising rules and sanctions for both preventing those harms and punishing those held responsible for them. In the classical model of crime–responsibility–punishment, criminal law is a liberal institution that holds accountable those who intentionally cause harm. Criminal harm is not only conceived as a threat to the security of the victim as liberal subject, but also to the security of the liberal state as a collective, and it is prosecuted and punished as such.

In the neo-liberal era, this model is being radically transformed. Traditional legal principles and practices related to *actus reus* (a specified criminal act) and *mens rea* (intention to commit this criminal act) – used to hold people responsible for criminal activity and to justify prosecution and punishment – are being eroded or eliminated altogether. There is a dramatic rise in strict liability offenses, and many due process standards of justice are diminished or eliminated in the name of risk management and, increasingly, uncertainty (Ashworth 2003). This changing role of criminal law, as it articulates with the other legal forms and infrastructures of risk management, is the subject of the following inquiry.

Precautionary Logic

The politics of uncertainty, conducted through the sciences of risk and in law, expresses increasing doubt about the capacity of liberal governments to govern the future and provide security. Indeed, in many quarters there is radical doubt, radical uncertainty, suggesting the ungovernability of modern societies (Stehr and Ericson 2000).

This radical uncertainty is expressed to a degree in the precautionary principle in law: "In cases where there are threats to human health or the environment the fact that there is scientific uncertainty over those threats should not be used as *the* reason for not taking action to prevent harm" (Fisher 2001: 316; see also Sunstein 2005). The precautionary principle in law addresses how corporate decision-makers are to balance science, scientific uncertainty, and normative considerations in their exercises of discretion. It emphasizes caution about legal reasoning with respect to the factual claims of science: "in cases of scientific uncertainty legal certainty cannot depend on factual certainty" (Fisher 2002: 17). It urges caution in legal processes with respect to the design of regulatory regimes, the allocation and exercise of discretion, and judicial review of administrative discretion. It also urges caution regarding administrative constitutionalism: how much legal authority should be given to the administrative branch of government to regulate uncertainty in the context of issues arising from the limits of science.

The precautionary principle carries legal authority in many jurisdictions. It is included in treaties and statutes and mobilized in case law. It has resulted in caution with respect to product development and marketing, cleaner production techniques, environmental impact assessments, adjusting procedural fairness in light of uncertainty, giving business licenses for restricted periods, banning activities, new forms of monitoring and audit, and specialized courts (Fisher 2002: 12). While the courts have recognized the principle as a justification for upholding precautionary decisions in regulatory environments, they have not gone further and accepted it as a justification for intensive review of administrative discretion. The reluctance to undertake such review is based on the view that the courts do not have the institutional expertise or constitutional competence for this task (Fisher 2001). Furthermore, to go this far, to try to convert precaution from a legal principle to a legal standard, would create enormous trouble for the courts, regulators, and regulated. Fisher (2001: 327) cites Talbot, J. in the Australian case of *Nicholls v Director General of National Parks and Wildlife Service* [(1994) 84 LGERA 397 at 419]: while the precautionary principle "may be framed appropriately for the purpose of a political aspiration, its implementation as a legal standard could have the potential to create interminable forensic argument."

Of course, this legal reticence to enforce precaution does not halt interminable forensic argument about scientific uncertainty in political culture. Beyond the precautionary principle in law, there is a deeper precautionary logic pervading the politics of uncertainty which "requires an active use of doubt, in the sense Descartes made canonical in his *Meditations of First Philosophy*. Before any action, I must not only ask myself what I need to know and what I need to master, but also what I do not know, what I dread or suspect. I must, out of precaution, imagine the worst possible, the consequence that an infinitely deceptive malicious demon could have slipped into the folds of an apparently innocent enterprise" (Ewald 2002: 286).

Precautionary logic is the logic of uncertainty. It confronts the limits of science and technology: the point at which science and technology no longer have a capacity to produce useful knowledge about the frequency and severity of risks; and the point at which science and technology are themselves producers of new uncertainties with catastrophic consequences. As such it is a logic beyond cost–benefit analysis, which uses knowledge of risk to understand the tradeoffs involved in risk-taking: "we take the risks and pay the price." Precautionary logic focuses on uncertainties that have no price, because the catastrophic loss of treasured lives, environments, and property is deemed beyond financial compensation. Precautionary logic is also beyond loss prevention through risk management, which presupposes scientific knowledge of risk and a capacity for technical control.

Precautionary logic fuels suspicion. It urges everyone "to anticipate what one does not yet know, to take into account doubtful hypotheses and simple suspicions. It invites one to take the most far-fetched forecasts seriously, prediction by prophets, whether true or false . . . Decisions are therefore not made in a context of certainty, nor even available knowledge, but of doubt, suspicion, premonition, foreboding, challenge, mistrust, fear, and anxiety" (ibid.: 288, 294). As in the tale of Moby Dick, malicious demons are identified, resentment of them is deemed virtuous, and relief is found through a culture of blame:

> The White Whale swam before him as a monomaniac incarnation of all those malicious agencies which some deep men feel eating in them, till they are left living on with half a heart and half a lung . . . All that maddens and torments; all that stirs up the lees of things; all truth with value in it; all that cracks the sinews and cakes the brain; all the subtle dimensions of life and thought; all evil, to crazy Ahab, were visibly personified, and made practically assailable in Moby Dick. (Melville 2003 [1851]: 200)

Precautionary logic does not eschew science. Rather, it converts science to its uses. Science becomes both an object and an instrument of suspicion. There is a "disrupted relationship with science, such that we are now less interested in the confidence science provides than in the suspicions and doubts it can arouse both about what we know and what we do not know. With precaution, science becomes a principle of challenge" (Ewald 2002: 284).

While in many contexts, including in law, uncertainty has conventionally spelled innocence, within precautionary logic uncertainty is a reason for extreme preemptive measures for which designated agents are held responsible, and monitored and sanctioned accordingly. "The boundless nature of liability

leaves no room for innocence" (ibid.: 287). There is a new proceduralism based on close monitoring of the agents' behavior
and decisions in which "verification of the observance of decision-making procedures takes on paramount importance"
(ibid.). This proceduralism is characterized by precaution:
being cautious even about how one is being cautious. There is
also a new sanctioning of responsibilities which escapes refer-
ence to anything but uncertainty: as the person responsible for
precautionary measures, the designated agent is judged not
only by what she should have known but also by what she
should have suspected.

Counter-law

Precautionary logic leads to criminalization through counter-
law. There are two types of counter-law. Counter-law I takes
the form of laws against law. New laws are enacted and new
uses of existing law are invented to erode or eliminate traditional principles, standards, and procedures of criminal law
that get in the way of preempting imagined sources of harm.
Counter-law II takes the form of surveillant assemblages.
New surveillance infrastructures are developed and new uses
of existing surveillance networks are extended that also erode
or eliminate traditional standards, principles, and procedures
of criminal law that get in the way of preempting imagined
sources of harm.

Counter-law I, using laws against law, is an obvious and relatively easy way for political authorities to try to maintain the
upper hand in the politics of uncertainty. Criminalization
through counter-law I is especially compelling when there
has been a catastrophic failure in a risk management system
for which the government is held responsible. Catastrophic
failures expose not only the limits of the risk management
system, but also the myth of governability. Counter-laws that
intensify criminalization are passed as *the* strongest statement
of authoritative certainty by government, even while government authority and certainty may be at its weakest.

Counter-law I exhibits the disturbing "tendency of government to propose the creation of new crimes without strong and principled justifications" (Ashworth 2000) when viewed from the template of traditional criminal law. It also involves efforts to counter the traditional distinctions between the different legal forms of criminal, civil, and administrative law. The traditional demarcations between legal forms, enunciated through the distinctive principles and procedures of each form, are now viewed as a problem to be overcome. "[N]ew variations of liability are devised so as to circumvent or minimize the scope of the principles that are identified as obstacles" (Ashworth 2004: 265). There is a proliferation of new forms of civil measure to address new imaginaries of harmful behavior that traditionally would have been within the purview of criminal law (Crawford 2003). There is also an expansion of the regulatory state in which criminalization based on precautionary logic has become pervasive.

Counter-law measures are also transforming criminal law itself, causing leading legal scholars such as Ashworth (2000) to ask, "Is the criminal law a lost cause?" In order to facilitate preemptive strikes against Moby Dicks – for example terrorists, sexual predators, welfare cheats, corporate fraudsters, and "anti-social" underclasses – substantive laws are reformed and reinterpreted within a precautionary logic. Due process standards evaporate, and sentencing structures are creatively devised to facilitate ease of prosecution, conviction, and incapacitation.

The legal transformation through counter-law is not only a response to scientific uncertainty about risk, but also to the law itself as a source of uncertainty. For example, when it sustains high standards of due process, evidence, proof, and culpability, criminal law creates a great deal of uncertainty in the capacity of the criminal justice system to prevent, discover, build a case against, and successfully prosecute criminal behavior. In the precautionary urge for greater certainty in crime control, these standards of criminal law are weakened, the lower standards of civil and administrative law are substituted, and law is devised to underpin the surveillant assemblage as the second form of counter-law.

Counter-law I is officially expressed as a "state of exception" (Agamben 2005). Normal legal principles, standards, and procedures must be suspended because of a state of emergency, extreme uncertainty, or threat to security with catastrophic potential. The legal order must be broken to save the social order. The legal norm is suspended and separated "from its application in order to make application possible," an application that serves "to make the effective regulation of the real possible" (ibid.: 36). The legal fiction of a duality between norm and reality is discarded, leaving only real hard decisions in the face of uncertainty without any encumbrance from law. "The normative aspect of law can thus be obliterated and contradicted with impunity by a governmental violence that – while ignoring international law externally and producing a permanent state of exception internally – nevertheless still claims to be applying the law" (ibid.: 87).

The key point about counter-law I, documented in the following chapters, is that the state of exception is not an exception at all, but has become the normal state. As Agamben documents, since World War I, across Western countries and through all legal forms

> the state of exception tends increasingly to appear as the dominant paradigm of government in contemporary politics. The transformation of a provisional and exceptional measure into a technique of government threatens radically to alter – in fact, has already palpably altered – the structure and meaning of the traditional distinction between contractual forms . . . The declaration of the state of exception has been replaced by an unprecedented generalization of the paradigm of security as the normal technique of government. (ibid.: 2, 14, 87)

The paradigm of security entails incessant elaboration of "rules about exceptions to rules" across all legal forms (Edgerton 1985). It also involves a parallel elaboration of the surveillant assemblage within the institutions of civil society.

Beneath the legal form that enunciates rights and obligations on all parties to the legal relationship, there is a disciplinary apparatus based on surveillance (Foucault 1977). Foucault invokes Bentham's liberal social imaginary of the panoptic workhouse and prison as a "house of certainty" (ibid.: 202), but extends it to the minute practices of surveillance and regulation in all social institutions. This extension still bears the penal imprint of the panopticon and as such entails processes of criminalization in everyday life. The prison, and the criminal law and criminal justice system more generally, are "reinscribed in non-juridical systems" (ibid.: 22). These systems embed "a whole new system of truth and a mass of roles hitherto unknown in the exercise of criminal justice. A corpus of knowledge, techniques, 'scientific' discoveries is formed and becomes entangled with the practice of the power to punish . . . [a] scientifico-legal complex from which the power to punish derives its basis, justification and rules, from which it extends its effects and by which it masks its exorbitant singularity" (ibid.).

Foucault points to an underlying logic of precaution in these systems, and to their malicious demon or Moby Dick character, which he expresses as "the attentive 'malevolence' that turns everything to account. Discipline is a political anatomy of detail" (ibid.: 139). While surveillance infrastructures develop within each institution to meet its peculiar needs, there is also an inter-institutional "swarming of disciplinary mechanisms" or surveillant assemblage in which "the closed apparatuses add to their internal and specific function a role of external surveillance, developing around themselves a whole margin of lateral controls." Foucault uses the example of schools that not only produce knowledge for control of children but also of their "parents, to gain information as to their way of life, their resources, their piety, their morals . . . [to] exercise regular supervision over them" (ibid.). Similarly, he observes that hospitals form a center of medical observation and statistics about populations in the outside community.

This development of knowledge about populations within and across institutions constitutes "biopower" (Foucault

1991) – a kind of power of biographical knowledge – as the necessary correlate of discipline. Surveillance, defined simply as the production of knowledge about populations useful in their administration (Giddens 1985; Dandeker 1990; Haggerty and Ericson 2006), serves not only the negative purposes of control, but also the positive purposes of the security and prosperity of populations. Seen in this way, surveillance is central to the conception of policing that has been at the heart of liberal social imaginaries from their inception in the 18th century (Radzinowicz 1956: iii, 417–38; Oestreich 1982; Andrew 1989; Pasquino 1991; Foucault 1991; Ericson and Haggerty 1997; Taylor 2004). Coincident with the early modern conception of policy, policing referred to a body of knowledge and regulation regarding security and prosperity. It was underpinned by "police science," a branch of political economy practiced by Beccaria, Bentham, Colquhoun, and Adam Smith, among others. Known also as the "science of government" and the "science of happiness," police science aimed to address "everything . . . unregulated, everything that can be said . . . to lack order or form" (Pasquino 1991: 111). For example, among the thousands of German works on police science was Frank's six-volume *System for a Complete Medical Policing*, which included detailed regulations designed to "prevent evils through wise ordinances," and covered every then imaginable aspect of health care. Van Justi, in his 1768 treatise entitled *Eléments généreaux de police*, said that "the science of policing consists . . . in regulating everything that relates to the present condition of society, in strengthening and improving it, in seeing that all things . . . contributed to the welfare of members that compose it." Karl Marx, writing in 1843, restated the 18th-century view that "[s]ecurity is the supreme social concept of civil society, the concept of police, the concept that the whole society exists only to guarantee to each of its members the preservation of his person, his rights, and his property" (Marx 1967: 236).

Conceived in this way, policing is integral to every institution and relations among institutions, and it has no obvious limits. It entails a perpetual and infinite thirst for knowledge of potential harms as a capacity to overcome uncertainties and underpin security.

> Police power must bear "over everything" . . . it is the dust of events, actions, behaviour, opinions – "everything that happens," the police are concerned with "those things of every moment," those "unimportant things." With the police, one is in an indefinite world of a supervisor that seeks ideally to reach the most elementary particle, the most passing phenomenon of the social body . . . the infinitely small of political power . . . what were registered in this way were forms of behaviour, attitudes, possibilities, suspicions – a permanent account of individuals' behaviour. (Foucault 1977: 213–14)

The police power is perfected when it results in self-policing among members of the population. The liberal social imaginary of the "house of certainty" is a house of discipline as self-policing. The individual who knows she is seen through by the surveillant assemblage, who recognizes her visibility, will internalize the gaze. That is, she will not only assume responsibility for the constraints of power, but will have that power inscribed in her to the point where she polices others as well as herself.

> He who is subjected to a field of visibility, and who knows it, assumes responsibility for the constraints of power; he makes them play spontaneously upon himself; he inscribes in himself the power relation in which he simultaneously plays both roles; he becomes the principle of his own subjection. By this very fact, the external power may throw off its external weight; it tends to be non-corporal; and, the more it approaches this limit, the more constant, profound and permanent are its effects: it is a perpetual victory that avoids any physical confrontation and which is always decided in advance. (ibid.: 202)

As this liberal social imaginary developed in the modern era, "what we got was not a network of agape, but rather a disciplined society in which categorical relations have primacy and therefore norms" (Taylor 2004: 66). The norms of surveillant assemblages, of policing and discipline, comprise counter-law II.

> The disciplines should be regarded as a sort of counter-law . . . whereas the juridical systems define juridical subjects according to universal norms, the disciplines characterize, classify, specialize; they distribute along a scale, around a norm, hierarchize individuals in relation to one another and, if necessary, disqualify and invalidate . . . they effect a suspension of the law that is never total, but it is never annulled either. Regular and institutional as it may be, the discipline, in its mechanism, is a "counter-law." And, although the universal juridicism of modern society seems to fix limits on the exercise of power, its universally widespread panopticism enables it to operate, on the underside of the law, a machinery that is both immense and minute, which supports, reinforces, multiplies the asymmetry of power and undermines the limits that are traced around the law . . . hence the affirmation that they [the disciplines] are at the very foundation of society, and an element in its equilibrium, whereas they are a series of mechanisms for unbalancing power relations definitively and everywhere; hence the persistence in regarding them as the humble, but concrete form of every morality, whereas they are a set of physico-political techniques. (Foucault 1977: 221–3)

In the following chapters I analyze criminalization and the politics of uncertainty in relation to both forms of counter-law. In counter-law I, new legislation proliferates and existing law is reconfigured, with the explicit intention of undermining the principles, standards, and procedures of criminal law. In counter-law II, surveillant assemblages also proliferate to the same effect. Both forms of counter-law are intimately connected to the neo-liberal search for security in the face of uncertainty as the basic condition of human knowledge.

Four fields of security are analyzed. Chapter 2 focuses on national security, asking how are we to know the possible harms of terrorist activity and use that knowledge to preempt terrorism. Chapter 3 focuses on social security, asking how are we to know and regulate the appropriate levels of health and welfare benefits to ensure that benefits remain in place without mortgaging the lives of future generations through debt financing. Chapter 4 focuses on corporate security, asking how are we to know and regulate the future liabilities posed by public and private sector corporate entities – regarding, for example, defective products and services, environmental harms, failures in technology and fraudulent practices – in ways that will both protect us from those harms and ensure sustainable futures. Chapter 5 focuses on domestic security, asking how are we to know and regulate the future harms posed by dispossessed individuals and whole underclasses for whom security is only a yearning, never a fact, and uncertainty is based on timelines of hours and days rather than months and years. In each chapter I show that, in the context of the uncertainty and insecurity that characterize neo-liberal politics at the beginning of the 21st century, criminalization through both forms of counter-law is a dominant political strategy.

The Two Leviathans

In each chapter I also show that criminalization through counter-law tears at the fabric of civil society that the neo-liberal state is supposed to be making tight-knit. I argue that in its exceptional efforts to criminalize as a response to uncertainty, the state helps manufacture malicious demons that resemble the biblical social imaginary of Leviathan as a sea monster.

Who can open the doors of his face?
  Round about his teeth is terror. . .
His breath kindles coals.
  And a flame comes forth from his mouth
In his neck abides strength
  And terror dances before him. . .

When he raises himself up the mighty are afraid;
  At the crashing they are beside themselves;
Though the sword reaches him, it
  Does not avail
  nor the spear, the dart, or the javelin.
He counts iron as straw,
  And bronze as rotten wood
The arrow cannot make him flee;
  For him slingstones are turned to stubble. . .
Behind him he leaves a shining wake;
  One would think the weak to be hoary.
Upon earth there is not his like,
  A creature without fear
He beholds everything that is high;
  He is the king over all of the sons of pride
                              (Book of Job 41: 14–34)

This Leviathan of the biblical social imaginary was represented in the emblematic literature of the 17th century by
the theological enemies of Thomas Hobbes (Farneti 2001;
see also Bayatrizi 2005) (illustration 1:1). This Leviathan *is*
uncertainty, a monstrous body that leaves only death and
destruction in its wake. Like the smoldering twin towers of
the World Trade Center, this imaginary signifies catastrophe
and the need for precaution at all costs.

The Leviathan of the biblical social imaginary contrasts
sharply with what the theological enemies of Hobbes were
responding to, namely his book *Leviathan* (1651). Hobbes'
book was a seminal expression of the liberal social imaginary,
visualizing a state that looks after both the physical security
(police and military) and prosperity (policing and political
economy) of the population. The frontispiece to *Leviathan*
depicts this liberal social imaginary beautifully (illustration 1:2). Leviathan is the embodiment of the population, a
people unified in life with their leader. Indeed the frontispiece shows the population forming the body of Leviathan,
including its outstretched and embracing arms. Leviathan is
headed by a slightly smiling face that, along with the sword

Illustration 1.1   *The Leviathan* © Tommy Castillo

Illustration 1.2   *The Leviathan frontispiece*
Frontispiece to 'Leviathan or the Matter, Forme and Power of a
Common Wealth Ecclesiasticall and Civil', 1651, by Thomas
Hobbe by English School, (17th century) Private Collection/ The
Bridgeman Art Library

and staff of office, appears protective and benevolent. Beneath the Leviathan as body politic is the product of the collective endeavors: a prosperous land of undulating hills, rivers, farms, roads, and a citadel. Underpinning this landscape are the nascent liberal institutions and technologies imagined to constitute this orderly state of certainty.

I argue that in manufacturing suitable enemies as malicious demons and criminalizing them through both forms of counter-law, the state transforms itself into the Leviathan of the biblical social imaginary. It enacts new laws against law and extends surveillant assemblages that engulf all imaginable sources of harm: terrorists, health and welfare system cheats, corporate executives whose operations are implicated in catastrophic loss, and underclass populations that signify disorder and decline. "It is as if the suspension of law freed a force or a mystical element, a sort of legal *mana*" (Agamben 2005: 51). The Leviathan of the liberal social imaginary is not only tarnished, but begins to unravel, as selected populations are criminalized in ways that create terror, insecurity, injustice, and diminished prosperity. Uncertainty ends up proving itself.

2
National Security

Terrorism and the Politics of Uncertainty

Terrorism *is* the politics of uncertainty. For example, Jihadist terrorism targets the values, science, technology, and law of Western risk societies, seeking to transform them into uncertain societies. Terrorists are in the business of uncertainty, playing on randomness to keep whole populations in fear, anticipation, and disestablishment. They underscore the potential ungovernability of modern societies, how those with little power can work cheaply and efficiently against powerful institutions to destroy.

Terrorists stage destructive events that ensure they will live on in the "vast metaphorical spectator spaces" of mass media (Taylor 2004: 170). These events strike at the Western liberal valorization of life at all costs and an orderly death. They do so by making death unpredictable, irrational, and highly symbolic (Bayatrizi 2005). Terrorists transcend life as order, security, prosperity, and freedom by glorifying a different symbolic state: a destiny, a cause, a pride, a sacrifice (Baudrillard 2003: 68).

Suicide bombers construct the Western obsession with uncertainty and fear of death as weakness and even cowardice, juxtaposed to their fearless embracing of death (Reuter 2004: 15). Often supported by family and community, theirs is a spiritual mission in which martyrdom and the afterlife rise above any desire to survive. The spiritual instructional manual for the 9/11 attack on the World Trade Center informed participants, "You will notice that the plane will stop, then will start to fly again. This is the hour in which you will meet God." The al-Qaeda ideology of destruction, while rooted in the Islamic tradition, ignites followers from different nations and backgrounds. To the extent an al-Qaeda network exists, it is mainly in the form of dispatching its own loyalists to scenes of local conflict where natives are converted to the view that their struggle is part of a global clash of civilizations. "Thus, injustices perpetuated in Chechnya or on the West Bank can stir up hatred within Morocco and Saudi Arabia, and unintentionally provide aid and comfort to opportunists who stoke the flames of righteous anger everywhere" (Reuter 2004: 18). This disparate nature of al-Qaeda has led Burke (2004) to conclude that it is more an ideology than an organization. There was an al-Qaeda infrastructure in Afghanistan, but it has been destroyed and many of bin-Laden's associates are on the run or have been detained or killed. However, the ideology remains strong and is spreading well beyond any link to bin-Laden or his immediate associates. Indeed bin-Laden has become part of the ideology, in the sense that his role model is used to advance the "Jihadi International" cause.

While rich with myths and symbols that make it seem highly irrational in the context of Western liberal conceptions of life and death, the bin-Laden model is highly rational. Indeed the myths and symbols are a crucial part of the rationality, mobilizing adherents to strategic action that one CIA analyst views as exhibiting "brilliance, eloquence, sanity, religious sincerity, [and] astute tactical skills" (Scheuer 2004).

The rationality includes methods and targets of attacks that provide poignant reminders of the limits of scientific and technological efforts at risk management. Many attacks, most spectacularly 9/11, involve the use of science and technology against itself. Science and technology simply rewards the suicidal will. All attacks expose the limits of risk assessment and management in conventional terms of frequency and severity

(Ericson and Doyle 2004b). Frequency is extremely difficult to ascertain for a given target. Terrorism is intentional catastrophe, and the same target can be struck repeatedly or not at all. Severity is also extremely difficult to estimate. Moreover, the consequences of a terrorist attack are assumed to be so severe that terrorism by definition is a risk beyond price.

The rationality also includes methods and targets of attack that provide poignant reminders of the limits of law in risk assessment and management. The new asymmetries of power between nation-states in conflict with non-nation-state actors blur the boundaries between war and peace, and with them the laws of war and domestic law enforcement. There is a new sense of permanent war and absence of peace requiring new laws of both war and domestic peacekeeping. The deterrent capacity of the legal power to punish is destroyed because terrorists express a desire to die. The relationship between law, power, and the state is radically reconfigured as an integral part of terrorism as intentional catastrophe.

> [Terrorists] annihilate the entire logic of power, since no credible threat can be made against someone who has no desire to survive. All of our notions of security and our civilization have been based on this unspoken assumption, which we heretofore have believed to be self-evident. For example, consider that for airport security checks, up until now, the only precaution thought necessary was the matching of every piece of luggage with an on-board passenger, since, as everyone knew, no one would think of blowing themselves up in midair. Or so we thought. The presumption of individual self-interest and fear of death underlies the function of the market economy and the power of the state: suicide bombers cancel these out. Deterrence, punishment, and retaliation all become meaningless when faced with an aggressor who will impose the utmost penalty for himself at the very moment of his victory. (Reuter 2004: 3)

Terrorism makes precautionary logic obvious. Following 9/11, political speech in the USA took a dramatic turn aimed at making precautionary logic part of everyday life. President Bush hit home in various sound-bites the need to preempt the terrorist threat "before it fully materializes." His then National Security Advisor, Condoleezza Rice, declared that extraordinary police and military mobilization against terrorism is necessary before the "smoking gun becomes a mushroom cloud" (Janus 2004: 577–8).

Investigations of the failure to prevent the events of 9/11 focused on the problems of bureaucracy, communication, and tunnel vision in the FBI, CIA, and other security agencies, and stressed the need to exercise the catastrophic imagination as a crucial ingredient of future security. The 9/11 Commission Report (Kean and Hamilton 2004: 339) said the 9/11 attacks reflected security agencies' failure of "imagination – the lack of organizational capacity to imagine such an attack." Ironically, it recommended efforts to bureaucratize imagination: "It is therefore crucial to find a way of routinizing, even bureaucratizing, the exercise of imagination" (ibid.: 334). While a bureaucratized imagination seems paradoxical, what is being recommended is the embedding of precautionary logic in the security systems of organizations. In all of their planning, strategies, and practices, security agents are to imagine the Leviathan of the biblical social imaginary, a sea monster intent on leaving tsunami-like destruction in its wake.

Precautionary logic has become central to the US politics of uncertainty, feeding into and fed by other features of its political culture. There is a concerted effort to conflate the need for precaution at home with precautionary strikes against terrorism abroad. This conflation was a key feature of Bush's strategy in the 2004 presidential election, continuing the post-9/11 campaign to simultaneously terrorize the American population into the precautionary logic of homeland security, and populations in Iraq and elsewhere in the Middle East through preemptive attacks.

This conflation of security at home with aggression abroad is effected through the view that the United States is at war with terrorists however defined. The USA has long used "war on" metaphors to identify suitable enemies and justify extreme security measures against them: "the war on crime," "the war on drugs," even "the war on poverty" when welfarism had a glimmer of hope in the American political culture of the 1960s. "The war on terrorism" in some respects encapsulates all of these "war on" campaigns because it is not only directed at foreign enemies and global security, but also at enemies within, blurring into precautionary approaches to domestic crime, drugs, welfare fraud, and anything else signifying moral degeneracy (see chapter 5; Barak 2005).

Agamben (2005) links the pervasiveness of "war on" metaphors in American culture to the fact that the sovereign power of the president is based in declared emergency linked to a state of war.

> [O]ver the course of the twentieth century the metaphor of war becomes an integral part of the presidential political vocabulary whenever decisions considered to be of vital importance are being imposed. Thus, in 1933, Franklin D. Roosevelt was able to assume extraordinary powers to cope with the Great Depression by presenting his actions as those of a commander during a military campaign . . . President Bush's decision to refer to himself constantly as the "Commander in Chief of the Army" after September 11, 2001, must be considered in the context of this presidential claim to sovereign powers in everyday emergency situations. If, as we have seen, the assumption of this title entails a direct reference to the state of exception, then Bush is attempting to produce a situation in which emergency becomes the rule, and the very distinction between peace and war (and between foreign and civil war) becomes impossible. (ibid.: 21–2)

Richard Clarke, a former member of the US Security Council, even argues that al-Qaeda is a "phantom enemy" manufactured through the precautionary logic of instrumental politicians: "those with the darkest imaginations become the most powerful" (Clarke 2004). Raban (2005: 22) observes there is now "a world of chronic blur, full of slippery words that mean something different from what they meant before September 2001." It is the blur of a war on everything, envisaged by US military officials long before 9/11:

> In broad terms, fourth generation warfare [involving a nation-state in conflict with a non-state actor] seems to be widely dispersed and largely undefined; the distinction will be blurred to the vanishing point. It will be nonlinear, possibly to the point of having no defineable battlefields or fronts. The distinction between "civilian" and "military" may disappear. Actions will occur concurrently throughout all participants' depth, including their society as a cultural, not just a physical, entity. Major military facilities, such as airfields, fixed communications sites, and large headquarters will become rarities because of their vulnerability; the same may be true of civilian equivalents, such as seats of government, power plants, and industrial sites (including knowledge as well as manufacturing industries). Success will depend heavily on effectiveness in joint operations as lines between responsibility and mission become very blurred. (Lind et al. 1989: 22–6)

Fundamentalist religiosity is also integral to precautionary logic in American political culture and the war on everything that flows from it. Radical political conservatism is entwined with a religious ethos powered by disgust with all manner of moral degeneracy believed to characterize Western societies. In this respect at least there is an affinity with militant Islamism. As Moyers (2005) observes, the religious right has become a powerful force in US electoral politics. Before the 2004 elections, 186 members of Congress were backed by the religious right, a number that has increased since the election. In the Senate, 45 members are similarly backed.

The religious right also has an enormous mass media infrastructure to ensure a strong presence in public culture, including approximately 1,600 Christian radio stations and 250 Christian television stations. There are also thousands of assembly halls in which church as theater is performed to live audiences. The *Toronto Star* church theater critic, Tom Harper, attended a one-day conference at a Baptist church in

Florida on the theme, "Left Behind: A Conference on Biblical Prophecy about End Times" (ibid.). He described conference speeches as full of "venom and dangerous ignorance" about a range of suitable enemies, including Islam as "a Satanic religion" and Muslims who intend "to impose their religion on all of us." A "final" war was said to be inevitable, but believers in the church's "Rapture" do not have to worry because sometime in the next four decades they will be swept to heaven. In this rapturous mindset, there is no need to worry about myriad sources of catastrophic loss or even where oil supplies will come from beyond the next four decades. The apocalypse was foretold in the Bible and believers will rise above it all, just as the terrorists of 9/11 imagined they would take a second flight that day to meet their God.

Counter-law I: Laws Against Law

Counter-law flourishes in this political culture of precautionary logic and war on everything. As Robert Cheaney (2004) wrote in "The sleeper scenario: terrorism-support laws and the demands of prevention," there is an imagined need to develop enabling legal regimes to aid in the search for malicious demons everywhere. "[T]he overriding priority of the Department [of Justice] since 9/11 is to prevent attacks before they occur using all available tools . . . [these tools will produce] significant internal incentive [for security officials] to expand their capacity for prevention" (ibid.: 578).

Following 9/11, the US government moved swiftly to enact counter-law. The primary move was the enactment of the USA Patriot Act – The Uniting and Strengthening of America by Providing Appropriate Tools Required to Intercept and Obstruct Terrorism Act 2001 (Pub. L. No. 107–56, 115 Stat 272) – codified in various sections of the United States Code.

The USA Patriot Act erases established principles, standards, and procedures of criminal law in the name of national security. It places no limit on presidential authority to criminalize those deemed "unlawful enemy combatants," including

US citizens. "Unlawful enemy combatants" is a dangerous offender-like status that criminalizes suspects for imagined future harm they might cause rather than past crime. People can be assigned this status on the basis of categorical suspicion: the wrong face in the wrong place at the wrong time. There is also suspicion by association: someone is suspected because they know someone who is suspected. Otherwise legitimate acts of non-violent political dissent may also be constituted as dangerous. The president is sovereign, the sole power for the real hard decisions that escape the law even as they carry the legal imprint of the USA Patriot Act.

Unlawful enemy combatants can be held without specific charges and for an indefinite period. At the beginning of 2005, only 4 out of 549 prisoners held for two to three years at the Guantánamo Bay detention camp had been charged with a specific offense. The designation of enemy combatant is made at hearings held by military Combatant Status Review Tribunals (CSRT). The suspect is not allowed a lawyer, only a personal military representative who is a military officer without legal training and obliged to serve his superiors who run the CSRT. Witnesses may be called, but only as screened by the military and said to be available. Stafford Smith (2005: 44) observes that the CSRT process "is just another form of interrogation . . . They've been interrogating these guys for two to three years, and now they send someone in who they say is your Personal Rep, and he gets to ask you more questions, and then he goes back and reports to the other side." At the beginning of 2005, there had been CSRT hearings for 440 suspects and 439 were deemed unlawful enemy combatants subject to indefinite detention.

Unlawful enemy combatants are subject to extreme interrogation tactics, including torture. While initial revelations of torture in the mass media suggested that it occurred in isolated cases involving aberrant security operatives – more dangerous offenders – it is now clear that torture was carefully planned as an integral component of the counter-law infrastructure. Greenberg and Dratel (2005) have published over 1,000 pages of legal memoranda documenting how the US government argued away laws and conventions against torture. In spite of its enormous expenditure on sophisticated surveillance technology and networks, the US government did not have adequate intelligence on Jihadist terrorism. Information extracted through torture of captured terrorist suspects was to be the answer to the information deficit. The best legal minds in the Justice Department and Defense Department were mobilized in a manner akin to how corporate lawyers help their clients overcome legal obstacles to the interests they wish to pursue (see chapter 4). Dratel (2005: xxii) refers to this as "the 'corporatization' of government lawyering: a wholly result-oriented system in which policy makers start with an objective and work backward, in the process enlisting the aid of intelligent and well-credentialed lawyers who, for whatever reason – the attractions of power, careerism, ideology, or just plain bad judgment – all too willingly failed to act as a constitutional or moral compass that could brake their client's descent into unconscionable behavior constituting torture by any definition, legal or colloquial."

The legal memoranda show how the US government internalized the view that the Third Geneva Convention rules on who is a soldier, spy, terrorist, or innocent, and how the issue is to be decided by a competent tribunal, was not applicable to what they planned. Against the advice of Secretary of State Powell and the long history of US policy and practice in this area, the White House proceeded to legitimate torture. In a memorandum to President Bush, White House Counsel Alberto Gonzales argued:

"[T]he nature of the new war [on terrorism] places a high premium on . . . the ability to quickly obtain information from captured terrorists and their sponsors in order to avoid further atrocities". . . He said this "new paradigm renders obsolete Geneva's strict limitations on questioning of enemy prisoners" and made other Geneva provisions "quaint" . . . Seven months later Assistant Attorney General Jay S. Bybee hardened the "constitutionally dubious" argument into a flat assertion of presidential immunity from legal restraints on torture. In a memorandum to White House Counsel Gonzales, Bybee said that in a war like the one against terror, "the information gained from interrogations may prevent future attacks by foreign enemies. Any effort to apply [the criminal law against torture] in a manner that interferes with the President's direction of such core war matters as the detention and interrogation of enemy combatants thus would be unconstitutional." The argument got further elaboration in a memorandum of March 6, 2003 . . . from an ad hoc group of government lawyers to Secretary of Defense Donald Rumsfeld . . . "Congress may no more regulate the President's ability to detain and interrogate enemy combatants," it argued, "than it may regulate his ability to direct troop movements on the battlefield." So presidential power overrode the International Convention Against Torture, to which the United States is a party, and the Congressional statute enforcing the convention. (Lewis 2005: xv)

Donald Gregg, a former national security adviser to the US government, subsequently wrote an article in the *New York Times* in which he made it clear that torture of enemy combatants is a product of this counter-law rather than of a few bad apples in the military. In his view, the legal memoranda "cleared the way for the horrors that have been revealed in Iraq, Afghanistan and Guantánamo and make a mockery of the administration's assertions that a few misguided enlisted personnel perpetuated the vile abuse of prisoners" (cited by Lewis 2005: xvi).

The legal memoranda document not only the desire to abrogate the Geneva Convention, but also strategies to place detainees beyond the reach of any court of law, and to absolve security operatives implementing the policies of liability for war crimes (Dratel 2005). The Guantánamo Bay detention camp location was chosen not only as a secure site, but also because it could be purported to be outside the jurisdiction of US courts and perhaps any other courts. Various legal analyses were undertaken "to give the policy architects and those who implemented it the benefit of the doubt on issues of intent and criminal responsibility while at the same time eagerly denying such accommodations to those at whom the policies were directed. Such piecemeal application of rights and the law is directly contrary to our principles: equal application of the law, equal justice for all, and a refusal to discriminate based on status, including nationality or religion" (ibid.: xxi).

Some aspects of this law against law have considerable support in prominent legal and academic circles (e.g., Dershowitz 2002; Ignatieff 2004; Posner 2004). For example, Posner (2004) invokes law and economics language to argue that "marginal costs" of civil liberties have increased significantly since 9/11, and that there is a need to formulate a new threshold in cost–benefit tradeoffs that preempts "Johnny-one-note civil libertarians uttering fallacious slogans" with their "bromides about free speech" and obsession over "coercive interrogation." Posner prefers the "war on" metaphors of American political culture as a way to instill precautionary logic and justify laws against law.

> It has been a commonplace since Thomas Hobbes wrote *Leviathan* that trading independence for security can be a profitable swap . . . In wartime we tolerate all sorts of curtailments of our normal liberties . . . conscription, censorship, disinformation, intrusive surveillance, or suspension of habeas corpus. A lawyer must say that this is because war is a legal status that authorizes such curtailments. But to a realist it is not war as such, but danger to the unusual degree associated with war, that justifies the curtailments. The headlong rush of science and technology has brought us to the point at which a handful of terrorists may be more dangerous than an enemy nation because the terrorists (unlike an enemy nation) may be undeterrable, may have both the desire and the ability to cause a global catastrophe, and may be able to conceal not only their plans and their whereabouts but their very existence from the world's intelligence services. (ibid.: 216, 230)

Posner's will includes legalized surveillance and restriction on a wide range of people in everyday life. For example, he feels scientists should be legally subjected to surveillance and enforceable standards of preventive security in order to preempt the threat that they will become the accomplices of bio-terrorists, unwittingly or otherwise. University students from suspect countries need to be subject to enhanced security screening. One-half of all foreign students return home, and "it is doubtful that all those who [do so have] . . . by virtue of their sojourn in the United States, become inoculated against rabid anti-Americanism" (ibid.: 232).

The USA Patriot Act includes unprecedented powers of surveillance. Based on the premise that malicious demons might be sleeping anywhere, law enforcers are given sweeping access to private spaces, places, and communication networks. In this legislation, the old model of resourceful police intelligence is replaced by one of universal suspicion that spells the end of innocence: everyone is suspect and treated as such to a degree; everyone is on a continuum of risk.

There is a legalization of access to communication and database infrastructures that might yield signs of suspicious activity, for example those of telephone companies, Internet Service Providers (ISPs), libraries, retailers (e.g., book stores, travel agencies, car dealers), and schools (e.g., under a "foreign student monitoring program"). Restrictions are eased regarding court orders and warrants to search for information. For example, court orders pertaining to telephone communications are extended to cover email and Internet communications, and to cover the entire country rather than only the judicial district in which the order is issued, which was the previous practice. ISPs are given incentives to provide access to information about their customers even without a court order. Incentives include holding them immune from legal liability if they provide such access in "good faith" with government, and offering them compensation for costs associated with their assistance.

The USA Patriot Act also provides for the widening of surveillance powers under the Foreign Intelligence Surveillance Act. For example, there is a widening of the duration of court orders, the scope of access to private sector business records, access to email, and "roving surveillance" schemes. The much laxer legal standards of the Foreign Intelligence Surveillance Act regarding physical searches, wiretaps, and access to private sector databases are extended to criminal investigations as long as domestic law enforcers can argue that there is an element of foreign intelligence gathering in their investigations.

While using the USA Patriot Act and related legislation to legalize its access to the spaces, places, and communications of other entities, the US government has simultaneously tried to draw the veil of administrative decency over its own operations. For example, in signing a November 2002 bill related to federal law enforcement activities, President Bush attached a statement regarding reporting obligations laid down by Congress in which he asserted his presidential authority "to withhold information 'the disclosure of which could impair foreign relations, the national security, the deliberative processes of the Executive, or the performance of the Executive's constitutional duties,' as defined in each case by the President" (Whitaker 2006: 153–54). There is growing recognition that this asymmetry of knowledge and power violates US First Amendment constitutional rights of free speech and access to information (Janus 2004: 579). Total information awareness is for some and not others.

This national security regime of law against law is designed to cast the net as widely as possible, identify suitable enemies, not worry about false positive identifications, drop any pretense of due process of law, and effect summary justice through incapacitation, torture, and elimination. It ignores *actus reus*, the legal principle that criminalization must be based on a specified criminal act. Indeed, there is not even a pretense of what might be termed *probabilis reus*: criminalization on the basis of actuarial knowledge of risk. There is only the law against law principle of *finus reus*: when criminalization appears necessary for national security, no other justification is needed and established legal principles are preempted, finished (Brodeur 1981; Brodeur and Leman-Langlois 2006).

In the aftermath of 9/11, the US government used a variety of other legislative maneuvers to circumvent normal legal process. While most laws against law were designed to ferret out and criminalize terrorists, there was also swift counter-law action to protect selective aspects of the economy. For example, extraordinary steps were taken to protect the airline industry, which was already in difficulty before 9/11. In addition to liabilities for the four airplanes destroyed and lives lost in 9/11, the industry suffered an immediate decrease in passenger traffic. The Air Transportation Safety and System Stabilization Act (ATSSSA), passed by Congress within twelve days of 9/11, provided a number of temporary financial measures to bail out and stabilize the industry: $5 billion direct compensation; $10 billion loan guarantees for both 9/11 costs and any subsequent terrorist attack; a $100 million liability cap on future terrorist attack claims; discretionary reimbursement of airline insurance premium increases; discretionary reinsurance protection; and an interim insurance program (Campbell 2002; Standard and Poor's 2002: 4).

The most extraordinary provision of the ATSSSA was the Victims' Compensation Fund (VCF). This provision was designed to compensate victims of 9/11 in a direct and timely manner, as an alternative to the tort liability system. Anyone who suffered personal injury in the terrorist attacks of 9/11, or beneficiaries of those who experienced wrongful death, could apply to the VCF. Since the claim was payable by the US Treasury, the VCF was not really a "fund" or insurance but simply a contribution to disaster relief. The VCF payment was reduced by collateral sources available to the claimant, such as life and health insurance, pension benefits, and specified charitable donations the victim received from the Liberty Fund or similar sources.

If the victim or beneficiary opted for the VCF, they were required to relinquish any right to sue through the tort liability system. As such, the VCF arrangement was consistent with the many other laws against law following 9/11 that short-circuited legal process or avoided it altogether. The events of 9/11 precipitated *the* mass tort of all time, and the

VCF provided an alternative that would preempt the extra-ordinary legal, time, and psychic costs of litigation. The fact that if litigated, all cases would be assigned to one court, the Southern District of New York, ensured a crippling backlog of cases. Indeed, cases from the 1993 terrorist attack on the World Trade Center were still pending in this court when the 2001 attack occurred!

The VCF was the "purest" no-fault statute ever adopted in the United States. The statute was drafted by leading repre-sentatives of the plaintiffs' bar, a group that would benefit enormously from litigation. The plaintiffs' bar cooperated in the VCF process because it felt it had no choice but to do so. Indeed, it not only helped to develop the VCF alternative to the tort system, but also offered free legal services to victims and their families as a gesture of solidarity.

On one view the VCF was "an unprecedented social welfare relief program" (Campbell 2002: 211). It was the first direct obligation federal bill since Medicare 36 years earlier, social security being the only other direct obligation provi-sion in US history. The official in charge of the program called it an "Unprecedented expression of compassion on the part of the American people to the victims and their families . . . designed to bring some measure of financial relief to those most devastated by the events of September 11 . . . [and] an example of how Americans rally around the less fortunate" (ibid.: 15–16).

The VCF was also an example of how Americans rally around their less fortunate industries, providing a form of socialism for business enterprise. The VCF was a crucial ingredient in efforts to bail out the airline industry, as signi-fied by the fact that it was included in the ATSSSA. The ATSSSA capped airline liability for 9/11 to their insurance coverage at the time. In effect, the VCF provided a federal immunity to commercial entities (airlines) for state-based tort claims, dispossessing the states of legal jurisdiction. In the legal opinion of some, the fact that taking the VCF option preempted the victim's right to sue also made it unconstitutional.

Many other strategic uses of law have developed in the ongoing "war on terror" campaign. For example, Welch (2002, 2005) reveals how the US Justice Department initially charges some terrorist suspects with immigration infractions under civil law in order to circumvent the due process standards of criminal law that might be invoked by defense attorneys if there were criminal proceedings. Indeed, under US immigration law, unlike criminal law, those arrested are not entitled to legal aid attorneys and many are thereby immediately rendered defenseless.

Counter-law II: Surveillant Assemblages

As we have already documented, laws against law help to support the surveillant assemblages of national security. However, these assemblages are based on additional foundations. Existing technologies are reconfigured and new technologies are invented to facilitate surveillance. Similarly, existing organizational arrangements are reconfigured and new organizations created to enhance surveillance and visibility. These technological and organizational transformations in turn mobilize both private sector entities and individual citizens as an integral part of the national security surveillant assemblages.

The technological infrastructures for surveillance have greatly expanded in the name of national security (Levi and Wall 2004; Amoore and De Goede 2005; Bennett 2005). Caught up in the marketing of (in)security following 9/11, organizations bought into an array of surveillance technologies aimed at monitoring people and lethal weapons. According to the publisher of the new *Homeland Defense Journal*, "The Sept. 11 attacks will be the biggest catalyst for US technological innovation since the Soviets launched their Sputnik Satellite in 1957, spurring the competing US space program" (Krane 2002: D16). In the year following 9/11, technology companies opened sales offices in Washington and staffed them with retired military and security officials. The big players included Microsoft, 1BM, Dell Computers, and Oracle Corporation, which proposed a national identity card and database. Smaller firms also saw the opportunity for expansion. For example, "Visage Technology Inc., a small Massachusetts company that makes drivers' licenses, used a post-Sept. 11 investment of $25 million to purchase a biometrics firm, open an office with a view of the US Capitol and recruit John Gannon, a former deputy director for intelligence at the CIA, as a board member. The company hopes to sell face recognition kiosks to government" (ibid.).

There is of course a long history of developing the latest technologies of surveillance and identification in the name of national security. For example, J. Edgar Hoover gained control of the fingerprinting system as part of establishing the FBI as a domestic surveillance agency in the 1920s (Cole 2001: 246–7). Hoover's dream of total information awareness "saw universal fingerprinting as the key to a national web of individualized surveillance, under his personal control" (ibid.). While his dream was never fully realized, Hoover did manage to develop the largest fingerprint file in the world through the requirement of the Alien Registration Act (1940) that all immigrants and other "aliens" be fingerprinted. "Hoover returned fingerprinting to its origins, as a mechanism for state monitoring and surveillance of citizens, especially those deemed foreign, politically radical, or otherwise dangerous" (ibid.).

The key difference in the contemporary era is the capacity to combine different surveillance technologies into a surveillant assemblage, yielding new forms of knowledge and control. A single surveillance technology such as a CCTV camera is usually a mile wide but only an inch deep because it does not in itself provide detailed knowledge about the person whose behavior is being momentarily captured and made visible. However, when combined with other technologies – for example, combining digitized CCTV systems with computer databases – depth and intensity of surveillance are achieved. In particular, new computer-based systems of data matching and data mining create new patterns of human traces – a person's "data double" (Haggerty and Ericson 2000) – that can identify them as a particular type of person, suspicious or otherwise. Many surveillant assemblages that were originally developed in commercial contexts to market segment consumers are also models and sources for population data potentially useful in national security contexts (Amoore and De Goede 2005; Turow 2006; Gandy 2006). For example, insurers use data matching and data mining systems to identify "prospects as suspects" (Ericson, Doyle, and Barry 2003: chap. 7) – insurance applicants they should not insure – as well as those who are suspected of making fraudulent insurance claims (ibid.: chap. 9). The technological infrastructures and algorithmic models used in this commercial context of identifying suspects have applications to any effort to identify suspicious behavior.

The new surveillant assemblages of national security post-9/11 seek both breadth and depth. Breadth is to be achieved through CCTV systems that aim to protect key urban venues in ways similar to the systems that proliferated in the UK in the wake of IRA terrorism. For example, "[a]ided by a federal grant of $5.1 million, the city of Chicago is spending $8.6 million on a system of smart video cameras, equipped with software that will raise the alarm when the cameras spot people loitering, wandering in circles, hanging around outside public buildings, or stopping their cars on the shoulders of highways" (Raban 2005: 25). The aim is to ensure that "Anyone walking in public [is] to be almost constantly watched" (*New York Times*, September 21, 2004). Depth is signified by the very name of the FBI's CARNIVORE "super search engine which, when installed on Internet service providers, is capable of trolling through email traffic and flagging communications of interest to the agency based on the identities of senders and receivers, keyword recognition, and so forth" (Whitaker 2006: 143). Breadth and depth are achieved through surveillant assemblages that cast nets for all manner of possible threats to homeland security, hoping to land big fish as well as the small fry.

The Department of Homeland Security is the co-sponsor, with the FBI and the Justice Department, of Operation Predator, intended to track down pedophiles via their use of the Internet – presumably because pedophiles, whose civil liberties are held in high esteem by almost nobody, are indeed guinea pigs for a more sweeping exercise in cyberspying that might net terrorists . . . our e-mails, shared files, and visits to suspect Internet sites are obviously more likely to identify us as al-Qaedist than any tendency we may exhibit to wander in circles in front of tall buildings. When FBI director Robert Mueller announced that Operation Predator "sends a clear message that the digital environment will not offer sanctuary to those pedophiles who lurk in peer-to-peer networks. We will identify you. We will bring you to justice," it seems improbable, given the DHS's involvement in the scheme, that he had pedophiles only, or mainly, in mind. (Raban 2005: 25; see also Janus 2004)

While electronic surveillance technologies have the breadth to traverse organizational boundaries and the depth to make visible previously unknown spaces and population profiles, they do not do so on their own. Organizational change occurs in conjunction with technological change, and the transition is not straightforward.

The US government created the Department of Homeland Security as an umbrella organization for bringing closer together a number of different security-related organizations, including the FBI and CIA. This organizational change is a means of trying to break down divisions between different government agencies that have worked semi-autonomously and at times in competition and conflict with each other. It also serves to advance the conflation of war abroad and war on threats to domestic security at home, including but not limited to the war on terrorism. Furthermore, it seeks to break down barriers that separate databases in different government agencies, in order to bring together information from counterintelligence investigations of foreign threats and ordinary domestic criminal law enforcement. The view is that borderless threats require borderless law enforcement across organizational entities nationally and internationally, and across categories of citizens and non-citizens.

The US government imagines a global surveillance state. This was symbolized in the Total Information Awareness (TIA) Program logo of an eye at the apex of a pyramid scanning the globe, accompanied by the slogan *Scientia ist potentia*, knowledge is power. The TIA program was housed in the Defense Advance Research Projects Agency (DARPA) and headed by Vice Admiral John Poindexter, infamously known for his involvement in the Iran Contra affair. DARPA's TIA plans for omniscience met with resistance across the political spectrum on the grounds that they signified the end of privacy. The TIA began to backtrack on its more ambitious claims; however, further concern was raised when Poindexter proposed a terrorism risk catastrophe bond market in which investors would speculate on future terrorist activity and profit if a catastrophe did not occur within the period during which the bond was held. The hope was that this futures market in terrorism would extend surveillance capacity because investors would demand better data to predict terrorism futures, and these data could in turn be used in the national security effort. For many, including then Deputy Defense Secretary Donald Rumsfeld, this proposal was the final indicator that the TIA program had become a political liability. Poindexter was dismissed and the program was terminated.

As Whitaker (2006) observes, the termination of the formal TIA program did not in any way stop other TIA-like initiatives. For example, DARPA also created Lifelog, "which seeks to amass every conceivable bit of information that can be gathered from every source (including audiovisual sensors and biomedical monitors) about an individual's life, and download it all into a vast, searchable database" (ibid.: 158–9). In the spring of 2003, the FBI and CIA jointly created the Terrorist Threat Integration Center to integrate information from all available foreign and domestic sources for possible signs of terrorism.

The effort to connect the surveillance infrastructures of national security and domestic security has led to an organizational and operational blurring between them (see also chapter 5). For example, in at least 75 cases identified by the Foreign Intelligence Surveillance Act review court, the FBI was said to have misled the court in its justifications for electronic surveillance (Whitaker 2006). In particular, the FBI justified electronic surveillance applications in the name of foreign threats to national security but used intelligence gathered for bringing charges in domestic criminal cases. The US Justice Department appealed this decision to the new Foreign Intelligence Surveillance Court of Review, and this court concluded that amendments to FISA under the USA Patriot Act permit such criminal prosecutions as long as the surveillance also has a significant foreign intelligence purpose. Attorney General John Ashcroft declared that this was a new legal permit for criminal investigators and intelligence agents to collaborate, and announced plans to intensify covert surveillance operators through designated intelligence prosecutors in each federal court district as well as a new intelligence warrant unit in the FBI. Ashcroft later "revealed that he had personally authorized secret electronic surveillance and physical searches without immediate court oversight in 170 'emergency' cases since the 9/11 attacks – more than triple the emergency searches authorized by other attorneys general over the past 20 years (Schmidt 2003)" (Whitaker 2006: 151).

There was a simultaneous effort to break down barriers to surveillance between government and private sector organizations, and among private sector organizations themselves. This effort was based on the view that Little Brother collaboration will yield more than the sum of its parts, a Big Brother surveillance infrastructure of total information awareness. The process began with the 9/11 investigation itself, which relied heavily on the data doubles of suspects in credit card, telephone, and air miles databases. It continued with an expansion of enabling regulations and technologies for surveillance in a wide range of private sector contexts. New air transportation information systems and screening procedures were developed to track the movement of people and goods

(Brodeur and Leman-Langlois 2006). Money trail surveillance by financial institutions, already in place regarding the drug trade and other forms of organized crime, was enhanced. With the aid of the USA Patriot Act provisions, financial institutions are enlisted in the government's money trail surveillance program on threat of severe sanction, including seizure of assets, for failure to cooperate. Many other fields of business enterprise have been enlisted, for example in creating surveillant assemblages that might identify financiers of terrorist activity or purveyors of nuclear, biological, and chemical materials.

On a different level, there is an effort to mobilize entire industries because of their key role at the foundation of surveillance infrastructures. One such industry is private security, which, because of its special legal access to private spaces on behalf of property owners, has a unique position as frontline "eyes and ears" in the national security effort.

Private security was a fast-growing and substantial part of the US economy prior to 9/11. One estimate of private security spending in the United States during the 1990s is $40 billion annually, with almost half devoted to private police staff and the remainder to preventive security technologies (Anderson 1999). The Organization of Economic Cooperation and Development (OECD) projected that private security would expand considerably following 9/11, with possible effects on economic growth and productivity: "A doubling of private security might reduce the level of potential output by 0.6 per cent after five years and the level of private sector productivity by 0.8 per cent" (2002: 136). The New York City Comptroller reported that, in 2001, over 1 percent of all workers in New York City were security guards. He observed that in the four years following the 1993 World Trade Center (WTC) bombing, there was a 22 percent increase in spending on private security guards. Assuming the same level of growth over four years following 9/11, the additional cost would be about $1 billion. The Comptroller also noted that some of this post-9/11 increase in private security would be driven by contract stipulations of the insurance industry.

"Security-related spending, however, is a cost that may be seen as an investment because it helps to narrow the future property/casualty [insurance] premium between NYC and other cities" (Thompson 2002: 22).

Joh (2004) documents the role of private security operatives in various contexts of terrorism-related security. For example, Disney World in Florida has an 800-member security force attuned to the post-9/11 environment. On the eve of the invasion of Iraq, the Federal Aviation Authority granted Disney World, as well as Disneyland in California, a no-fly zone as a precautionary measure. In an ethnographic study of policing in a large commercial complex in Manhattan, Joh found ongoing relations between city police and private security operatives regarding terrorism-related security threats.

At the same time private security operatives are sometimes viewed as a source of threat because of their intimate knowledge of, and access to, critical infrastructures, and the fact that they are often ill-trained, poorly equipped, inadequately regulated, and at the margins of the labor market. Private security operatives are said to be in need of intensified surveillance even as they are embraced as essential to surveillance infrastructures.

As indicated in the statement above by the New York City Comptroller, the private insurance industry is also a key player in the development of surveillance infrastructures. It has unique capacities to govern other organizations through contracts which define the meaning of terrorism and specify the security measures the insured must put in place to help preempt terrorism.

In the insurance world there is a marketplace of definitions of terrorism, open to negotiation depending on how insurers wish to participate in a specific terrorism risk with specific clients. For example, a reinsurance company I studied (Ericson and Doyle 2004a: chapter 5) created a very broad definition of terrorism as an opening position with which to negotiate contracts with primary insurers and in turn their clients. An executive involved in these negotiations said that, "we might throw out these words, then someone else might throw out another set of words to define terrorism, and we work through it . . . Everybody usually has a different point of view on things, which are guided maybe by corporate risk appetites and such." A colleague added, "There are as many terrorist exclusions in the marketplace as there are ceding companies. So at last count I think we were above 250 [companies]. So there's probably 250 some-odd wordings for terrorism exclusion in the current marketplace." He stated that the final definition of terrorism settled on for a given insurance contract depends on the other terms of the contract. "There's a lot of negotiation that goes back and forth with the companies depending upon our participation in the program, limits offered, attachment points, whatever, where we may come off some of those [definitions that exclude specific aspects of terrorism] objectives . . . Sub-limits are one of the ways to obviously reduce your exposures, to reduce your limits, then maybe we can give a little bit on the wording."

Insurance contracts also place terrorism-related preventive security requirements on the insured, with the capacity for detailed, on-site inspections for compliance. A senior executive of a reinsurance company explained to me how 9/11 changed the commercial risk underwriting environment in this regard.

It's impacted our whole underwriting process, where, before we renew reinsurance contracts, we ask for a lot more information from our clients . . . Stuff that before nobody would care to find out or ask about. Now it's being asked by the reinsurer, and in turn the insurance company needs to find out from the insured and make sure that information is kept up to date . . . You are also dealing with a very "live" [hard] market. This [9/11] came at the end of a very soft market. Typically in a soft market people don't dare ask a lot of questions, the client goes somewhere else . . . [T]he market started turning before 9/11 – 9/11 really pushed it up in a much more dramatic fashion. Now it's OK to ask ten, twenty, thirty questions before you renew your account, and get that information.

Another reinsurance executive said that his company was questioning ceding insurers about their clients' preventive security arrangements with respect to terrorism. This new vigilance was exercised in relation to all commercial reinsurance under consideration, but intensified if the buildings involved were deemed symbolic targets of terrorism.

> One of the first questions we ask our underwriters toward their clients is, "What do your clients do about the terrorism exposure?" . . . There's things you can do on an underwriting basis, on a loss prevention basis . . . to avoid a terrorist act. For example, you own a building and you have a security guard at the entrance, that will prevent a lot of unwanted people from wandering around the building. The WTC, the top door to the roof had been locked for some reason. A good loss control person, had he or she done a review, would have noticed the door probably should not have been locked, lives would have been saved . . . We have developed a number of detailed questionnaires . . . [regarding] accessibility, security, after-event evacuation procedures, those types of things.. . . And this target-class list . . . main targets of terrorism, many of those [questionnaires] have to do with security . . . precautions that are taken. We're just trying to limit the accessibility of these targets to outsiders, to people that we don't want in there. Inside concerns, how are you monitoring the inside of your plant?

In direct underwriting situations, some insurers send loss control engineers to field sites with detailed questionnaires addressing terrorism-related security arrangements. This assessment is used to decide whether terrorism coverage should be excluded entirely, or included at particular sublimits and prices. Agreed levels of surveillance personnel and technologies are negotiated in this process.

Insurance company executives I interviewed offered various examples of increased vigilance about commercial operations. A reinsurance company executive used the example of a trucking company and said that before 9/11 the drivers' licenses may have been checked annually for authenticity but now "we may come up with a recommendation that if you want us to reinsure your business, we want you to *insist* on having drivers' records checked on a quarterly basis. Because there is turnover and you never know who is going to drive a truck on a particular day. So in those cases, we would make a proactive check that they do so, and we would come back and follow up . . . We can certainly get off that business, or break the contract, if we don't like what we see." Another interviewee illustrated the point with "the courier company that couriers packages, or a small airlines company, I wouldn't necessarily exclude terrorism but I would ask questions. 'What have you done since 9/11 to increase your security? Do you check what's in the packages before they board the plane? How are your pilots trained? How do you screen people?' "

There is no doubt that business enterprise became more vigilant after 9/11. In a survey of chief executive officers asking them to identify "post 9/11 precautions," the following were mentioned most frequently: review of disaster plan (90 percent), background checks on contractors (51 percent), background checks on employees (39 percent), limiting staff on a single flight (36 percent), and considering alternative office space (35 percent) (Insurance Information Institute www.iii.org.25, April 2002). Organizations were urged to examine building infrastructures regarding their physical security features. With visions of the *Titanic* as *the* infallible technology that failed, it was pointed out that the WTC had been touted as "collapse proof." Those contemplating future high-rise construction were implored to take note of total loss risks, while those responsible for existing buildings were asked to address remedial measures that might reduce such risks. On a mundane level, advice flowed on the need for target hardening. "For instance, installing a film across windows can reduce the risk of injuries from flying glass. By putting a barrier around a building, a company can keep potentially dangerous cars and trucks away" (Green 2002).

The US government has also sought mobilization of all citizens in the national security surveillance effort. This mobilization is spearheaded by the US Department of Homeland Security (DHS) and its partner, The America Prepared Campaign, Inc. (APC) (www.ready.gov; www.americaprepared.org).

DHS has published a 200-page manual for citizens entitled, *Are You Ready? An In-Depth Guide to Citizen Preparedness*. This manual covers preventive measures and recovery plans regarding a wide range of catastrophic risks, including terrorism. In the section on terrorism, a photograph of the smoldering remnants of the WTC is placed in the center of a long definition and description of terrorism. This material makes it clear that terrorism refers to a very broad range of criminal activity and that the response to terrorism inevitably entails more criminalization.

> Recent technological advances and ongoing international political unrest are components of the increased risk to national security . . . Terrorism is the use of force or violence against persons or property in violation of the criminal laws of the United States for purposes of intimidation, coercion or ransom. Terrorists often use threats to:
>
> • Create fear among the public
> • Try to convince citizens that their government is powerless to prevent terrorism
> • Get immediate publicity for their causes
>
> Acts of terrorism include threats of terrorism; assassinations; kidnappings; hijackings; bomb scares and bombings; cyber attacks (computer-based); and the use of chemical, biological, nuclear and radiological weapons.
>
> High-risk targets for acts of terrorism include military and civilian government facilities, international airports, large cities, and high-profile landmarks. Terrorists might also target large public gatherings, water and food supplies, utilities, and corporate centers. Further, terrorists are capable of spreading fear by sending explosives or chemical or biological agents through the mail. (DHS 2004: 145. 148)

With targets as vague as "large cities," "large public gatherings," "water and food supplies," and "corporate centers," the citizen must be ready for the malicious demon of terrorism in all places at all times. The whole world is to be watched as if one is always in an airport security environment. Thus, *Are You Ready?* recommends adoption of precautionary logic at home, work, and play. For example, there is the admonition to "Take precautions when traveling. Be aware of conspicuous or unusual behavior. Do not accept packages from strangers. Do not leave luggage unattended. You should promptly report unusual behavior, suspicious or unattended packages, and strange devices to the police or security personnel" (ibid.: 148). The minutiae include 14 signs of what might make parcels suspicious.

- Are unexpected or from someone unfamiliar to you
- Have no return address, or have one that can't be verified as legitimate
- Are marked with restrictive endorsements such as "Personal," "Confidential," or "Do not x-ray"
- Have protruding wires or aluminum foil, strange odors, or stains
- Show a city or state in the postmark that doesn't match the return address
- Are of unusual weight given their size, or are lopsided or oddly shaped
- Are marked with threatening language
- Have inappropriate or unusual labeling
- Have excessive postage or packaging material, such as masking tape and string
- Have misspellings of common words
- Are addressed to someone no longer with your organization or are otherwise outdated
- Have incorrect titles or titles without a name
- Are not addressed to a specific person
- Have hand-written or poorly typed addresses

DHS has developed a Security Advisory System to mobilize citizens into precautionary activity. Treating the uncertainty of terrorism as if it is a risk, five threat levels are identified: severe, high, elevated, guarded, low (figure 2.1). "Risk includes both the probability of an attack occurring and its potential gravity. Threat conditions may be assigned for the entire nation, or they may be set for a particular geographic area or industrial sector. At each threat condition, government entities and the private sector, including businesses and schools, would implement a corresponding set of 'protective measures' to further reduce vulnerability or increase response capability during a period of heightened alert" (ibid.: 174).

As indicated in figure 2.1, citizens are to become more suspicious and vigilant at each threat level. Even when the alchemists of risk in the DHS give the green light to go about business normally because there is a low risk, normality includes joining community surveillance organizations such as Citizens Corps, Volunteers in Police Service, and Neighborhood Watch, and taking courses in emergency preparedness. This is because "There is always a risk of terrorist threat. Each threat condition assigns a level of alert appropriate to the increasing level of terrorist attacks" (ibid.).

The DHS and APC collaborate with a wide range of organizations in business enterprise, mass media, education, and communities to mobilize citizens as agents of surveillance. APC declares on its website that it "is an all-out drive to galvanize Americans to prepare themselves and their families." Skepticism, cynicism, and resistance among citizens is to be overcome through communication strategies that make people appreciate that knowledge is power, and that safety measures with respect to terrorism can be normalized in the same way as countless other such measures in everyday life (cf. Hunt 2003).

APC's website observes that citizens have an inclination to be dubious about the threat, given past US government efforts to spend trillions of dollars of citizens' money on the elusive pursuit of malicious demons. However, the war on terrorism is different because in this case the enemy is real.

Severe Risk

Complete all recommended actions at lower levels.
Listen to local emergency management officials.
Stay tuned to TV or radio for current information/instructions.
Be prepared to shelter or evacuate, as instructed.
Expect traffic delays and restrictions.
Provide volunteer services only as requested.
Contact your school/business to determine status of work day.

High Risk

Complete recommended steps at lower levels.
Exercise caution when traveling, pay attention to travel advisories.
Review your family emergency plan and make sure all family members know what to do.
Be Patient. Expect some delays, baggage searches and restrictions at public buildings.
Check on neighbors or others that might need assistance in an emergency.

Elevated Risk

Complete recommended steps at levels green and blue.
Ensure disaster supplies are stocked and ready.
Check telephone numbers in family emergency plan and update as necessary.
Develop alternate routes to/from work or school and practice them.
Continue to be alert for suspicious activity and report it to authorities.

Guarded Risk

Complete recommended steps at level green.
Review stored disaster supplies and replace items that are outdated.
Be alert to suspicious activity and report it to proper authorities.

Low Risk

Develop a family emergency plan. Share it with family and friends, and practice the plan.
Visit www.Ready.gov for help creating a plan.
Create an "Emergency Supply Kit" for your household.
Be informed. Visit www.Ready.gov or obtain a copy of "Preparing Makes Sense,
Get Ready Now" by calling 1-800-BE-READY.
Know where to shelter and how to turn off utilities (power, gas, water) to your home.
Examine volunteer opportunities in your community, such as Citizens Corps,
Volunteers in Police Service, Neighborhood Watch or others, and donate your time.
Consider completing an American Red Cross first aid or CPR course, or Community
Emergency Response Team (CERT) course.

Figure 2.1   *Citizen guidance on the Homeland Security Advisory
System*
Source: Adapted from Department of Homeland Security
(2004: 175)

Unlike the catastrophe of a nuclear war and the fruitless Cold War civil defense campaigns that accompanied that threat – *the consequences of certain kinds of terrorist attacks can be significantly mitigated if fear and panic are replaced by knowledgeable preparation* . . . A citizen education and preparedness campaign in the September 12th Era is not an abstract, feel good program. It will lessen psychic and economic damage. *And it will save lives. It is a real line of defense* . . . *Everything the Campaign does will have to overcome the obstacles of complacency, cynicism and ridicule.* Those behind the campaign know that they cannot fully avoid these reactions. They intend to face them head on by engaging the best creative and research minds in the country to craft messages that will break through. The Campaign must convey urgency, without fear. It must galvanize, not terrify.

APC Communications try to normalize precautionary measures with respect to terrorism as no different than what is already taken for granted in other safety environments, such as having smoke detectors in the home and wearing a seatbelt while driving. "Similar to the approach used by the seat belt and recycling campaigns of recent years, the objective of all America Prepared Communications is to build awareness of preparedness as a philosophy, to encourage Americans to integrate thinking about preparedness into their everyday lives, and to provide specific information and direction about actions to take to achieve peace of mind."

One APC ad campaign appeals to consumer identities. Each ad features a particular consumer item in a household closet or cabinet that has been consumed in excess: shoes, lipstick, compact disks, neckties. The picture of excessive consumption is overlain with "But Do You Have A [naming a security item]? READY.GOV. You have the things that make you happy. Get the things that make you prepared. Get a kit. Brought to you by The America Prepared Campaign Inc." One such ad is shown in illustration 2.1. The message is that overspent Americans (Schor 1998) should get their priorities right and redirect more of their disposable income to security

Illustration 2.1 *Advertisement: But Do You Have a Whistle?*
Reproduced by permission of Allison Phinney, Verified Identity
Pass, Inc.

products. This act is depicted as both good sense and good citizenship.

DHS and APC also operate through key institutions to galvanize citizens in the war on terror. One such institution is schools, which are seen as both vulnerable to terrorism and a site for mobilization of precaution against terrorist activity. For example, APC developed a Standard and Poor's-like rating of the 20 largest school districts in the US on their preparedness for a terrorist attack or other emergency. The school districts were graded as best, good, needs improvement, and failing, with the results published in a 70-page document and on the APC website. This shaming exercise was aimed at redirecting resources away from other education system expenditures and toward security products. While the chair of the APC states that one should not blame the victim – impoverished school districts that have already lost out through cutbacks and other neo-liberal government security spending priorities – he then proceeds to do precisely that. "Those who are failing should be embarrassed into improving. Indeed although there are no villains here, if the overall conclusions of the 9/11 Commission are to be taken seriously, we should hope that those responsible for schools that should be doing more will be embarrassed out of claiming a lack of resources or other priorities as excuses for not acting." Indeed it is especially embarrassing to be publicly scolded for not doing enough to protect the safety of children, even if it is at the expense of their education.

Another initiative used school children to mobilize their parents in the war on terror. Children were enlisted as "deputies" to recruit their parents for an educational visit to www.ready.gov, purchase of an emergency kit, and completion of a family communication plan in the event of an emergency. Two competitions were held, one for the school with the greatest number of parents enlisted in absolute terms, and one for the school with the greatest number of parents enlisted in proportionate or ratio terms, taking into account the school size. The prize in each case was $10,000 for the school library fund and having DHS Secretary Tom Ridge as school principal for a day.

DHS also mobilizes citizens through the newly created umbrella of Citizens Corps. Citizens Corps seeks to coordinate myriad surveillance and emergency response organizations already in place: police volunteers, Neighborhood Watch, Fire Corps, medical reserve corps, Senior Corps, AmeriCorps, Learn and Serve America, emergency response teams, and many others. "The mission of Citizen Corps is to harness the power of every individual through *education, training and volunteer service* to make communities safer, stronger and better prepared to respond to the threats of terrorism, crime, public health issues, and disasters of all kinds." This mission requires "*Personal responsibility.* Developing a household preparedness plan and disaster supplies kits, observing home health and safety practices, implementing disaster mitigation measures, and participating in crime prevention and reporting." As of March 2005, DHS claimed to have established 55 state and territory Citizen Corps Councils and 1,608 county, local, and tribal Citizen Corps Councils serving 189 million people, two-thirds of the US population.

There are many other accounts of community organizations forming around terrorism as a national security threat. For example, operating under the motto, "Watching America with Pride, Not Prejudice," and using the acronym CAT eyes, the Community Anti-Terrorism Training Institute formed as an "anti-terrorist citizen informant program [and is] being adapted by local police departments throughout the East Coast and parts of the Midwest" (Takei 2003). Commenting upon this development, Whitaker (2006: 159–60) observes that "The program's founder ambitiously envisions an eventual 100 million informers, a ratio of watchers to watched of about one to two, as compared with the East German *stasi* ratio of one to eight."

As indicated by the above "mission" and "personal responsibility" statements of Citizen Corps, DHS and APC initiatives are not limited to terrorism as a national security threat. Rather, they address myriad domestic security threats and problems, a point that is taken up in more detail in chapter 5. DHS and APC websites and published materials make it clear that while terrorism is the primary spur to intensified homeland security, there are many other threats to homeland security: bullying, child abuse, drunk driving, Internet-based threats, television-based threats, rape, substance abuse, tobacco abuse, and family communication breakdown, to name a few. "Governing through terrorism" (cf. Simon 1997, 2006; Ferguson 2005; Altheide 2006; Welch 2006) mobilizes citizens against the uncertainties of many other "terrors" in everyday life.

The Two Leviathans

Jihadist terrorism is a real threat. National security efforts to address this threat produce myths. These myths in turn constitute new realities of crime, risk, and uncertainty.

The war on terror perpetuates myths that seem more associated with the Leviathan of the biblical social imaginary. First, there is a belief that the Jihadist Leviathan is a fearless demon bent on death and destruction. Its power to create tsunami-like waves of devastation is underpinned by imaginary networks that are global in their reach. Second, the entire terrorist movement can be toppled if only the heads of its mastermind monsters can be decapitated. During the 2004 presidential election debates on television, even the Democratic Party candidate John Kerry was scripted to repeat at many junctures, "We will *kill* the terrorists. We will *kill* the terrorists. We will *kill* the terrorists." Third, there is a need for preemptive war abroad in the name of preventing attacks at home. National security cannot be separated from global security. Fourth, there is a new doctrine of *parens patriae* regarding homeland security: citizens are children in need of constant protection from danger, precautionary moral lessons, and surveillance.

These myths of the war on terror constitute new realities. There is the reality of counter-law I, laws against law, which undermine the principles, standards, and procedures of democratic legal institutions that have been foundational to the enactment of the liberal social imaginary. There is the reality of counter-law II, surveillant assemblages that not only counteract democratic legal institutions but also substitute a new basis for governing that is patently undemocratic in its mobilization of categorical suspicion, suspicion by association, discrimination, decreased privacy, and exclusion.

Happily there has been some democratic resistance. There are mounting court cases and some legal decisions freeing some terrorist suspects and placing some limits on laws against law (Janus 2004: 579). There was successful resistance to the original Total Information Awareness initiatives (Whitaker 2006). But the war on terror continues to use both forms of counter-law more or less unabated, to the point where the USA begins to resemble the Leviathan of the biblical social imaginary more than the Leviathan of the liberal social imaginary (Ferguson 2005). Indeed, given US aspirations to be a global Leviathan, its myths of terror – malicious demons, leaders to be decapitated, wars to be fought abroad in the name of security at home, and the need for *parens patriae* – extend around the world, accompanied by the new realities of counter-laws I and II.

As we have already seen, the national security regime of counter-law reaches into other fields of security provision and in turn draws upon them. In the USA and elsewhere, precautionary logic and its embodiment in the two forms of counter-law were well entrenched in other fields of security long before 9/11. At the same time, these other fields of security have taken on new forms in the wake of 9/11.

3
Social Security

Social Benefits Fraud and the Politics of Uncertainty

National security is widely regarded as *the* field in which criminalization through counter-law is required. Under neoliberal governments, social security has emerged as another field in which criminalization through counter-law is deemed necessary. Ashworth (2003: 34) asks, "What kinds of justifications for extending the criminal law beyond direct victimizing harms may be accepted? There are some general obligations of citizens that are so important that the criminal sanction may be justified to reinforce them. A core of offenses against state security may be justified on these grounds, as may offenses against the taxation and benefits system, so long as the thrust of the minimalist principle (last resort, significantly reprehensible conduct) is kept in view."

Over the course of the 20th century, Western nation-states expanded their social security benefits systems based on an ethos of spreading risk, solidarity, and welfare. For example, disability insurance arose as an important institution for addressing the uncertainties of routine engagement with science and technology, especially while at work and driving. Seen as an unfortunate by-product of modern technological progress, personal injury accidents were met with compassionate compensation to victims. Income support schemes such as unemployment insurance and welfare benefits were devised to help those who experience the uncertainties of local labor markets and health-related problems that impair their earning capacities. Ideally, these social security programs ensure that people do not become totally destitute, and therefore more criminally inclined, and thus alleviate the need for expenditures on other forms of security such as the police and criminal justice system.

At the beginning of the 21st century, social security systems are strained and part of the politics of uncertainty. This politics is focused on the capacity to know appropriate levels of social security benefits. The capacity to know is limited in two interconnected ways. First, in many fields of health and welfare provision, the medical and human sciences have very limited ability to assess a person's incapacity and need for benefits. Second, there is uncertainty about how to frame the benefits system in sustainable ways: how can the system ensure reasonable benefits without mortgaging the lives of future generations through debt financing?

In neo-liberal regimes, the dominant response is to reduce benefits by both limiting eligible disabilities and restricting the terms and conditions of benefits where eligibility remains. Benefits are constructed as temporary, exceptional, and abnormal. Integral to this construction is a strategy of treating some disability and welfare statuses as if they are criminal. This criminal association is meant to convey that the person receiving social benefits is a social enigma, someone to be stigmatized and scrutinized for being a drain on collective prosperity. It legitimates treating everyone in the status as a potential source of fraud, and paves the way for a regime based on laws against law and surveillant assemblages.

Many fields of social benefit provision face conundrums regarding eligibility of claimants and how to decide reasonable levels of benefits. One especially difficult area is provision for soft tissue injuries arising from vehicle accidents (mainly whiplash associated disorders [WAD]) and work accidents (mainly lower back pain associated disorders)

(Shorter 1992, 1994; Malleson 2002; Duncan 2003; Ericson and Doyle 2004a: chap. 3). There is a wide range of illnesses associated with these injuries that can rarely be assessed on the basis of directly observable evidence, and there is little consensus on what constitutes successful medical treatment. Medical practitioners, underpinned by personal injury lawyers, invent new disabilities that are easy to imagine but impossible to prove, and the meaning of disability is negotiated in each local insurance-medical-legal context.

All institutional players in the disability benefits relationship – insurers, various health professionals, and lawyers – understand that their collective micro-negotiations constitute the realities of disability in the face of uncertainty. This fact is made starkly evident in the publication of two special issues of *Recovery: A Quarterly Journal of Roadway Causes, Injuries and Healing* (1998, 1999). The first special issue is entitled "Truth." The opening editorial of this special issue declares what the truth is: "Whiplash consumes more money and probably creates more frustrations over certainty than any other injury . . . the truth – the ultimate truth – is not knowable . . . Perhaps humility in the face of the unknowable is exactly what's needed to enable us, separately and together, to step away from our fixed positions – our bastions of illusion – and communicate more effectively. Genuine dialogue can help us to function a little more practically (and truthfully) and work toward common solutions."

The second special issue is titled "The Uncertainty Principle" and opens with an editorial, "Inexplicable Conditions." Among the contributors to this special issue is Professor Hillel Somner of the University of Manitoba, who also served as medical coordinator for Manitoba Public Insurance, the government motor vehicle insurance corporation. "Nowhere else in medicine is there as large a gap between what we think we know and what we can prove as in the area of musculoskeletal disorder" (Somner 1999: 26). In fact, the gap is a chasm. Although insurance claims for whiplash form a multibillion-dollar industry, "There is no population-based study of WAD which provides an estimate of actual risk"

(British Columbia Whiplash Initiative 1997: 8). A task force on WAD, established by the Quebec government motor vehicle insurance corporation, documented that the voluminous medical literature "has been polluted by the fashion to publish biographical papers – 'what do I do in my practice' – that offer no proof of either the reliability, validity or true efficacy of the practice" (Spitzer et al. 1995: 8). Similarly, Malleson, a psychiatrist with decades of experience seeing disability claimants in clinical settings, states, "[A]lthough these articles are often published in reputable medical journals, the extensive literature is filled with scientifically spurious studies. One misleading study after another shows how doctors and lawyers managed to finesse whiplash from a trifling injury into a permanent disability that keeps both doctors and lawyers gainfully employed. One Danish doctor, for example, titled his medical journal article, 'With Whiplash, the Future Comes from Behind' [Durr 1994] . . . Much medical whiplash literature is like medieval scholasticism. It matters more that a recognized authority has affirmed something to be true than that it actually is" (Malleson 2002: 5, 109).

Workers' compensation insurers address the same uncertainties regarding spinal injuries. For example, back pain affects 80 percent of adults at some point in their lives (Sullivan, Stainblum, and Frank 1997: 20). "In the United States, it is the second most common reason for work absenteeism [and] the third leading cause of total work disability" (ibid.). The rate of lower back pain is increasing substantially, yet the etiology is uncertain.

Typically there are no specific diagnoses; no constellation of reliable physical signs (i.e. objective evidence of injury), and up until recently, little consensus on appropriate care . . . Back pain falls somewhere between an accident, injury and disease . . . The absence of a specific causal event and the emphasis placed by adjudicators on "objective" physical evidence of disease, often stands in the way of compensation, particularly with respect to soft tissue injuries . . . [It is] multifactoral in origin . . . and therefore the search for a specific precipitating event may be fruitless in the majority of cases . . . Dissatisfaction with job status, performance of repetitive, monotonous tasks and self-reported fatigue at the end of the day have also been associated with greater disability and absenteeism due to back pain. (ibid.: 20–1; see also Sullivan 2000)

The history of workers' compensation is characterized by an increasing variety of disabilities that are invisible. Compensation schemes were started in relation to visible physical injuries, but then spread to soft tissue injuries, stress, and environmental exposures. As the director of compensation services for a workers' compensation board related to me in an interview, "The Board is challenged ever more to sort out between, 'if I'm really not just feeling great, is it because my work is not making me feel great? My boss? My relationship? Or the building?' "

The conundrum facing disability benefits systems is captured in the term "somatoform": complaints by patients for which there is no apparent physical illness. Health service professionals have a propensity to underwrite culturally legitimate somatic claims for a number of reasons. First, they are socialized to be sympathetic to patients. Second, they have ongoing relationships of trust with patients that lead them to dispense helpful diagnoses and treatments routinely. Third, health service professionals are well aware of the limits of medical science. In the absence of objective evidence, they go with the flow of medical consensus as shaped by insurance benefit and legal systems. Fourth, they are backed by enormous resources, largely from public and private insurance schemes, that facilitate invention of diagnoses and treatments that seem legitimate at the time. Treatments proliferate to the point where they make the diagnoses to which they refer seem obvious in retrospect. With respect to somatoform illnesses in particular, treatment often underscores the imagined physical basis of the illness for both patient and doctor (Shorter 1992, 1994). "In our society, nothing defines the diagnoses more than the treatment: 'No treatment, no illness!' . . . In treatment, the power of mystery often wins out over the transparency of science" (Malleson 2002: 65,

367). Fifth, following upon the heavily resourced infrastructure, the health professions are iatrogenic, generating business in order to expand their enterprises as well as, hopefully, the well-being of their patients. In this respect, "Human bodies and car bodies are similar. All the pre-accident damaged and malfunctioning parts get lumped in with damage caused by the accident. Again like body shop owners, health care practitioners are on the lookout for work – and often again like body shop owners, almost double their charges when an insurance company pays" (ibid.: 197). Sixth, medical practitioners are always half-watching in terms of another show, namely, the involvement of lawyers and the law. On the one hand, they fear malpractice suits. On the other hand, they appreciate that lawyers also participate in the invention and perpetuation of disabilities, contributing to nomogenesis in tandem with iatrogenesis. Lawyers are business partners in the spinal injury enterprise, quick to engage new medical diagnoses and treatments and to build claims for compensation. Indeed, they are key participants in the process through which particular diagnoses and treatments become institutionalized and legitimate, and therefore a routine part of disability benefit compensation.

This medical-legal-insurance environment is characterized by a politics of uncertainty in which disability is a "moral battle" (Sontag 1979, 1989) fought via classification schemes, metaphysical language, legal regulation, and fiscal constraints. Physicians struggle with the believability of patients' claims; lawyers with efforts at claims suppression by insurers; insurers with how to manage their loss ratios in the face of iatrogenic health services and nomogenic legal services; and claimants with insurance, medical, and legal obstructions that seem to impair them more than their disabilities. Illnesses, and social benefits to help address them, rise and fall according to this politics of uncertainty. As Duncan (2003: 466) observes regarding workers' compensation systems:

> It is necessary to view their existence as a social event, the observation of which is occasioned by a certain stage in the evolution

of industrial processes, political strategies in the confrontation between labour and capital, and the current development (or uncertainty) of medical knowledge. At the same time, bio-political interventions are mounted to include or exclude – but in any event, to control – those who suffer from such "epidemics." Policy makers fund the expansion of new fields of medical knowledge and clinical practice which will justify the maintenance of boundaries between those bodies deemed "unable to work" and those deemed "able but unwilling."

The cost of disabilities arising from work-related and vehicle accidents forms a significant part of all Western political economies. In the United States, the annual national claims costs for whiplash are estimated to range up to $18 billion annually, while in Britain a recent estimate is £3.1 billion (Malleson 2002: 10, 28). In the United States, between 1980 and 1993, the rate of bodily injury claims arising from vehicle crashes rose from 17.9 to 29.3/100 insured vehicles, and the likelihood of such a claim being filed in a crash that also involved a property damage claim increased 64 percent (ibid.: 254). In the Canadian province of British Columbia, the government motor vehicle insurance corporation paid out personal injury claims of $1.185 billion in 1995, or roughly 1 percent of provincial Gross Domestic Product (GDP). Almost three-quarters of these claims were for whiplash-associated disorder injuries. A research organization funded by this insurance corporation reports that on average each whiplash claimant sees a family physician 5 times, a physiotherapist 38 times, and a chiropractor 42 times (Physical Medicine Research Foundation 1997). A leading actuarial expert with knowledge of this insurer's operations said that for 1997, bodily injury claims were about $1.3 billion, of which $.5 billion went to pay the "subjective" injuries. She said an average automobile insurance policy in the province carried a $600 annual premium for bodily injury risks, and "about $250 of that is for stiff necks and sore shoulders."

It has been well documented that whiplash claims rates vary enormously across jurisdictions. For example, in the mid-1980s, Victoria, Australia and New Zealand were similar in size and standard of living. They also had similar rates of rear-end collisions, but the rate of whiplash claims in Victoria was 800 percent greater than in New Zealand, and the amount paid for whiplash injury was 300 percent greater (Malleson 2002: 32, citing Awerbuch 1992; Mills and Horne 1986). In Canada, even provinces with government-run motor vehicles insurance corporations vary enormously in whiplash claim rates. For example, in 1997 the rate per 100,000 in Quebec was 70, Manitoba 700, Saskatchewan 800, and British Columbia 1,600 (Malleson 2002: 297). In the United States, bodily injury [BI] claims, three-quarters of which involve whiplash, also vary substantially across jurisdictions. For example, "In 1993, North Dakota had 5.6 BI claims per 100 property damage claims, while Massachusetts had 34.8; both are no-fault states. Wyoming had 17.6 such claims compared to California's 60.7; both are *tort* states" (ibid.: 256). In the UK, whiplash claims were not prevalent during the heyday of the National Health Service. Physicians were paid either a salary or on a patient per capita basis, and therefore had no incentive to promote whiplash-associated disorders. However, in the 1990s the National Health Service faltered and there was an expansion of private health insurance that pays on a per service basis. Whiplash became a lucrative source of work for the private health services and claims multiplied (ibid.: 26–7).

Such variability across jurisdictions, and within the same jurisdiction over time, also occurs with respect to work injuries and how they are compensated (Sullivan 2000; Malleson 2002; Ericson and Doyle 2004a). This variation indicates that the acceptance of disability claims and willingness to compensate them is an artifact of the politics of uncertainty in each local insurance-medical-legal system context. It also suggests that, in spite of the rise of a strong neo-liberal ethos across Western jurisdictions, there remains considerable welfarism in some jurisdictions. Nevertheless, the overall trend at the beginning of the 21st century is to try to reduce and limit benefits with considerable stringency.

The neo-liberal response to the uncertainties of benefits systems is to hand more risk back to those who are supposed to be protected by such systems (Baker and Simon 2002). Benefits system providers in both public and private sectors decrease their risk-taking on behalf of the collective in the name of their own responsible risk management. In an interview with me, a leading university-based actuarial scientist had the following observations on the changes he witnessed in Canada over the 1980s and 1990s:

> The whole idea of insurance works on the pooling of risk . . . Those categories of the collective were very broad even fifteen years ago . . . You'd have to have a couple of claims in a short period of time to see your premium change very much. Now it is going with the philosophy of the rest of society that you are responsible . . . The whole concept of a pure accident is almost disappearing. There is no pure accident any more. If you have a claim, you are partly at fault. And you need to change risk categories . . . [This is a] move to more slicing and individualization, and more and more passing the responsibility back to the claimant. If it goes too far people will say that this isn't insurance any more . . . As soon as I have a claim my premium goes up. So over the next six years I pay the claim. Well heck, I can run my bank account to do that.

This shifting of risk to the individual has been underpinned by the concept of "moral hazard" advanced by neo-liberal economists and the law and economics movement (Baker 1996; Ericson, Barry, and Doyle 2000; McClusky 2002). A generous benefits system is seen as providing too much protection to claimants, reducing incentives to return to full productive work, and increasing incentives for exaggeration of incapacities and outright fraud. A related argument is that the resulting "social inflation" of benefits system costs reaches the point where such costs reduce the number of jobs available and affordability of goods, creating ever-increasing pools seeking disability and welfare benefits. This leads to the argument that a cutback in the benefits system will sustain employment and put more money in the hands of workers, including a greater capacity to self-insure through savings and private insurance markets.

Governments celebrate their cutbacks in social security benefits and associate them with increased productivity and well-being of the population. For example, in the context of a special section on Canada in the *Financial Times* of London (May 25, 1999), the Government of Canada took out paid advertisements to declare to the international business community that it had the best economic growth record and best business costs of any country in the Group of Seven states. As part of this declaration, it proudly announced that "Canada's [social] programme spending as a percentage of GDP has declined from more than 16 percent in 1993 to 12.6 percent this year, and will continue to fall to 12 percent, the lowest level in 50 years."

Of course, handing more risk to individuals is a social security move that protects business enterprise at the expense of enterprising individuals. For example, in the case of workers' compensation benefits systems, there is a shift in risk taking and management from the employers, who hold the insurance contracts and are responsible for personal injury claims and preventive safety, to workers, who embrace more risk.

> Recent neoliberal political efforts to replace government security with market risk aim not to reduce social insurance as much as to redistribute it toward employers (and capital owners in general) and away from workers . . . [T]his double standard of risk privileges security for employers on the theory that too much risk bearing is harmful for those whose interests are most closely connected to society as a whole. In the prevailing neoliberal ideology, new conditions of global market interdependence make protections for capital owners, not workers, most beneficial. In this view, by reducing security in social insurance programs like workers' compensation in favor of policies supporting investors, we can better promote market growth that will bring the most security to workers and others in the long run . . . The labels "risk" and "security" do not objectively describe discrete

policy choices, but instead serve to prescribe a vision of community based on moral judgments about who deserves the costs and who deserves the benefits of social interdependence. (McClusky 2002: 146; see also McClusky 1998; Duncan 2003: 469)

McClusky (1998, 2002) documents how most states in the USA have rewritten their workers' compensation laws to impose substantive and procedural limits on benefits. The result has been a dramatic decline in compensation, and large numbers of the population dropping from middle-class stability to financial ruin.

A serious assault on government-backed social security provision has the effect of undermining the founding rationale for social benefits systems. Reconfiguration of law and law enforcement crackdowns mean that broad risk pools begin to evaporate. Instead of risk spreading, there are more specialized markets in insurance pools. These specialized insurance pools are segmented according to ability to pay steep premiums, as well as the ability to be good risks who do not make claims. Solidarity fractures as many are depooled from benefits systems entirely, while those remaining receive differential contract conditions and benefits based on their ability to pay. Human welfare responses recede and neoliberal deterrence models ascend. Each insured and professional service provider is expected to do his or her part to prevent claims arising in the first place and to reduce expectations for compensation when claims cannot be suppressed.

Criminalization is a key feature of both the rhetoric and reality of this benefits system crackdown. Criminalization includes stigmatization of the disability claimant status as "criminal." It also involves an enforcement crackdown on claims based on the premise that everyone is trying to cheat the system. As Duncan (2003: 272) points out, neo-liberal government makes individuals more autonomous and self-interested, and then tries to harness these attributes in systems of governance. However, this self-interestedness amplifies moral hazard which in turn fosters distrust regarding the self-governing capacities of the governed. In benefits systems, this distrust is especially focused on claimants, but it extends to medical, legal, and other professional service experts regarding their assumed thirst for competitive advantage and profit in what has become the business of social security. This culture of distrust fosters the perception that anyone participating in the system has "criminal" intentions and therefore preemptive forms of counter-law are necessary.

Recent analyses of reforms to the social security system in Ontario, Canada, document the ways in which being on social assistance is also stigmatized as criminal. Chunn and Gavigan (2004: 219) observe that in the contemporary politics of uncertainty over social security, the neo-liberal social imaginary has "shifted public discourse and social images from welfare fraud to welfare as fraud, thereby linking welfare, poverty and crime." They add that this "inordinate focus on 'welfare cheats' leads to the 'criminalization of poverty'." Their analysis is confirmed by Mosher and Hermer's (2005) report to the Law Commission of Canada, *Welfare Fraud: The Constitution of Social Assistance as Crime*:

> In undertaking the most significant reforms to Ontario's social assistance regime in decades, fighting welfare fraud was expressly identified as a central objective, and a vast array of new measures were introduced to assist the government to win this battle. "Welfare fraud" is now policed in such a way as to evoke a major crime against the public, one that is deserving of widespread condemnation and intensive policing and punishment. The impression that there is widespread defrauding of benefits by recipients has been so successfully installed in public discourse and government policy that social assistance is now primarily viewed not as a necessary form of support for those in need, but rather negatively, as a burdensome problem of regulation, policing and crime control. Those on social assistance, the far majority of them women and children, are widely viewed as morally suspect persons, criminals in waiting poised to abuse a public expenditure and trust. But in fact, much of the conduct so frequently characterized as "fraud" falls far outside the boundaries of formal criminal law to include virtually all situations where

a rule is breached. Moreover, because the welfare system is rife with literally hundreds of complex rules, errors on the part of both recipients and bureaucrats are not only common but unavoidable. Yet, it is often these unintended rule violations that are portrayed as the "fraud" within the system. (Mosher and Hermer 2005: 5)

These images of welfare as fraud slip into other fields of social security, including personal injury compensation (Lippel 1999, 2003). There have been widespread publicity campaigns that portray workers' compensation claimants as fraudsters, paving the way for radical law reforms that eliminate or restrict benefits (Ellenberger 2000), new surveillant assemblages to detect questionable claims (Eakin, Clarke, and MacEachen 2002), and a general chilling effect on legitimate claims (Hyatt and Law 2000). "The 'welfarization' of workers' compensation programs gives rise to stigmatization of injured workers, who are often illustrated in the media as fraudulent profiteers. This image may be internalized by the workers themselves. The historical link [of workers' compensation] to tort is long forgotten, to the point that an attitude of 'entitlement' is often perceived as pathological by compensation board doctors and other experts" (Lippel 1999: 538). Parallel criminalization campaigns with similar effects have also occurred in the field of personal injury claims arising from vehicle accidents (Ericson and Doyle 2003, 2004a: esp. 130–5, 2004c).

Of course, crime is an omnipresent reality in social security benefits systems. For example, a survey of 353 US insurers (Insurance Research Council/Insurance Services Organization 2001) revealed that the "soft-core" fraud problem of "average" claimants who exaggerate their losses is perceived as very costly. While antifraud publicity campaigns dramatize individual cases of wholesale "hardcore" fraud, such as staged auto accidents by personal injury rings (Dornstein 1996), the "soft-core" problem was seen as much more serious. Studies of bodily injury claims arising from vehicle accidents in Massachusetts (Weisberg and Derrig 1991, 1992) judged

31 percent (*n* = 597) of one sample and 47 percent (*n* = 1,154) of another sample to have involved dishonesty in the claim. Ethnographic research (Ericson, Doyle, and Barry 2003: chaps. 6, 9; Ericson and Doyle 2003, 2004a, 2004c; Ericson and Doyle 2006) also documents fraudulent practices throughout the insurance system, not only by claimants but also by insurers and those who provide professional services to them. Malleson (2002) offers further examples from clinical practice and secondary literature. Some of his illustrations are very colorful, for example how in Winnipeg "As a form of protest, 107 police officers called in sick on the same day. Faced with the threat of losing a day's pay, 91 officers produced a doctor's note certifying that they were sick" (ibid.: 63).

A great deal of this social benefit fraud is a product of the neo-liberal politics of uncertainty that condemns it, and the attendant counter-law measures that suppress it. This fact is recognized by benefits system operatives themselves. A sales manager for a disability insurer I researched said that the rightsizing of both state bureaucracies and business enter prises in neo-liberal regimes, as part of economic restructuring and declining incomes, can cause serious disabilities, as well as feigning of disabilities, and it is difficult to separate the two. "A recession triggers stress, which is a huge claims area for us: mental and nervous disorders, family break-up, drug and alcohol abuse . . . higher incidences of abuse of the [disability insurance] policy. You go to your doctor, you say, 'My back is sore.' They can't prove it, what am I, the insurer, to do? But your key motivation is to get money to pay your creditors . . . If we're entering a period of recession, we might have a different rate class for occupations that are sensitive: stockbrokers, real estate agents . . . [we might] adjust our rates to reflect the fact."

The vice-president of a large disability insurance brokerage I researched described two social security service agencies that saw their group disability insurance premiums triple because of high claims rates by employees. He said the claims inflation was directly attributable to the state's neo-liberal regime, which had cut back resources for these agencies at a time when they were experiencing greater demands because of rightsizing in all sectors:

> Because they're facing government cutbacks, funding cutbacks, increased utilization, more clients . . . mentally handicapped, physically challenged or underprivileged, or children's aid, all these groups are being tested to the maximum . . . And they get downsizing in those organizations too because they don't have the budgets anymore. They've had no pay raises in some cases for four, five years. Stress in society, double incomes, chasing the Joneses, trying to make ends meet . . . So people are either not coping with it or they don't see a favorable outcome and disability is their last straw so they jump at it.

The claims manager for another disability insurer I researched said that claims rates were especially high among working women with children. On relatively low employment incomes, this population seeks disability income as a temporary relief from work or as the answer to rightsizing. "Females . . . the ones from the east coast especially, I find them more difficult to deal with . . . So if the job isn't there anymore, or even if the job might be there, the person maybe tends to want to stay at home with their four little children. There isn't much to cause that person to want to go and get better, and they're going to have a bad back."

These views are consistent with the fact that all types of health and well-being are related to distribution of wealth (Evans et al. 1994; Wilkinson 1996; Sullivan, Stainblum, and Frank 1997; Sullivan 2000). When neo-liberal regimes intensify wealth inequality, disadvantaged populations, taught to be enterprising selves, try to restore some equity by turning to insurance resources such as those available in state and private disability insurance systems. An executive with an occupational health and safety research organization I studied made the following observation:

> If you look at the Canada Pension Plan in the last decade, there's been a doubling of people who have long-term disabilities

associated with soft-tissue injuries. When you pull that apart
demographically it turns out to be mainly older middle-aged
men . . . English-speaking origins, who are also the market casu-
alties in the labor market. So it is one way of insuring. And I'm
not trying to be cynical about this. People actually develop disabilities, there's a downward spiral in which if they didn't really
have some patho-physiological process before, they're going to
have one at the end of this. I think *the* big issue is all of these
mind-body conditions.

While social benefit fraud is embedded in some of these
structural features of neo-liberal politics of uncertainty, it is
also a product of enforcement crackdown efforts to discover
and suppress it. There is considerable fluidity in defining
precisely what is meant by fraud, and the scope of the fraud
problem is linked to how the boundaries of fraud are drawn.
Indeed, the prevalence of benefits system fraud is ultimately
unknowable, except to the extent that system operatives
make it a problem. As the social-reaction perspective indicates with crime in general (Ericson 1975, 1993), fraud is an
artifact of how the insurance industry organizes to deal with
it. As related by a senior official in an insurance private-
policing operation I studied, "The scary part is, as we continue to increase the fight, we continually uncover more and
more fraud. So people say, 'you are putting all these dollars
in there, but the problem is increasing.' You can't say something is fraudulent until you find it. There's been such a
growth in 'insurance fraud.' It has probably always been
there; it is just that more has been uncovered than ever
before."

Counter-law I: Laws Against Law

In this section I consider how laws against law are constituted
in two fields of social security benefits: disability arising from
personal injuries while at work or driving, and welfare assistance for those with employment and income problems.

Disability benefits systems

It should be kept in mind that no-fault disability insurance systems such as workers' compensation arose as a form of counter-law regarding problems with the tort liability system. The idea was that greater social solidarity, harmony, and well-being could be created by eliminating case-by-case litigation in favor of an insurance-based system. This system would provide the injured worker with health services as well as financial compensation to restore her to the station in life she had before her accident. Workers' compensation insurance was developed to spread disability risks across broad pools to protect both parties in the employment relationship. Employees are protected from the effects of work-related injuries that threaten their livelihood and socio-economic standing. Employers are protected from costly litigation and upheaval in the workplace that is likely to arise in each case of serious injury without a workers' compensation scheme. Such litigation would be anti-thera-peutic, pose uncertainty, and in many cases, threaten the via-bility of a business.

The problem is that uncertainty over what constitutes dis-abilities such as soft tissue injuries, and the elasticity of claims of fraud, promote a different kind of adversarialism between employers and workers. These new sources of adversarialism are compounded by the fact that in no-fault workers' com-pensation schemes, such as those that operate in Canada, it is employers who hold the insurance contracts and are there-fore responsible for losses and their impact on future insur-ance premiums and contract conditions. As a result, employers have a strong incentive to contest and suppress workers' claims, without fear of economic sanction if their efforts prove unjust. As Lippel (1999: 538) observes in the context of Quebec, "Today, contesting workers' compensa-tion claims has become a thriving industry. Medico-legal centers 'manage' compensation claims not only for large industries, but for small and medium workplaces for whom legislation regarding experience rating was specifically adopted in 1997. In theory, experience rating is designed to encourage prevention of work injury. In practice, it promotes the adversarial process, and encourages much of the behavior that is most damaging to the worker."

Adversarialism has intensified through the criminalization of disability claimants. In many jurisdictions there has been an escalation of both criminal and civil penalties against insurance fraud. For example, in the USA almost every state now defines insurance fraud as a felony rather than a misdemeanor, and has enacted legislation creating state-government fraud bureaus which are often jointly funded with the private insurance industry. However, most criminalization transpires through contract and administrative law mechanisms. These mechanisms of counter-law impose substantive and procedural limitations on benefits, enable more intrusive surveillance of claimants, require claimants to return to work even when they have not fully recovered, and entail looser application of rights and freedoms legislation compared to other fields of law (McClusky 1998, 2002; Lippel 1999, 2003; Ericson and Doyle 2004a: chap. 3).

To illustrate, we can consider the development of "work-hardening" regimes in personal injury benefits systems. The lack of knowledge about recalcitrant disabilities such as soft tissue injuries is used to justify work-hardening regimes. Instead of placing the onus on the insurance and health care systems to produce better knowledge for diagnosis and treatment, ignorance is confessed. This confession allows a shift to production and distribution of surveillance-based knowledge useful in getting the person back to work quickly. Surveillance-based knowledge shifts responsibility onto health professionals to do their part in the management of malingering, and onto the claimant to do her part in learning to risk-manage her pain at work. In many jurisdictions, such as British Columbia, workers' compensation legislation requires that if the person is deemed able to return to work, she must do so even if she has not fully recovered. This requirement is accompanied by a shift from a "vocational rehabilitation" model, in which the person is given time and rehabilitative services before returning to work, to a "disability manage-ment" model whereby the disability is risk-managed at work.

Return-to-work incentives are often built into individual insurance contracts. For example, the policyholder can be substantially underinsured in order to control malingering. One insurer I studied kept income replacement levels for a person on a disability claim to about half of the person's normal income on the experience that a higher level sub-stantially increases claims costs. This company also built a number of specific return-to-work conditions into the con-tract. In keeping with the "responsibilization" of the individ-ual characteristic of neo-liberal regimes, this package of conditions was called the "enterprise claims system." It was designed to reward the enterprising disability claimant with a series of benefits for returning to work quickly, and it was combined with a more stringent surveillance of the claimant to ensure that she was indeed enterprising rather than malin-gering. A company official described this surveillance as a move from a "paper audit" of paying a claim strictly on a reading of the contract to a "clinical audit" involving ongoing claims management of the disabled person's condition and return-to-work process. To facilitate this move to clinical audit, the company acquired another company with 3,500 employees who specialized in disability claims management.

As Lippel (2003) documents, these forms of contractual governance, and the surveillant assemblages they enable, are underpinned by a legal system that is less inclined to invoke high standards of rights and freedoms in this context com-pared to others. For example, in a case involving a worker charged under the penal provisions of workers' compensation legislation, a Quebec court rejected the Supreme Court of Canada standard for limiting the use of electronic surveil-lance devices.

> The court trivialized violations of privacy by the state in the context of regulatory offences, and concluded that the policing of injured workers does not require a vigilant respect of Charter [Canadian Charter of Rights and Freedoms] rights, given the

importance of the Workers' Compensation Board's mandate to manage public funds. The judgment regarding a regulatory offence under workers' compensation legislation may be subsequently invoked to deny benefits that the worker relies on for subsistence. It seems surprising that the context of workers' compensation would somehow reduce the state obligation to respect human rights provisions, given the importance of the consequence for the worker . . . Rights have been whittled away in the name of administrative needs of regulatory agencies. (Lippel 2003: 109)

The medical profession is centrally involved in the criminalization of disability claimants through its invention and enforcement of medical categories that pathologize the claimant as an undeserving fraudster. A wide range of "illness behaviors" are used to designate undeserving claimants whose benefits should be restricted or cut off. The simplest definition of "illness behavior" is whatever is "dysfunctional" to the clinical eye as it is focused by the insurance system. A manual for clinicians dealing with whiplash claimants defines illness behavior as any effort to seek compensation that is unwarranted. This undue compensation-seeking is referred to as "secondary gain . . . consciously or unconsciously using or maintaining symptoms to obtain psychological, social, or economic advantage expressed in behaviour that appears to seek sympathy, manipulate others, avoid work or responsibility, or save face when expectations are too high." In clinical shorthand the claimant is said to suffer from "compensationitis" (Munglani 1999: 14), "dissimulation disorders" (Jonas and Pope 1985), or "factitious disorder." An insurance company's internal manual for clinicians defines factitious disorder as "A conscious or willful invention or distortion of symptoms to achieve secondary gain, usually a financial gain . . . [I]n malingering the person knows that they are faking an illness or injury, and why – usually for money or to avoid traumatization or abuse."

Another syndrome is "pain disorder" where it is determined that pain is largely related to "psychological factors." In extreme form it becomes "chronic pain syndrome" which is "a condition of its own" and not just an acute pain that lasts longer. An insurer's internal manual instructs clinicians as follows. "Patients' questions about the origins of pain are often really questions about the legitimacy of suffering. Restate questions about the origin of pain as questions about the nature of appropriate treatment." Apparently a lot of suffering is illegitimate and the appropriate treatment is to restrict benefits. Lists of clinical symptoms for chronic pain syndrome indicate that it is not really distinguishable from malingering or factitious disorder. Among the symptoms listed in the manual are: "dysfunctional or maladaptive behavior; reinforced by iatrogenic, and/or psycho-social stressors; often related to secondary gain (social, family, vocational or financial); often provides the rationalization for quitting an unpleasant work situation, retirement, or breaking a workaholic pattern; pain may provide expectations for financial rewards through a legal and insurance or compensation system; may result from complications arising from the involvement of various professions, such as medical, legal, insurance."

Chronic pain syndrome is in turn construed as influencing diagnoses of fibromyalgia. The manual states that fibromyalgia may be caused or aggravated by malingering. An associated cause is "litigation; the stress of having to 'prove' one's dysfunction and to live with it could be a factor." The clinician is charged with the responsibility of trying "to control the issues of secondary pain for gain behaviour. The rewards of pain and dysfunction can be powerful mediators for pain behaviour."

The clinical task is to redefine chronic pain as "activity intolerance" and therefore not a disability at all (Fordyce 1995). This paves the way for return-to-work programs and cessation of benefits. Resistance entails further criminalization through medical-legal labels, applied by both clinicians and lawyers to "economically dictated behavior" (Lippel 1999: 529). Through these labels the claimant is cast into the status of an abnormal person who violates the conditions of the insurance contract, which alone is to dictate when the sick role may be granted. The person is stigmatized with a criminal-like status, and through this status, threatened with severe penalties, including loss of further treatment and financial compensation, exclusion from future acceptance into disability insurance programs, and, in the extreme, criminal prosecution. All of these labels are codes for an undeserving claimant, continuing "the tradition of building moral hazard into a quasi-pathology, a form of neurosis which delays the normal medical-rehabilitation process" (Duncan 2003: 464).

These practices institutionalize suspicion in the disability claims process to the point where there is a presumption of fraud. This "decline of innocence" (Ericson 1994) shifts the burden of proof onto the claimant, and gives rise to a strong blame-the-victim approach. The former chief actuary of a vehicle insurance company said in interview with me that all claimants are treated as "fraudsters," leading insurers to take "financially the most expedient view of the claim. I will squeeze, extract, cajole; I'll do anything I can to keep the costs of the claim down. And I'll squeeze the customer, *victim*, in the process." In another interview, a former adjuster for a vehicle insurer concurred, saying his company's routine practice in personal-injury claims was "to deny until they hire a lawyer. So there's no question they were entitled to benefits, it's just denied them and hope they go away." A claims analyst for another vehicle insurer said in interview that at the height of traumatic experience, the accident victim is blamed for not having prevented the accident in the first place and then for exaggerating his or her suffering.

> The number one complaint people have with the claims process is that they're being treated as criminal: that essentially they're not being given the benefit of the doubt and that they're presumed guilty, and it's up to them to prove their innocence . . . Especially after they've had a crash, they need some support mechanism, not being interrogated . . . [w]hat it revolves around is the perception that people don't trust us because they feel we

don't trust them, and it's the trust issue that's absolutely central to all this insurance business . . . They want to feel that we are delivering on a promise. Because people are not actually buying a product, they're buying security, and they want to make sure that if something happens to them . . . in fact we'll be there for them. It's the gap between the expectations and the actual realities of what happens when you actually have a claim that sets off the negative reactions.

Lippel (1999) describes the full force of this counter-law system as it operates in the workers' compensation arena. She observes that there is structured inequality whereby the disability claimant is stigmatized as a fraudster and not given access to legal justice, whereas the benefits system operatives engage in similar self-interested economic behavior and reap rewards as effective risk managers and legal regulators.

> At times a "no-fault" system can be even more anti-therapeutic than the tort system, as it may re-introduce victim-blaming behavior without providing the victims with the benefit of "having their day in court" or blaming those responsible for injury. The current system is imbalanced. Claimants cannot discuss the reasons why they blame the employer yet many workers' compensation systems allow evidence of claimant's negligence and encourage blaming behavior on the part of employers, evaluating physicians and adjudicators. When a claimant exaggerates symptoms to manage compensation he is labeled a malingerer. When employers or insurers indiscriminately contest or refuse claims to reduce costs they are labeled as effective managers. Behavior designed to maximize institutional profit is not considered to be pathological. (Lippel 1999: 540)

This system of laws against law works routinely and systematically on a *sub rosa* level. However, there are occasions when it rises to the surface and law injects some balance, albeit only in the isolated case. The routine and systematic nature of counter-law operating over a long period of time is illustrated in a 2001 opinion by the Utah Supreme Court in *Campbell v. State Farm Mutual Automobile Insurance Company No. 981564.* State Farm is well known for promoting consumer trust in itself. For decades it has used the same advertising slogan, "Like a good neighbor, State Farm is there." As it turns out, for decades State Farm was not a good neighbor and was not there when needed. Indeed, its operatives collectively exhibited insurance company equivalents of "compensationitis," "dissimulation disorder," and "factitious disorder." In affirming a $145 million punitive damages judgment against the company, the court stated that

State Farm repeatedly and deliberately deceived and cheated its customers . . . for over two decades, State Farm set monthly payment caps and individually rewarded those insurance adjusters who paid less than the market value for claims . . . Agents changed the content of files, lied to customers, and committed other dishonest and fraudulent acts in order to meet financial goals . . . For example, a State Farm official in the underlying lawsuit in Logan instructed the claim adjuster to change the report in State Farm's file by writing that Ospital was "speeding to visit his pregnant girlfriend." There was no evidence at all to support that assertion. Ospital was not speeding, nor did he have a pregnant girlfriend . . . The only purpose for the change was to distort the value of the assessment of Ospital's claims . . . State Farm's fraudulent practices were consistently directed to persons – poor racial or ethnic minorities, women, and elderly individuals – who State Farm believed would be less likely to object or take legal action . . .

Second, State Farm engaged in deliberate concealment and destruction of all documents related to this profit scheme . . . State Farm's own witnesses testified that documents were routinely destroyed so as to avoid their potential disclosure through discovery requests . . . Third, State Farm has systematically harassed and intimidated opposing claimants, witnesses, and attorneys. For example, State Farm published an instruction manual for its attorneys mandating them to "ask personal questions" as part of the investigation and examination of claimants in order to deter litigation . . . The record contains an eighty page report prepared by State Farm regarding De Long's personal life, including information obtained by paying a hotel maid to disclose whether De Long had overnight guest in her room . . . There was also evidence that State Farm actually instructs its attorneys to employ "mad dog defense tactics" – using the company's large resources to "wear out" opposing attorneys by prolonging litigation, making meritless objections, claiming false privileges, destroying documents, and abusing the law and motion process.

Taken together, these three examples show that State Farm engaged in a pattern of "trickery and deceit," "false statements," and other "acts of affirmative misconduct" targeted at "financially vulnerable" persons.

Welfare benefits systems

New laws against law are also evident in welfare benefits systems. In what follows I focus on recent law reform in Ontario, Canada, drawing in particular upon the analyses of Chunn and Gavigan (2004) and Mosher and Hermer (2005).

In 1997, the Government of Ontario enacted radical laws against law to restructure its welfare benefits program (Social Assistance Reform Act, 5.0 1997, c. 25 enacting Ontario Works Act, 1997, 5.0 c. 25, 51 and Ontario Disability Support Program, 1997, 5.0. c. 25, 5.2). As signified by the title of the Ontario Works Act [OWA], this legislation was designed to shift social security from a welfare needs-based system to one of temporary assistance to the unemployed person actively committed to seeking work. Section 1 of the OWA provides a clear statement that one must be a responsible and enterprising neo-liberal citizen in order to be deemed eligible for social assistance. The OWA's purpose is to establish a program that: "a) recognizes individual responsibility and promotes self reliance through employment; b) provides temporary financial assistance to those most in need while they satisfy obligations to become and stay employed;

c) effectively serves people needing assistance; and d) is accountable to the taxpayers of Ontario."

Parallel to work-hardening regimes in disability insurance contracts, the OWA requires eligible claimants to return to work as expediently as possible under rigorous contract terms and conditions. The OWA creates a "participation agreement" between the eligible claimant and government through which the claimant agrees to participate in designated "employment assistance" activities.

> Employment assistance activities include "community participation" and any of the following "employment measures": job searches; literacy screening, testing, assessment, or programs; basic education and job-specific skills training; employment placement; screening for substance addiction; or participation in a program to complete high school or to develop parenting skills. In addition, every participant has an obligation to make reasonable efforts to accept and maintain employment "for which he or she is physically capable"; and if employed part-time, to find full-time employment; if employed and still eligible for assistance, to find employment to increase his or her income. The failure to comply or to make reasonable efforts will result in the cancellation of benefits for a three or six month period (depending on the circumstances). (Mosher and Hermer 2005: 21–2)

A number of other regulations were developed to enforce this work-hardening regime. For example, a "quit/fire" regulation (OWA, 1997, O. Reg. 134/98) requires termination or suspension of assistance if the claimant resigns employment without just cause or is dismissed from employment with cause. Regulations also restrict benefits in particular circumstances. For example, in 1995, prior to the OWA, the Government of Ontario amended the regulatory definition of "spouse" for social assistance purposes, creating a presumption that anyone of the opposite sex who shares a common residence is a spouse. This definitional change alone resulted in 10,013 claimants being cut off social assistance, of whom 89 percent were women and 76 percent single mothers

(Little 1998). There have been subsequent definitional changes that further restrict benefit eligibility of spouses (*Falkiner v. Ontario 2002*).

Counter-law to restrict benefits was accompanied by deep cuts to benefits available (Mosher and Hermer 2005: 20). In 1995 the government cut the benefits budget by 21.6 percent, and it offered no increases over the subsequent eight years. The then Minister of Community and Social Services expressed the government's sensibility by suggesting "that people could get by through measures such as negotiating for discounts on things like dented tins of tuna or buying food in bulk. He also maintained that because those on welfare had been given three months notice on the rate cuts, they had adequate time to prepare for the cuts" (ibid.: 21). Taking inflation into account, the decline in purchasing power of welfare benefits between 1995 and 2002 was 34 percent. In 2003, a single person in Ontario received benefits that equaled 35 percent of the poverty line; for a single parent with one child, it was 56 percent. With such levels of impoverishment guaranteed by the social assistance regime, there is likely to be a violation of regulations, including creative forms of fraud.

The government used the specter of widespread benefits system fraud as the over-arching feature of its counter-law regime. Drawing on the rhetoric of "zero tolerance" that was popular in public order policing at the time, the government pursued a crackdown on claimant fraud. This zero tolerance approach was symbolized by legislation enacted in April 2000 that made a claimant convicted of benefits system fraud permanently ineligible for future benefits. Although a new government repealed this provision in December 2003, it was successful in underpinning the precautionary regime of fraud control. As Chunn and Gavigan (2004: 232) state, "The lifetime ban upon conviction for welfare fraud arguably ensures a lifetime of (secondary) punishment (without parole) and unameliorated poverty upon such a conviction." The rhetoric of zero tolerance is accompanied by zero law, that is, law against law.

The "governing through fraud" frame legitimates the entire counter-law regime of criminalization: the exclusion of large numbers of claimants who would have been included under the former welfarist needs-based system; keeping benefit levels well below the poverty line; and enabling laws against law and survcillant assemblages that police eligibility continuously. The continuous monitoring of claimants as suspected fraudsters is deemed necessary because welfare is now conceived as temporary social assistance enabling an expedient path to self-sufficiency.

Such extraordinary monitoring requires extraordinary resources. Hence, the government expanded its special investigations unit of Eligibility Review Officers (EROs). By 1998–9, there were 300 EROs, up 80 percent from 1987, and an additional 100 positions were funded in 2000. Additional funds were also provided for development of an informant system called the Welfare Fraud Hotline, a Welfare Fraud Control Database, dedicated criminal prosecution efforts against alleged fraudsters, an annual audit published as the *Welfare Fraud Control Report*, and other measures aimed at policing welfare recipients more than providing for them.

This process of criminalization rarely results in actual criminal convictions for fraud. Rather, criminalization is embedded in an administrative regime of counter-law in contracts, regulations, and surveillant assemblages. This regime includes over 800 administrative rules regarding eligibility criteria, such as alternative sources of income, efforts at skills training and employment seeking, and compliance with surveillance such as drug testing and disclosure of personal information. As described in a recent report by Member of Provincial Parliament Deborah Matthews (2004: 25):

> Many of those rules are punitive and designed not to support people, but rather to keep them out of the system. Because there are so many rules, they are expensive to administer and often applied inconsistently from one caseworker to another, even within the same office. Further, the rules are so complicated that

they are virtually impossible to communicate to clients, and it takes years to train a caseworker.

Violation of these rules is typically treated as an act of criminal fraud even when it clearly is not.

[T]here are substantial and on-going reporting requirements, including, for example, the obligation to report a change in circumstances or the receipt of income. If a recipient has failed to report as required, this is commonly characterized as fraud. Yet, in many of these instances, the conduct falls far short of what is actually necessary to satisfy the *Criminal Code* test for fraud. A related error that is commonly made where a recipient says she didn't know or didn't understand the rule in issue (for example, that she didn't understand that most loans are considered income and are thus reportable), is to respond with the invocation that "ignorance of the law" is no excuse. But this is an incorrect application of the doctrine; her lack of knowledge of the rules is not being invoked to argue that she did not know the law of fraud and hence cannot be guilty of fraud, but rather to negate the *mens rea* of the offence. Yet, over and over, we heard of instances where recipients were threatened with fraud charges (and often agreed to terminations and over-payments as a result) or were charged with fraud and plead guilty in precisely these kinds of circumstances. The misapprehensions as to what conduct actually constitutes criminal fraud are rife throughout the social assistance system, and perhaps more distressingly, can also be found within the criminal justice system itself. (Mosher and Hermer 2005: 78)

Descriptions of how this rule system is used indicate that everyone operates with the presumption of fraud. For example, welfare caseworkers have been transformed into policing agents more than social workers helping with skills training and employment. Based on focus-group research, Herd and Mitchell (2002) describe a system that "is more concerned with surveillance and deterrence, than it is with assisting people to find employment" (p. 8), which leads to treating "everybody like they're cheating the system" (p. 33). Mosher and Hermer (2005) interviewed both welfare caseworkers and claimants who held similar views. One of their caseworker respondents observed "that hardly any of her clients now refer to their welfare workers as their 'social workers' as they did formerly; rather welfare workers have become much more closely associated with police officers. Fraud is now *the* focus of the system, explained another" (ibid.: 55).

While criminal prosecution of fraud is rare statistically, when it does occur there is a policy of using the fraud provisions of the Criminal Code of Canada (CCC) rather than those available in the OWA. The January 2004 "Controlling Fraud Policy Directive #45" of the Ontario Ministry of Community and Social Services states that where there is "sufficient evidence to suspect an intent to commit fraud the case *must* be referred to the police for investigation under the Criminal Code." The OWA (s. 79) provisions for fraud carry a maximum penalty of a $5,000 fine or six months' imprisonment or both. The CCC (s. 380) provisions for fraud treat it as an indictable offense with a maximum penalty of 14 years' imprisonment if the subject matter of the offense is valued at more than $5,000; and as either an indictable offense with a maximum penalty of two years' imprisonment or as a summary conviction offense with a maximum penalty of six months' imprisonment where the value is under $5,000. Not surprisingly, there is enormous discretion on the part of police and Crown attorneys as to whether referred cases go forward. In some districts a threshold value such as $5,000 or $10,000 is established before a prosecution will be indicated, while in other jurisdictions even small values are subject to prosecution (Mosher and Hermer 2005: 75). In any case, this counter-law regime involves a transformation of regulatory infractions created through the OWA into CCC matters. As Chunn and Gavigan (2004: 230) note, "this shift in the direction of increased surveillance and criminalization of welfare recipients, notably women on welfare, illustrates that the (coercive form of) criminal law and (the regulatory form of) welfare law are inseparable."

As mentioned earlier, the actual number of criminal convictions for fraud is infinitesimal when viewed against the regulatory investigations of fraud that prove to be unfounded or result in administrative reduction or termination of benefits. For example, the *Welfare Fraud Control Report 2001–2* indicates there were 38,452 fraud investigations. In 25,636 cases (66 percent) fraud allegations were unfounded; in 12,816 cases (33 percent) social assistance was reduced or terminated; and in 393 cases (1 percent) criminal convictions for fraud resulted. These data indicating very high levels of unfounded accusations, and administrative solutions when founded, suggest that governing through fraud is a pervasive means of obtaining claimant acquiescence to surveillance and claims suppression more than criminal conviction for fraud (for parallels in the case of insurance fraud, see Ericson, Doyle, and Barry 2003: chap. 9; Ericson and Doyle 2004a, 2004c). As we shall see in the following discussion of how the welfare benefits surveillance system actually operates, all claimants are nevertheless criminalized in ways that fundamentally transform social security regimes.

Counter-law II: Surveillant Assemblages

Disability benefits systems

Surveillance regarding disability claims is managed by case coordinators working for the social benefits program. Case coordinators undertake direct surveillance themselves. They also mobilize other agents of surveillance, including health-care professionals, citizen informants, and private police.

Case coordinators are charged with inspecting the minutiae of the claimant's background and current activities. In practice, they are engaged in physiognomy, the "ancient art or science of judging an interior reality by an external appearance . . . color of the face . . . passing expressions, bodily form or posture" (Graham 1979: 35; see also Rivers 1994). This practice is based on the view that disability claimants routinely express somatoform ailments that must be seen through in order to accelerate their return to work and suppress claims costs. The task is one of "building strong and healthy egos" in claimants on the view that accident victims have "suffered more from the so-called emotional maladjustments or personality defects that accompanied their physical impairments than from the impairments themselves" (O'Brien 2001: 7). The following extract from an insurance company's manual for disability case coordinators reveals both the depth of inspection and the way in which the facts discovered are to be valued with an eye on reducing claims costs.

An accurate observation of the insured's environment, family dynamics as well as verbal and non-verbal behaviour will assist in developing the foundation for the insured's rehabilitation planning . . . Listen to your clients and be attentive not only to what they say but even more so to what they do not say. Non-verbal clues, body language and voice tones often say more than words . . . It is always important to ascertain the insured's family, social, employer, recreational, community and other networks, and the degree to which each network influences the insured . . . The multicultural milieu . . . requires rehabilitation staff to be culturally competent . . . [e.g.] An insured who has limited English or none at all, will likely have less appreciation for the intent and the value of medical or rehabilitation services . . . Some minority groups are disproportionately represented at the lower end of the economic spectrum and in the ranks of the unemployed. Their socioeconomic conditions, which may be characterized by poor housing, behavioural problems in children, dissatisfaction with social situation and health problems, may affect their medical and rehabilitation needs as well as service delivery . . . An individual with a value system which puts an extraordinary emphasis on the medical model of care will be less likely to respond to active rehabilitation . . . Family values of certain cultural groups may interfere, if not completely hinder the rehabilitation process. Independence, which is often the primary goal of most rehabilitation programs, may not necessarily be important to some cultural groups who may have a tendency to protect and care for an injured member.

Physicians and other healthcare professionals, working under the Hippocratic oath, may also have a tendency to protect and care for the injured. Therefore, the case coordinator must be vigilant about the health services being recommended and associated costs, and mobilize the service providers as an integral part of the surveillant assemblage. Medical practitioners are required to use their clinics as a surveillance site for differentiating the deserving disabled from the undeserving. This includes ferreting out signs of claims fraud: "malingering," "compensationitis," "factitious disorder," "compensation neurosis," "activity intolerance," and so on. As such, medical practitioners are drawn into the legal-administrative framework of disability management and assigned medical policing tasks that are well beyond their professional training and competence (Malleson 2002; Duncan 2003; Ericson and Doyle 2004a: chap. 3).

A description of one clinical site is illustrative (for a fuller description, see Ericson and Doyle 2004a: 155–66). In order to effect better claims management and fraud detection, a workers' compensation insurer contracted to have disability claimants tested on a new computer-based surveillance technology that I will refer to as Precision. Precision is used to put the claimant through a series of physical tasks in order to measure levels of functional impairment and the pain associated with each task. It also runs a series of reliability and validity checks on the claimants' efforts in testing in order to detect possible faking. As such it functions as a lie detector of the body, used in determining levels of insurance compensation as well as denial of further benefits if the threshold for disability is not reached or fraud is detected.

The detection of fraud occurs through a number of additional investigative technologies and practices in the clinic and beyond. The claimant is subject to being watched for telltale signs at every step of the way, both in approaching the testing center and during the test. A Precision program administrator remarked in interview:

> You've never seen so many knee braces and wrist braces brought out of mothballs when you come in for [a Precision] impairment rating. Everybody has got one. I mean you get people walking in with dual knee braces – and they've got blisters walking from their car to the building because they hadn't worn them for a year and a half – but they've got them on because a lot of people perceive this is a pot of gold at the end of the rainbow. The intent of the Precision system is not to catch the system magnifiers, it's to give a truly accurate reflection what findings are on that particular day . . . The clinician that actually conducts the test makes ongoing comments regarding the client's behavior, from the moment of hitting the door until leaving. So, for instance, the patient was unable to bend over during the test; however, I noted that they had no difficulty bending to tie their shoes when they got dressed after their examination.

During a demonstration of Precision to me, a technician said that she constantly looks for signs of faking during tests. For example, during a hand-grip dynamometer testing she looks for "whitening of the fingertips" as well as "accessory muscles activating in the forearms, activation of musculage all the way up. Some people, all you see is a bit of gripping, and some people it is just hard to tell." The technician can turn on a surveillance camera during testing to capture any behavioral subtleties.

Monitoring begins before a claimant even enters the clinic. Surveillance cameras are available in the clinic parking lot and corridors to capture bodily movements that do not match what the Precision testing records. During one of my observation sessions with Precision operators, a woman was detected as a "symptom magnifier." She claimed that she could not move her neck because of a cervical injury, but three signs counteracted this claim: she drove her car a long distance to the clinic; she moved her neck considerably during the examination; and she was put under video surveillance in the parking lot and again she displayed ample mobility with her neck.

The claimant may also be the target of photo surveillance in his everyday routines before and after the Precision testing day. A technician said she had recently tested a claimant who subsequently claimed that his disability had been aggravated further by the testing itself. Photo surveillance by an undercover operative was used to belie this claim. "The guy said he couldn't crawl out of bed the day after I examined him. Two days later, he was filmed coming in first in a Rambo-esque archery tournament, in which he traveled in camouflage fatigues and crawled across all kinds of terrain."

Disability insurers operate their own in-house private police departments called Special Investigation Units (SIU). In Canada and the United States, there has been a massive expansion of these units in the past 20 years, much of it directed at policing disability claims fraud (Dornstein 1996; Ericson, Doyle, and Barry 2003). For example, between 1992 and 1997, one major American insurance company increased its SIU from 300 to 1,200 investigators, and developed its own training academy for investigators. A Canadian provincial government motor vehicle insurance corporation I studied expanded its SIU to 50 investigators and six managers by the late 1990s, all of whom were former public police officers. It developed subsidiary units, including one dedicated to bodily injury fraud, one dedicated to material damage fraud, and one that used a dataveillance (data matching and data mining) system to risk profile potential fraudsters for further investigation. A bodily injury investigator and a material damage investigator were assigned to each of its decentralized claims centers to investigate fraudulent files identified by adjusters.

In addition to working with case coordinators, healthcare professionals, and insurance adjusters to identify fraudulent claims, SIUs mobilize citizens as agents of surveillance. Through publication of trend data on the scale of disability claims fraud, news stories that dramatize the prosecution of major fraud, and brochures and posters asking citizens to call a tip-line to report on their fellow workers, friends, and neighbors, SIUs encourage routine surveillance by everyone. The appeal is that those who cheat the benefits system are victimizing everyone in the insurance pool. In the case of vehicle insurance, the fact is that everyone is paying hundreds of dollars annually for the damages lottery of personal injury claims, especially regarding whiplash. In the case of workers' compensation insurers, while employers and employees are paying directly for the damages lottery of personal injury claims, every consumer is as well, because the cost of insurance is embedded in the price of goods and services.

An example of the recruitment of informants is provided in a poster distributed by the National Insurance Crime Bureau in the USA. The poster shows a person grimacing in excruciating pain. Indeed the pain is so severe that the eye, cheek, and side of the face are badly disfigured and have an inhuman texture. However, this person has not become badly disfigured and dehumanized by real pain and suffering, but rather by fraud. The word "fraud" is repeated on several levels and with different sizes on the poster, indicating that this is a problem with many layers that need to be peeled back through surveillance to achieve criminalization. Furthermore, each letter in the word "fraud" is shot through with tiny holes to connote that deception must be seen through with microscopic inspection. This poster gives yet another twist to the legendary State Farm Insurance slogan, "Like a Good Neighbor, State Farm is There." The good insurance citizen is urged to see through the pain of fellow workers and neighbors in this way, and "report the rip-off" to the NICB tip-line with a possible reward up to $1,000.

Benefits system citizenship in this form does prove helpful to SIUs. A bodily injury investigator for a government auto insurer I studied said that 14 percent of his unit's caseload derived from informant tips. A workers' compensation insurer I studied worked with Crime Stoppers and, according to an SIU officer interviewed, received 40 to 50 tips each month, some through Crime Stoppers, others provided directly to the SIU.

SIU-coordinated surveillance depends most heavily on proactive approaches, in particular photo surveillance. Photo surveillance involves undercover operatives trying to capture disability claimants on camera doing things that seem to belie their claims of injury. The practice is extensive, involving not only in-house SIU operatives but also private investigators on contract to the insurer and/or employer of the suspected claimant. For example, in the Quebec workers' compensation system, between 1998 and 2002, photo surveillance was conducted on an average of 1,042 injured workers each year. On average, 55 percent of these cases were contracted out to private investigators. In 1995, the British Columbia government motor vehicle insurance corporation used contract private investigators on 4,400 disability case photo surveillance assignments at a cost of $8 million. This custom accounted for the livelihood of about 80 percent ($n = 600$) of registered private investigators in the province. In the United States, there are "tens of thousands of private investigators working on contract to insurers . . . [The company] Photo Surveillance . . . has more than 100 agents nationwide completely outfitted with custom vans, cameras, and in some cases, camouflage jumpsuits designed to look like shrubbery" (Dornstein 1996: 332).

Photo surveillance has two main purposes. First, it is an effort to document that the disability claimant is actually working in gainful employment and therefore committing blatant fraud. Second, and much more commonly, it is used to contend that the person's condition is less serious than claimed in order to contest benefit levels or deny compensation altogether. In this regard, video evidence of an allegedly feigned disability is often used as a bargaining tool to effect a final claims settlement or withdrawal of the claim. If this tactic fails, it is used in evidence in administrative tribunals or arbitration hearings.

Among disability insurers, photo surveillance is normalized as good management practice. In place of the uncertain knowledge of medical science, the iatrogenic tendencies of medical practitioners, and the nomogenic tendencies of legal practitioners, insurers substitute the more certain knowledge of video evidence that helps them assess the credibility of claims and control social security inflation. Photo surveillance is also a tool in adversarial efforts to deal with recalcitrant claimants who are uncooperative or test their legal rights. Lippel (2003: 102) reports that it is more likely to be used in workers' compensation cases in which the worker does not keep appointments, complains about a case coordinator, complains about compensation payments, or fails to comply fully with rehabilitative and return-to-work regimes. In the arena of personal injury arising from vehicle accidents, it is more likely to be used when a claimant proceeds to litigation, and when the behind-the-scenes adversarial battle for an out-of-court settlement intensifies (Ericson, Doyle, and Barry 2003: chap. 9).

Photo surveillance is facilitated by the fact that law treats it as a regulatory matter. As such, it is not subject to criminal law protections such as those relating to reasonable and probable grounds for believing that an offense has been committed, the need to obtain a search warrant, or criminal standards of proof. Indeed, the law reinforces the practice through court decisions and judicial praise for it. A recent Quebec Superior Court judgment (*Dugnay v. Plante et le Tribunal du travail*, DTE 2001 T-1023, (CSQ)) declared, "Covert shadowing and surveillance, or their spectre, particularly when practiced without warning, constitute a pragmatic method to promote respect for the law." Referring to this practice as "the criminalization of convalescence," Lippel (2003: 112) observes that "video surveillance is permissible while it would be illegal to use the same techniques to catch criminals . . . consequences are often much more serious for an injured worker than those affecting many accused under the Criminal Code. Loss of economic support, stigmatization and humiliation, in a context in which health and self-esteem are often extremely fragile, are all serious consequences."

Lippel (2003: 98) interviewed injured workers who "feel they are treated like criminals. One of the reasons given for this relates to the activity of private detective agencies hired to shadow the worker covertly." Moreover, as in the case of

welfare benefit investigations, a great deal of this criminalization is unjustified. In the case of the Quebec Workers'
Compensation Board, anywhere from one-third to one-half
of photo surveillance assignments yield no justification for
suspension of benefits (Lippel 2003: 112).

Photo surveillance operatives sometimes use illegal and
unethical practices that constitute entrapment, harassment,
and unreasonable invasion of privacy. Entrapment can be as
simple as letting the air out of the claimant's car tires in the
hope that she will stoop down to inspect the damage, or better
still try to repair the tire, and be caught on film doing so.
Lippel (2003: 105) reports an American case in which "the
detective befriended an injured worker and invited her to
Disneyland, where he then filmed her enjoying herself and
making gestures that were inconsistent with functional
limitations recognized by the compensation authority."
Harassment is constituted by persistent spying even when the
effort continues to be unproductive. Lippel obtained copies of
a photo surveillance operative's reports to his client, a
workers' compensation board (WCB), that indicate a vindictive as well as overly persistent approach to an injured worker.

> The first report praises the WCB for targeting this particular
> worker, as "[they] have a very large family out there and they are
> always into something like this. I can almost guarantee you are
> correct in questioning this claim." Over several weeks, the detec-
> tive failed to identify any untoward activity, and he became
> increasingly frustrated at his failure to find anything suspect. ". . .
> so far I have spent about 16 of the hours you approved watching
> this guy's place and all I have on him is a couple of trips to the
> local store and one trip to [the local village]."
>
> Nevertheless, the detective suggested that surveillance be con-
> tinued. ". . . I notice that he heats with wood so he will also have
> to start looking for the winter's supply of firewood very soon. I
> am in the area a lot anyway, so I will keep an eye (overall) on his
> place at no charge to you. If he is there or if he is doing some-
> thing then I will start the clock on your time and stay on him.
> (ibid.: 104)

Invasion of privacy is also common. Photo surveillance operatives have been known to use infrared camera and other penetrating technologies to peer into the homes of suspects. In one notorious case in Quebec, the investigator used an infrared camera to film a suspect making love to his wife. This evidence of the suspect's physical abilities was actually submitted to the workers' compensation review board (Lippel 2003: 104)! There are many reports of investigators using false pretenses to gain entry to a home, for example as a salesperson, or expressing interest in buying or renting the property (ibid.; Lowther 1996). Collecting information extraneous to investigations, and for investigative purposes beyond detection of disability claims fraud, is also commonplace. Again it appears that "factitious disorder" is as much an issue in claims suppression by benefits system operatives as it is in claims magnification by the disabled person.

Photo surveillance, combined with other counter-law practices of disability insurers, can have perverse effects. A disability benefits system that is supposed to help the person restore her health and return to work as quickly as possible engages in practices that have the opposite effect. The following case description by Lippel is illustrative.

> A woman was profoundly depressed after having been scalped in an extremely serious work accident, serious depression, and the film shows her leaving her apartment, which is something her case workers were encouraging. They kept saying, "Try to go out, try not to have agoraphobia," which is what she had. So the woman actually manages to get out, and then they film her, so is she ever going to go out again, this woman? What are we doing to these people? And the reason this woman is being filmed is that . . . she's going to be a very costly claim, because she's very seriously disabled. (Canadian Broadcasting Corporation 2004: 98)

Perversities of counter-law also pervade disability claims management in the vehicle insurance system. When there is a personal injury claims crackdown, those deemed to be threats to the integrity of the insurance risk pool are punished through the insurance contract. Insurance availability becomes more selective and exclusive according to ability to pay. Some people deemed threats to the integrity of the benefits system are unpooled into specialized market segments where they pay extraordinarily high premium rates and receive very unfavorable contract conditions. Others are depooled from the availability of any insurance, forced to take the risk of driving without insurance (Ericson, Doyle, and Barry 2003: chap. 7). In Ontario, it is estimated that 10 to 15 percent of all drivers, or about one million people on the roads, drive without insurance. In addition to the potential personal liability they face, this significant proportion of the Ontario population is engaged in the criminal offense of driving without insurance on a daily basis. The government response is further criminalization of this depooled population, which is disproportionately poor but usually in a situation where a car is needed for work (ibid.). "In Ontario, the government has just introduced fines of up to $50,000 for driving without insurance coverage, fines intended to discourage the million Ontario drivers who now either can't afford their sizable premiums, or who optimistically hope to get by without paying. The whiplash lottery may be fun, but not, I expect, at the cost of no longer being able to afford to keep the family car on the road" (Malleson 2002: 264).

Welfare benefits systems

Surveillance in the welfare benefits system scans for signs that the claimant is obeying the terms of the "participation agreement" contract and therefore on her way to being an enterprising neo-liberal citizen. Ironically, the structure of this system fosters forms of enterprising behavior that are forbidden by the contract. Given that benefit levels are far below the poverty line, the claimant is forced into various forms of enterprise to make ends meet: begging for alms from family and friends or on the street; seeking odd jobs, preferably those that pay in cash to avoid detection by the welfare and tax authorities; and seeking a partner for shared shelter and support. However, these activities are seen as grounds for reducing and terminating welfare benefits and, if they have not been reported properly, as grounds for punishing the claimant as a fraudster. When other sources of support, however meager, can bring the claimant closer to the poverty line, the system pulls the plug and punishes, thereby ensuring that she has an even greater struggle to get by.

Mosher and Hermer (2005: 46–7) observe that in the Ontario welfare benefits system "behavior which in any other context would never attract criminal investigation – in fact, behavior which is frequently lauded – becomes the object of suspicion, interest, interrogation and potential sanction: a regular meal at a friend's house; an evening out on a date or a visit to your parent's home; or the payment of your hydro bill by your parents." There is intensive surveillance of intimate relationships for possible criminal charges if the person is materially benefiting from this relationship in ways that are not approved (ibid.: 70–1). Herd and Mitchell (2002: 48) describe a claimant's account of what she was required to report as income offsetting benefits, and what the surveillance infrastructure scanned for in this regard.

> [Gifts] had to be reported. Shoes, and various items like that, you were supposed to report at the dollar value. You were allowed a birthday gift and a gift at Christmas. One of the things that I always remembered on that list was that if you were invited to someone's house on a regular basis for a meal, that meal is a reportable item. Like if every Sunday you went to your Mom's for dinner, you were supposed to say to them, "I had a dinner at my Mother's 3 Sundays this month and the value of the meal was $8.95 or whatever." If you got taken to a restaurant on a regular basis, that was a reportable item . . . One of the few things that was excluded was gifts from the food bank, but you were allowed one visit a month and no more than a certain dollar value.

This surveillance infrastructure is coordinated by eligibility review officers (EROs), who have full legal powers to mobilize surveillance, including the capacity to obtain and effect search warrants. Regulation 134/98, section 65, stipulates that an ERO can: "a) subject to subsection (2), enter any place that the officer believes on reasonable grounds contains evidence relevant to determining a person's eligibility for payments under an Act set out in subsection 58(2) of the O.W.A. 1997; b) inquire into all financial transactions, records and other matters that are relevant to the investigation; and c) demand the production for inspection of anything described in clause (b)." Subsection 2 states, "An officer shall not, without the consent of the occupier, exercise a power to enter a place that is being used as a dwelling except under the authority of a search warrant."

Subsection 5 declares that, "If an officer makes a demand, the person having custody of the things shall produce them to the officer." Finally, subsection 11 indicates that, "An officer may require information or material from a person who is the subject of an investigation under this section or from any person who the officer has reason to believe can provide information or material relevant to the investigation."

There is also an obstructing the investigation provision. OWA (5.79(3)) makes it an offense for anyone to obstruct any authorized person pursuing an investigation, for example, by giving false information. Thus, family, friends, neighbors, landlords, employers, teachers, and others who do not voluntarily inform on suspected welfare cheats as an act of good neo-liberal citizenship can be compelled to do so on threat of also being subject to criminalization.

The primary method of obtaining information is from the claimant herself. As a condition of the "participant agreement" contract, the claimant must consent to self-surveillance at the outset and on a continuous basis.

[O]ne need provide information to verify: birth; marital status; support; immigration status; income; property; debts; S.I.N. [Social Insurance Number]; health card; sponsorship; bank accounts; receivables; funds in trust; boarder; accommodation; school attendance for dependent children; employment; and education status ... checks with Employment Insurance,

Equifax Credit, and Canada Customs and Revenue Agency are mandatory and checks are made with the Ontario Student Assistance Program, the Ministry of Transportation [driving record] and M.E.C.C.A. (enforcement of support orders) as appropriate . . . not uncommonly, the O.W. [Ontario Works] office is in a position where it could quickly access information (because of the consent form or information sharing agreement), yet nevertheless requires recipients to obtain documentation. For recipients, accessing the required documentation can be anything but quick: they may have to deal with an unyielding bureaucracy; or make repeated visits; and/or incur transportation, childcare and other costs. (Mosher and Hermer 2005: 47, 52)

Beyond compelling self-surveillance in these forms, the welfare benefits system seeks informants to be "eyes and ears" on its behalf. An informant tip-line tries to mobilize participants in the everyday life of the claimant to be on the lookout for behavior that, in any other context, would be viewed as healthy and essential to well-being: gift giving, family meals, intimate partnerships, income supplements. According to the *Welfare Fraud Control Report 2001/02*, there were 35,593 welfare fraud complaints of which 6,527 (18.3 percent) derived from the tip-line. Obviously the deputization of neo-liberal citizens to be on the lookout for threats to their tax dollars among the impoverished had a substantial payoff in work for investigators. While these snitches undoubtedly assumed that they were contributing to the integrity of the welfare system, they were at the same time undermining its integrity by fueling the perception that everyone on welfare is suspect and all welfare itself is a fraud against the corporation of neo-liberal citizenship (Chunn and Gavigan 2004: 229–30).

EROs also mobilize the surveillant assemblage of information sharing agreements and "consolidated verification procedures" with other state and non-state entities. In Ontario, there is legal authority to establish information sharing agreements with the Canadian federal government, other provincial governments, and ministries and agencies of the Ontario government. The consolidated verification procedure system provides a database of risk factors that "red flag" potential fraudsters for further investigation. Similar to such systems in the insurance industry and other financial institutions (Ericson, Doyle, and Barry 2003), this system uses moral risk indicators of living beyond one's apparent means, malingering, and tell-tale household arrangements to indicate who should be investigated, penalized, or excluded. For example, higher risk indicators include high accommodation costs in proportion to income, being on welfare benefits for an extended period, and living with others (Mosher and Hermer 2005: 46).

Similar to the situation of disability claimants described in the previous section, welfare claimants experience forms of entrapment, harassment, and invasion of privacy. There is an ERO program of random home visits, with or without notice, in which consolidated verification procedure risk criteria are sometimes used to identify targets and justify particular forms of scrutiny (ibid.: 46–7). The surveillance infrastructure in general is experienced by claimants as based on continuous entrapment, harassment, and invasion. "[V]irtually everyone on welfare struggles to survive and comply with this intense and unrelenting web of surveillance, experiencing ongoing and profound violations of privacy and living in fear of a 'fraud' allegation. Moreover, very substantial numbers of recipients are subjected to fraud accusations and resulting investigations in which they are frequently put in the humiliating position of having to explain why they are managing to survive on benefits which are acknowledged to be wholly inadequate" (ibid.: 14).

Welfare surveillance infrastructures have perverse effects. The greatest perversion was introduced at the beginning of this section: the claimant is contractually obligated to become an enterprising neo-liberal citizen, but is at the same time forced to engage in forms of entrepreneurship that, while acceptable and even lauded in other contexts, are suppressed and criminalized in this context.

A second perversion derives from the ways in which surveillant assemblages erode community solidarity and limit
the prospects of the claimant for full community membership. As Mosher and Hermer (2005: 55–6) document, the
informant system breeds malicious reporting of claimant
behavior: false reports are made by abusive partners seeking
further control, landlords pursuing evictions, and vindictive
neighbors. The informant tip-line sometimes rings with
gossip that is corrosive of community. The claimant is too
often silenced, fearful that any words or actions might be
taken and used as evidence of fraud against her. As in other
total information awareness campaigns, both the target population and those mobilized as informants live in a climate of
fear and suspicion.

A third perversion is embedded in the cost–benefit framework that is so dear to this counter-law regime of risk and
regulation. As Chunn and Gavigan (2004: 232) observe, the
added costs of the return-to-work programs and surveillant
assemblages, including regulatory staff, may well exceed what
is saved through cutbacks and case-by-case claims suppression. In 2002, a conservative estimate for the administrative
cost of the Ontario welfare infrastructure was $18.7 million.
While one will never know how much money this infrastructure saved by intimidating the destitute into not press-
ing their claims, it is easy to calibrate the benefit that would
have accrued if this money had been given to them as part of
their effort to inch closer to the poverty line.

The Two Leviathans

Social benefits fraud is a real threat. Social security efforts to
address this threat produce myths. These myths in turn constitute new realities of crime, risk, and uncertainty.

The over-arching myth of the war on social benefits fraud
is that all social benefits are a kind of fraud against the well-
being and prosperity of society as a whole. In making pain-
staking distinctions between the deserving disabled and poor

and those who are undeserving, the social security system criminalizes all benefit claimants as threats to its integrity. Claimants are the suitable enemy, the malicious demons who threaten to drag down the entire social body as visualized in the neo-liberal social imaginary. They are the Leviathan of the biblical social imaginary, sea monsters who soak the population of resources they have rightfully gained as enterprising neo-liberal citizens.

Social benefits fraud is a product of the myths and realities of the neo-liberal politics of uncertainty. As we have seen, neo-liberal policies intensify wealth inequality and make more people destitute. Benefits system operatives themselves describe how neo-liberal policies increase benefits system claims, including fraudulent claims as the "last straw."

Neo-liberalism does include a program of wealth redistribution, but it is socialism for business enterprise. As McClusky (2002) shows in the case of changes to workers' compensation schemes in the USA, there has been more social security for employers, while employees are forced to embrace more risk, including that of permanent disabilities that have driven significant numbers of the population from middle-class stability to financial ruin.

When placed in desperate financial straits, benefits system claimants face excruciating moral conflicts. When does the noble motive of preserving one's health and that of one's children through cheating, secrecy, and lying outweigh one's moral commitment to the integrity of the social benefits system? Similar rationalizations of self-interest versus the public good are made by individuals in other contexts of less need, for example when crossing borders and reporting to customs officials, or when filing income tax returns. At the level of corporate entities, politicians cheat, maintain secrecy, and lie for what they regard as noble motives of security and prosperity (Bok 1979, 1982). Police authorities do the same, especially in cases of national security. Private corporate executives also rationalize cheating, secrecy, and lying in the context of noble motives to protect corporate security interests (especially profit-making and avoiding liability for harms) and personal interests (what they feel they deserve in compensation packages for being so instrumental in helping their organization to be profitable and to avoid liabilities).

David Matza (1957) taught us long ago that such techniques of moral neutralization arise in all personal and institutional spheres of decision-making to rationalize that which, when viewed in isolation and the abstract, is immoral, and often criminal, conduct.

Neo-liberal government makes both individuals and corporate entities more autonomous and self-interested. Ironically, success in this regard amplifies the moral hazards which neo-liberal government condemns and seeks to control. Relatively autonomous and self-interested, people do have less inclination to help governing institutions protect against losses. This inclination leads the governing institutions to distrust the self-governing capacity of the governed and to intensify criminalization through counter-law in an amplifying spiral.

Distrust and the urge to criminalize in the social benefits system is compounded by uncertainty among experts over what conditions are deserving of benefits. Disability benefits fraud is a conundrum because of the limitations of medical knowledge as to what constitutes a disability for insurance purposes, and what treatment and financial compensation are therefore reasonable. Welfare benefits fraud is a conundrum because of the limitations of social caseworker knowledge as to whether a person receiving welfare benefits has other viable means of support, or could be taking more initiative to "work harder" and become self-sufficient. In both cases of social security provision, the parameters and levels of fraud are a fluid, not a solid. Fraud is a direct product of how the social security system seeks to define and control it.

Faced with both the broader neo-liberal politics of uncertainty and professional experts' uncertainty over the problems they are supposed to remedy, benefits system operatives opt for "governing through fraud" as a means of claims suppression and cost control. In the case of disability claims, medical experts are mobilized as agents of surveillance and to manufacture and apply criminal labels of fraud: illness behavior, secondary gain, compensationitis, dissimulation disorder, factitious disorder, pain disorder, chronic pain syndrome, malingering, and activity intolerance. These labels make the myths of rampant fraud stick in particular cases, thereby affirming the reality.

In the case of welfare claims, casework professionals mobilize institutional databases, as well as family and friends of the client, for vigilance about signs of fraud. Every move of the claimant to supplement benefit levels that are well below the poverty line is subject to intense scrutiny as possibly illegal. Ironically, while the system contractually obligates the claimant to become an enterprising citizen, the meager benefit levels force her to engage in forms of entrepreneurship that, while accepted and even lauded for citizens in other contexts, are suppressed and criminalized in this context. The system criminalizes anyone who fails to give off the proper signs of becoming an enterprising neo-liberal citizen, that is, someone who works constantly at self-betterment as defined within the strict parameters of the system. The myth of widespread fraud becomes a reality.

While it criminalizes with severe sanctions – loss of income and support, loss of social legitimacy, being on a probationary status of citizenship that is indeterminate – this system does not meet the standards of criminal law. Rights are taken away in the interest of administrative convenience of regulatory agencies governing through contracts. As we saw in the case of photo surveillance, practices do not meet criminal law standards regarding reasonable and probable grounds for believing an offense has been committed, the need to obtain a search warrant, and criteria of admissible evidence. Photo surveillance has even been lauded by the courts as a means of promoting respect for the law among people who would surely be fraudsters otherwise.

Such institutional support for governing through fraud in the social security system guarantees the success of claims suppression. At the same time, there is ample evidence that the systematic denial of claims has adverse health, well-being, and prosperity effects on the claimant. These effects often compound the problems the social security system is supposed to ameliorate. As Lippel (2003: 97) concludes, "The use of surveillance techniques in the context of social security legislation not only represents, in many cases, a violation of fundamental rights, but also contributes to the stigmatism of all injured workers and constitutes an impediment to successful and rapid rehabilitation from injury. The influence of economists and their concept of 'moral hazard,' which promotes system design that discourages reliance on benefits, is seen as a possible explanation for the apparent tolerance of practices that would be judged illegal in other contexts."

The myths of social benefits fraud constitute the realities of a counter-law regime that undermines the principles, standards, and procedures of democratic legal institutions that have been foundational for social security as envisaged since Hobbes' Leviathan. The institutionalized suspicion, denial of rights, discriminatory practices, unreasonable invasions of privacy, and social exclusion resulting from this counter-law regime indicate that the state as Leviathan is beginning to resemble the original biblical representation of the sea monster. In exercising its catastrophic imagination and instituting a precautionary regime in the name of protecting the integrity of the social security system from benefits fraud, the state leaves death and destruction in its wake. Some victims have chosen suicide (Chunn and Gavigan 2004; Mosher and Hermer 2005). Among those who choose life, there is often only a vicious swirl between destitution and prostitution.

4
Corporate Security

Corporate Liabilities and the Politics of Uncertainty

Corporate activities with potential for catastrophic loss are at the forefront of the politics of uncertainty and urge to criminalize. For example, controversies rage over the security of food supplies (Schwartz 2003), pharmaceutical products (Angell 2004), medical services (Baker 2005), nuclear, biological, and chemical production (Fortun 2001; Beamish 2002; Petryna 2002), financial institutions (Pauley 1997; Schiller 2003), and environments (Stehr and von Storch 1999; Tsing 2005). These controversies focus on the "manufactured uncertainties" (Beck 1992, 1999; Giddens 1990, 1994) of public and private corporate activities, and the threats they pose to the lives and livelihoods of innocent people.

There is a particular concern about the manufactured uncertainties of multinational corporations. Comparing their annual revenues with nation-state gross domestic product (GDP), multinational corporations constitute 51 of the world's largest 100 economies (Wells and Elias 2005: 147–8). However, when it comes to redressing the harms involuntarily imposed, these corporate entities lack democratic processes of accountability parallel to those of Western nation-states. They often escape responsibility for fair compensation of victims and for new precautionary measures to minimize future harms.

The politics of uncertainty focuses on the reluctance of governments to improve democratic processes of accountability within corporations. Indeed, states have typically supported specific corporate interests through their approaches to corporate regulation. Company law grants limited liability to private corporations, giving them many rights and few responsibilities. Tort remedies for involuntary harms often fall below expectations because the legal process is arduous, damage awards are unpredictable, and the deterrent effect is minimal. Companies often fail to introduce adequate safety measures following a loss, seeing the occasional catastrophic consequences of their activities as a cost of doing business (Atiyah 1997; Bell and O'Connell 1997). Criminal law remedies are viewed as limited for a number of reasons, in particular the difficulty in attributing responsibility for the harms caused to specified members of the corporate entity, or to the corporation itself as a "legal person" (Harvard Law Review 2001a). These problems in seeking legal remedies are compounded in the context of multinational corporations causing harms across borders. While there are some tort remedies – for example the Alien Tort Claims Act in the USA, which permits people abroad to initiate private tort suits against US corporations for human rights violations – these are limited in use and impact. The fundamental problem is that "International law has neither articulated human rights obligations of corporations nor provided mechanisms to enforce such obligations" (ibid.: 2025–6).

The politics of uncertainty compels changes to both national and international legal regimes to make corporate entities more responsible for the harms they impose. Contrary to Giddens (1990, 1994) and Beck (1992, 1999), who contend that manufactured uncertainties exclude the identification of responsible parties, the political trend at the beginning of the 21st century is to identify responsible parties and make them accountable through imaginative uses of counter-law. This responsibilization strategy is based on the view that possible outcomes in the world are amenable to human decisions and interventions, if not through the sciences and technologies of risk, then through precautionary legal measures aimed at preemption of harm. It is also based on the view that while science and technology have made many things safer and better, there is inequality in this respect that needs to be redressed. Corporate entities often improve their own security at the expense of ordinary people. We have already considered one example in chapter 3, regarding changes to workers' compensation schemes in the USA that provide more security to corporate entities at the expense of their employees. But the examples are legion, leading to the fact that trust in corporate entities is at an all-time low (Bakan 2004).

The politics of uncertainty places new demands on both political and corporate authorities to demonstrate their vigilance in addressing sources of catastrophic loss. Within a precautionary logic, they are asked to severely restrict, or even prohibit, corporate activity believed to be linked to the possibility of catastrophic loss. When catastrophic loss occurs, they are to provide extraordinary levels of compensation, both in recognition of the harm inflicted and as a punitive reminder of the need for more precaution. As Power (2004: 41–2) observes, "A wider set of risks and dangers facing individuals is being increasingly perceived as 'involuntary,' imposed by business and public organizations who must be made responsible. Indeed, if all risks were thought of in this way, all law would be compensatory law. It may be that a growing understanding of many risks as involuntary and compensatible provides the cultural climate for the social amplification of risk and for the necessary legalization of organisational life."

In the politics of uncertainty over corporate security, compensation alone is deemed insufficient. All law cannot be compensatory law because the loss has no price for those whose lives and livelihoods are destroyed. Criminalization is turned to, involving new forms and combinations of criminal, civil, and administrative law. Criminalization is aimed at retributive punishment of those held responsible when things go wrong, not only through extraordinary compensation awards, but also through fines and imprisonment. Criminalization is also intended to prevent things from going wrong: threatening to punish and stigmatize responsible parties for failures in risk management.

It should be kept in mind that corporate regulation has been the most significant domain of public policing historically (Smith 1978). "The business regulatory agencies grew to be more significant law enforcers than the police because the corporatization of the world in the 20th century changed the world to a place where most of the important things done for good or ill in the world were done by corporate rather than individual actors (Braithwaite and Drahos 2000)" (Braithwaite 2003: 10–11). State regulatory institutions started out as more punitive (Carson 1979; Braithwaite 1985), but became less so with the evolution of insurance, tort remedies that relied heavily on insurance, and compliance models of law enforcement. While there have been a few control waves of more punitiveness over the 20th century, the general approach of regulatory law enforcers has been one of compliance rather than punitive deterrence (Reiss 1984; Hawkins 2002). However, at the beginning of the 21st century, there is a new punitiveness based on precautionary logic, and a new regulatory environment aimed at instantiating this logic in the everyday life of organizations.

This new regulatory environment entails more and different forms of regulation than occurred in the past. Under neoliberal governments, market fundamentalism has been fostered, including greater privatization of formerly public corporate entities. Contrary to conventional wisdom that market fundamentalism entails deregulation, the opposite has occurred (Ayres and Braithwaite 1992; Power 2004; Hutter and Power 2005). Enterprising corporate entities are seen by state authorities as requiring more regulation to keep markets fair and competitive, and to facilitate safety measures in the new environment of entrepreneurial risk-taking. At the same time, and also contrary to conventional wisdom, corporate entities themselves often demand more regulation as a means of disciplining the "freer" market and maintaining a viable playing field among competitors. Indeed, in many spheres of business enterprise, the regulated entities collectively pay for the state regulatory agency's operations. The state governs corporate enterprise, but in turn corporations also govern the state (Braithwaite and Drahos 2000; Ericson, Doyle, and Barry 2003: chap. 5).

Osborne and Gaebler (1992; see also Braithwaite 2003) depict this new regulatory environment as one in which the state now "steers" private corporate activity rather than "rows." However, it is doubtful that the state did much rowing in most spheres of corporate activity historically. Moreover, in the new regulatory environment, the state often does much more than steer. Through new regulatory regimes and the surveillant assemblages they enable, the state frequently channels corporate activities into narrow grooves of routine conduct. State and industry regulators map out the approved channels of corporate activity and leave any steering capacity remaining to the corporate actors. This steering capacity is more akin to that required on a canal boat moving from lock to lock than on a supertanker in high seas.

This regulatory environment creates a radically new and expanded role for public administration. Risk assessment becomes not only a tool for converting uncertainty into risk, but also a way of governing corporate entities and their decision-makers (Fisher 2003). The thrust of this corporate governance is the translation of the real risks the organization faces into organizational surveillance mechanisms, such as early warning and compliance audit mechanisms.

> Thus many risks can be, and are being, operationalised as organisational processes of control, e.g. BSE and farm management systems, GM crops and traceability systems, earthquakes and emergency services/building regulations, terrorism and the organization of security and intelligence services . . . Organisational translations of risk into internal controls are necessary conditions

of possibility for risk-based regulation, and hence for the successful operation of the risk management state. Internal control is thereby the state in organisational miniature. (Power 2004: 24)

Through legalization of these internal control systems, the state enhances its place *within* corporate governance structures. Internal control systems of private corporate entities are thereby made visible for ongoing public policy and law reform initiatives. These internal control systems help stabilize the macro-politics of uncertainty by routinizing a micro-politics of surveillance and visibility (Haggerty and Ericson 2006). This micro-politics is aimed at providing reassurance about corporate security, and the effectiveness of state government in helping to "guarantee" this security.

Historically, law enforcement has been a "last resort" in seeking corporate compliance (Hawkins 2002). In the new regulatory environment, law is increasingly seen as a first resort, both to hold authorities responsible when a catastrophe occurs and to further institutionalize surveillance and visibility in the everyday priorities of organizations. A catastrophic event demands an authoritative response, and law is turned to as an expression of authoritative certainty and closure. Law helps to impose meaning on uncertainty, especially law that criminalizes through increasing punitiveness and more minute controls of decision-makers deemed responsible for safety.

In what follows I examine innovative uses of counter-law in the field of corporate security. New laws against law are being devised to criminalize officials deemed responsible for the catastrophic consequences of corporate practices, even if they had no direct control over, or knowledge about, these practices, and even if these practices were widely regarded as acceptable before the catastrophe. These new laws against law have effectively criminalized a few political and corporate authorities, and played their part in the symbolic politics of uncertainty. However, criminalization at this level is nascent, and its long-term influence on legal forms and corporate security is unclear.

The real legal revolution is taking place at the level of counter-law II, the surveillant assemblages that now govern the minutiae of corporate conduct. Surveillance infrastructures regarding corporate security have greatly expanded and intensified in the new regulatory environment. Through these infrastructures the state is omnipresent in private corporate life. At the same time, the corporate world is being turned inside out, made more publicly visible than ever before. As we have already observed in the spheres of national security and social security, there are real effects of such counter-law with regard to institutionalized suspicion, denial of rights, discriminatory practices, unreasonable invasions of privacy, exclusion, and unintended consequences.

Counter-law I: Laws Against Law

It is widely acknowledged that criminalization of corporate liability for harm has increased across Western nation-states in the past decade (Wells and Elias 2005). However, there is variation in the legal mechanisms used to criminalize. For example, in most countries of Western Europe, criminal law addresses individual human agents, and criminal liability of groups has been unacceptable as a matter of principle. Therefore administrative law is typically used as a preferred route to impose corporate sanctions. At the same time, as we shall see, some of these jurisdictions are devising innovative approaches to criminal law to control the behavior of corporate entities. In Anglo-American common law jurisdictions, there is more scope for criminalizing groups, and a mix of approaches to criminalization involving criminal, quasi-criminal, and administrative procedures and sanctions. This mix also includes new laws against law that erode established principles, standards, and procedures of criminal law.

Criminal law is premised on individual culpability for wrongdoing. This premise is challenged when the wrongdoing results from corporate activity that is organized and collective. The challenge is even greater when the corporate wrongdoing involves members of different organizations. For example, in corporate fraud cases such as Enron, the parties to the scandal included not only directors and officers of the company, but also accounting firms, banks, investment dealers, and other financial industry organizations. In the criminal law model of individual culpability, the enforcement task is to identify parties directly responsible for the wrongful harms caused and to punish them. This task is fraught with difficulty in the corporate context because the wrongdoing is typically a product of organizational cultures, inter-organizational systems, and collective decisions. There is a tendency to find a few individual malicious demons and scapegoat them in order to reproduce myths of control and accountability, when the real problems lie in the structure, organization, and regulation of corporate entities. The result can be unjust criminalization of selected individuals who may not have directly participated in, or even had direct knowledge of, the wrongful practices, and, if they did, may have been conducting business as usual in a corporate culture that did not define the activity as having harmful consequences.

The alternative to criminalization based on individual culpability is to reconceptualize the corporate entity as a legal person. As Hutter (2005: 82) observes, "recently there has been a discernible pressure to target the corporation and to call the body corporate to account." Legal fictions are created to anthropomorphize the corporation as if it is a rational entity that can be held responsible for its thoughts and actions. In the extreme, the corporation is depicted as pathological in its pursuit of self-interest and profits, the Leviathan as sea monster that must be criminalized in order to halt the devastation it leaves in its wake (Bakan 2004).

A less extreme view is the argument that while criminal law principles and doctrines keep the individual at the forefront, group liability has actually emerged in various practical contexts of criminal law. Many jurisdictions have recognized the criminological truism that a great deal of criminal activity is group based in, for example, organized crime syndicates, motorcycle gangs, drug distribution networks, and local criminal subcultures. Criminal law has responded to this reality through new laws aimed at criminal organizations, for example regarding seizure of the proceeds of crime and other assets. The same logic can be used to devise new criminal, quasi-criminal, and administrative laws that criminalize corporate entities.

> Group based liability is uncomfortably accommodated rather than clearly embraced. Yet in practical terms its significance is hard to overstate. It is not just aiding and abetting or participatory liability that we need to include here, but inchoate forms such as incitement and conspiracy which assume more than one "player." In regulatory law corporations are often prosecuted and competition law seeks to control cartels. There is a centrality to groups in criminal law practice that is denied by its relative marginality in theoretical accounts. (Wells and Elias 2005: 164)

As Wells and Elias also point out, the International Criminal Court provides another example of efforts to target the organization, planning, and incitement of offenses more than the actual direct perpetrators of crime.

Of course, the theoretical and doctrinal aspects of criminal law are not separate from practice but are in a dialectic with it. Questions of corporate personhood and law address not only the regulatory aspects of law but also its symbolic or expressive aspects in the politics of uncertainty. Defining the corporation in terms of personhood is a political matter because it signifies the nature of corporate membership in the political community and associated values, aspirations, identities, and responsibilities. This signification in turn has influence on the regulatory level, shaping corporate behavior and specific responses to it, including those that involve criminalization.

> Legal personhood is more than a metaphor; it becomes, in many cases, law's repository for expressions of anxiety about powerfully divisive social issues . . . In debates about corporate personhood, lasting terminological anxiety expresses the tension between the desire to stimulate the economy by granting

constitutional protections to corporations and the fear that unchecked corporate growth may have socially deleterious effects or that unchecked recognition of corporate personhood may cheapen our own. (Harvard Law Review 2001a: 1759–60)

Historically, the legal fiction of corporate personhood has given corporations recognition as bearers of certain rights, and much less recognition as bearers of legal obligations and thus entities that should be sanctioned for wrongdoing, criminal or otherwise. For example, in the USA corporate personhood has been used to grant corporations property rights, as well as Bill of Rights privileges with the exception of the Fifth Amendment right against self-incrimination. The Bill of Rights privileges require radical anthropomorphization of the corporation as having an autonomous existence prior to and separate from its creation by the state or the individuals who constitute it, and thus a unique entity deserving of rights protections.

As one commentator observes, American courts selectively deploy various approaches to personhood as a matter of political expediency. In the case of the US Supreme Court, there is a question of whether its "corporate personhood jurisprudence is purely result oriented. At least, it does not seem a coincidence that as the increasingly complex modern corporation has become increasingly dependent on Bill of Rights protections and the American economy has become increasingly dependent on corporations, courts have adjusted definitions of personhood to accommodate the modern corporation's need for the protections" (ibid.: 1754).

At the same time the USA is a leading nation-state in applying juristic personhood standards to corporate entities and regarding them as individuals liable for the acts and omissions of employees as agents (Lofquist, Cohen, and Rabe 1997). This "agency" or "vicarious liability" principle equates corporate culpability with that of an individual. In federal law, this principle is applied to the wrongdoing of organizational agents regarding strict liability offenses as well as those requiring *mens rea*. In criminal law, which is a matter of state rather than federal jurisdiction, this principle has been accepted for strict liability offenses. Some innovative theories of knowledge pertaining to imaginaries of corporate person-hood have been invoked to sustain legal actions. For example, it has been held that there is an aggregation of knowledge that can be imputed to the corporation that is the sum of what each actor knows in part only.

> [K]nowledge acquired by employees within the scope of their employment is imputed to the corporation. In consequence, a corporation cannot plead innocence by asserting that the information obtained by several employees was not acquired by one individual employee who then should have comprehended its full impact. Rather, the corporation is considered to have acquired the collective knowledge of its employees and is held responsible for their failure to act accordingly. (*US v. T.I. M.E.-D.C., Inc.* (1974) 381 F. Supp. 730 (WD Va.), at 738–9, cited by Wells and Elias 2005: 158)

The Australian Criminal Code Act 1995 reconfigures corporate liability by focusing explicitly on corporate culture and management systems. Section 12 of this Act provides that for offenses involving intention, knowledge, or reckless-ness, fault "must be attributed to a body corporate that expressly, tacitly or impliedly authorized or permitted the commission of the offence." One way of showing authoriza-tion or permission is to demonstrate that the corporate culture was the source of wrongdoing. Corporate culture is not only constituted by written rules and policies, but also by unwritten rules, policies, attitudes, and practices conducive to wrongdoing (Wells and Elias 2005: 158).

English law approaches corporate liability for wrongdoing in a somewhat different way. The agency or vicarious liabil-ity approach is limited to some regulatory offenses. Otherwise, "identification liability" specifies a limited group of company officers as representing the embodied knowledge of the company. The company is held liable for their culpa-ble transgressions, but not for those of other employees. In both vicarious and identification liability, any employee can be prosecuted individually, and the company can be held liable only if fault is established in one person.

In the past 20 years there have been innovative efforts to develop an English law of corporate manslaughter based on "management failure . . . conduct falling far below what can reasonably be expected of the corporation in the circumstances" (Wells and Elias 2005: 158; see also Wells 2001). This approach to criminalization emerged as a key strategy in the politics of uncertainty, an effort to give greater recognition to systemic sources of catastrophic loss. It was underpinned by public inquiries into disasters that also attributed blame at the organizational level; for example, the Steen Inquiry into the capsized ferry, *Herald of Free Enterprise*, the Fennel Report into the Kings' Cross Underground fire, and the Hidden Report into the Clapham Junction rail crash (Wells 2001; Hutter 2005).

The counter-law maneuver of corporate manslaughter within an identification liability framework has had limited effect. Only seven corporate manslaughter cases have resulted in convictions, all involving very small companies, such as an activity center determined to have been grossly negligent in the death of four teenagers on a canoe trip (*The Times*, July 15, 2005, p. 19). In contrast, corporate manslaughter charges against large railway companies and their officers after train crashes have not resulted in convictions. For example, following the Southall crash, one of the train companies involved was charged with seven counts of manslaughter through gross negligence. However, no convictions resulted because of legal difficulties in establishing negligence by any individual in the company, and in attributing intent to the corporate body. The company did plead guilty to regulatory offenses under the Health and Safety at Work etc. Act 1974, "but this was clearly viewed by the press, the families of those killed in the crash and the judge to be separate from the opprobrium which attached to more traditional criminal charges" (Hutter 2005: 84). Following the train crash at Hatfield in 2000 that resulted in four deaths, the rail maintenance company Balfour Beatty was charged with corporate manslaughter, as were five of its senior officers under identification liability. The prosecution contended that company employees systematically operated outside the rules of safety, and ignored warnings about a specific safety infrastructure problem. In July 2005, five months into the trial, corporate manslaughter charges against both the company and its senior officers were dismissed upon instruction from the judge to the jury.

In 2005, draft legislation was introduced to create a statutory offense of corporate manslaughter. This proposed legislation is intended to counter the legal conundrums of identification liability and the need to determine who is the "directing mind" of the company. The proposed legislation would find the company guilty of corporate manslaughter if the prosecution can prove that senior officers ran the company in such a way that its activities were systematically in breach of health and safety laws and therefore were grossly negligent in causing a person's death. The proposed punishment is fines without limit against the company. A *Times* editorial addressing this proposed legislation captures the continuing role of corporate manslaughter in the politics of uncertainty.

> The new law is largely symbolic and a sop to unions. Companies already face potentially unlimited fines under existing health and safety legislation for killing members of the public or employees. The emotive desire on the part of a deceased person's relatives to brand a company with the "corporate manslaughter" charge is what lies behind the move. This meets the instinctive and unfortunate view of many on the Left, which has lobbied for the new laws, that all corporations are intrinsically bad . . . The new law's application to public bodies is also problematic. Have ministers considered the potential embarrassment when an NHS [National Health Service] trust is branded a corporate killer after a patient dies from a hospital acquired infection? If business is concerned about the new law, the Government should be more so. (*The Times*, July 15, 2005, p. 19)

Government officials concerned about how the politics of uncertainty over corporate liability might affect them can derive lessons from France (Roussel 2002, 2003). During the 1990s in France, there was an acceleration of prosecutions of political authorities for failing to anticipate catastrophe and manage risks in a variety of fields: blood supplies, technological failures, financial service management, and so on. Prosecutions were brought through innovative uses of an ordinary law of criminal negligence originally intended to apply to road and occupational safety contexts. In the late 1990s, 54 parliamentarians were committed to trial and 14 were convicted and sentenced regarding various scandals of corporate security. There were many more prosecutions of politicians and officials at regional and municipal levels of government.

This criminalization was a desperate expression of authoritative certainty and responsibility through counter-law in conditions where other mechanisms of political authority and governance of uncertainty were lacking. For example, a prosecutor involved in the prosecution of three ministers in a blood contamination case posed the following series of questions:

> Who governs asks the victim of social risks? A science that is or claims to be irresponsible? An administration assigned to implement tests without controlling them? Political consultants with an uncertain status or without any status? Politicians that did not know? Who still governs if the judge becomes the arbiter of these illusive responsibilities? (Roussel 2003: 129)

Fortunately for them, politicians have control over the legislative process. In 2000, the Minister of Justice introduced a bill entitled "The Definition of Unintentional Offenses", aimed at curbing the mounting prosecutions against her colleagues for matters over which they had no direct knowledge or control. In introducing the bill, the Minister observed, "It is not fair that a mayor could be sentenced for homicide because a child had been electrocuted with a lamp post, installed 20 years before by his predecessors, even when he had never been alerted to the problem of this lamp post's maintenance." (ibid,: 134)

The prosecution of political authorities for failures in corporate security was intended to foster a precautionary environment. According to Roussel, this effort was largely successful. "After the mid-1990s, this field of criminal responsibility was reorganized around the notions of imprudence and precaution. Accusations of lack of 'precaution' . . . were increasingly invoked to stigmatize imprudent, risky, irresponsible behaviors" (Roussel 2003: 125–6). A new "politics of visible precaution" arose in which both corporate authorities and politicians engaged in dramatic rituals of preempting all manner of risk. For example, in the face of a foot-and-mouth disease outbreak in England, 50,000 French sheep were slaughtered even though no ill sheep had been detected in France. The French sheep were merely suspected of having the disease because they had been in contact with English sheep suspected of having the disease. Based on a precautionary view of suspicion by association, or what might be called "sheep terrorism," the "obvious" solution was a preemptive strike to hopefully eliminate the risk.

These myriad forms of criminalizing corporate and political authorities for failures in risk management run counter to established principles, standards, and procedures of criminal law. Authorities are deemed criminally responsible for errors and omissions at a great distance from them in terms of organizational hierarchy, knowledge, and geography. They are charged and punished retrospectively for actions which, in many cases, they regarded as the normal way of doing business. Caught up in "zero tolerance" waves of criminalization that are characteristic of the politics of uncertainty, they face demonization through zero law, law against law.

None of this denies that some corporate actors intentionally engage in criminal conduct and deserve to be criminalized, any more than one can deny the realities of terrorist activity or social benefits fraud. What is at issue here is the precautionary logic of these efforts to criminalize and its implications for criminal justice. Take the example of Enron. Enron had a fully developed corporate risk infrastructure that met state-of-the-art expectations at the time. While Enron criminal prosecutions are, at the time of writing, still in process, it is important to observe that many of the parties implicated were engaged in creative compliance accounting practices that were widely in use and remain so (McBarnet 2006). The criminal actions of a few members of Arthur Andersen, the accounting firm engaged by Enron, effectively destroyed an established global company and displaced the lives and livelihoods of thousands of its employees and their families. The shredding of accounting documents pertaining to Enron not only resulted in convictions, a $500,000 fine, and five years' probation for obstructing justice, but brought "into question the legitimacy of the entire global organization to practice audits. This seems to have happened because these specific actions were also regarded as reflecting a sys temic or cultural feature of larger firms. Timing was also critical: coinciding with the audit renewal season, clients left and the firm was effectively doomed" (Power 2004: 33).

The case of Barings Bank and its high-rolling Far East trader, Nick Leeson, also illustrates how normal business practices become redefined as criminally abnormal after a catastrophic loss. As Hutter and Power (2005: 14) observe, Leeson operated in a risk-taking climate of "notional normality" tolerated by senior management, but became notionally deviant in retrospect. Leeson was held primarily and criminally at fault for unauthorized trading, and he was imprisoned as a result. However, events "unfolded over a period of time in which senior management denial (Stein 2000) or ignorance, the overriding of formal controls and a culture of risk-taking combined to destroy the organization" (ibid.). Indeed, non-criminal investigations held others responsible for the collapse: the accounting profession excluded a former deputy chairman of Barings from membership in its professional association, disciplined the former finance director of Barings, and initiated proceedings against the accounting firm that audited Barings; the Securities and Futures Association initiated disciplinary actions against several former members of Barings senior management; and the Secretary of State for Trade and Industry brought proceedings in the High Court to disqualify several former Barings directors (Hutter 2005: 81).

Criminalization of corporate liability for harm through innovative laws against law has intensified over the past decade and will continue to be a key feature of the politics of uncertainty in the 21st century. Across jurisdictions, administrative procedures and sanctions are being replaced by criminal provisions, and there are new international conventions and human rights approaches to criminalizing corporate liability (Wells and Elias 2005; Harvard Law Review 2001b). However, as we have seen, those developments are nascent and vary across jurisdictions. Criminalization in this sphere remains highly selective and largely symbolic, feeding into the rituals of visible precaution that characterize the politics of uncertainty.

Criminalization of corporate liability for harm through new laws against law may nevertheless have influence at the level of corporate organization and decision-making. Combined with new surveillant assemblages for corporate governance analyzed in the next section, criminalization fosters greater prudence to anticipate harmful consequences of corporate activity and to take action to prevent it. Since harms can occur through systemic processes over which the individual corporate actor has little or no control, and yet he or she faces possible criminal sanctions when things go wrong, there is strong incentive to exercise extreme precaution. Uncertainty is to be managed by exercising the catastrophic imagination of worst-case scenarios, and by intensifying surveillant assemblages in the hope that those scenarios do not become real-life dramas.

Precautionary logic also pervades the new approach to criminal sanctioning in this sphere. The traditional criminal law framework of crime–responsibility–punishment is transformed. Strict liability replaces the conundrums of intention and guilt, and *actus reus* and *mens rea* are preempted. Responsibility remains relevant, but it is now responsibility to exercise extreme precaution in face of uncertainty and catastrophic imaginaries. Writing in the French context analyzed by Roussel, Ewald observes that

> the sanction escapes the reference to available knowledge, a standard of determined knowledge, whether one is judged not only by what one should know but also by what one should have or might have suspected. Here, precautionary logic, even if it extends the field of subjective responsibilities because it focuses on the act of decision, does not strictly speaking enter into the former logic of fault. The latter presupposes the existence of knowledge, which is absent here because one is *ex hypothese* uncertain . . . Under the old approach to responsibility, uncertainty of knowledge was innocence. The application of the precautionary principle gives a very different result: the uncertainty is not an excuse, but rather a reason for greater caution . . . sanctioning such "responsibility" can only lead to a considerable restriction of entrepreneurial effort . . . Is it not unjust to judge an act from the perspective of another state of awareness than that under which it was carried out? Is it fair, even for purposes of compensation, to appraise an act in accordance with suspicions and doubts that one is only capable of having after the event? (Ewald 2002: 287, 291)

Counter-law II: Surveillant Assemblages

In the sphere of corporate security, the real legal revolution, the real criminalization, is taking place at the level of counter-law II. The surveillant assemblages of corporate entities – early warning devices, regulations, inspections, audits, private policing – expand and intensify after each public drama of catastrophic loss and the politics of uncertainty it triggers. "Verification of the observance of decision-making procedures takes on paramount importance" (Ewald 2002: 287).

There is a proliferation of "organizing organizations" (Brunsson and Jacobsson 2000) charged with writing rules and standards for corporate entities, and thereby effecting warning, monitoring, inspection, and auditing mechanisms.

Organizing organizations include not only state regulatory agencies, but also professional associations, industry associations, insurers, and various private regulatory bodies. For example, the Sarbanes–Oxley Act (2002), passed to address the financial reporting scandals in corporate America, mobilizes layers of organizing organizations for minute surveillance of company directors and officers. Bodies such as the Committee of Sponsoring Organizations of the Treadway Commission (2004) provide guidance to companies on compliance with the requirements of the Act (Hutter and Power 2005: 25). Section 404 of the Act requires Security and Exchange Commission companies to have their internal control systems certified on a regular basis by management and auditors. This certification process focuses on the "internal weaknesses" of the internal control system, the revelation of which could negatively affect the company on equity markets and with rating agencies. "In a nervous, litigious climate, one might anticipate the mandated reporting of such control near-misses to lead to over-responsiveness and over-reporting by organizations . . . in a downward precautionary spiral. Thus, while re-organization processes relevant to organizational encounters with risk have usually been reactions to adverse events, neo-precautionary attitudes will drive 'anticipatory' responses" (ibid.: 27–8).

Power (2005b) offers a detailed examination of another agent of the corporate surveillant assemblage, the corporate risk officer (CRO). The CRO position was created and developed in the 1990s, especially in organizations faced with complex risk environments and the politics of uncertainty characteristic of such environments (Conference Board of Canada 2001). CROs are "merchants of norms" and risk management technologies, brokering within and between the corporate entity and organizing organizations that participate in their governance. This positioning creates a tension between the CRO's public role as a meta-regulator and private role as an agent of corporate management.

CROs represent the legal order of the organization to the outside world in general, and the organizing organizations in particular. As Power (2005b) observes, the very term "officer" signifies this legalism: how the role is partly embedded in the frameworks of the regulatory organizations, and how it is also part of the new legalization of corporate life. "The creation of new control agents reformats the 'moral economy' of an organization with a new set of corporate norms" (ibid.: 139). Internally, the CRO provides "organizational representations of externally encountered norms and rules" (ibid.: 137). He or she thereby helps legalize the organization (Sitkin and Bies 1994), imposing a "responsibility order" (Power 2005b: 148) of risk disclosure, sign-off, and vigilance. Much of this responsibilization is strict rule-based governance, requiring procedures to be followed on penalty of being reprimanded, demoted, or dismissed. But there is also a positive, compliance orientation in which employees buy into the regulatory regime. One approach in this regard is to foster an organizational culture in which employees accept "the business case for compliance," in other words how they can participate in " 'turning law into profit' [Weait 1993]" (ibid.: 138).

The CRO organizes the risk management technologies and processes within the organization. As *the* organizer of uncertainty, the CRO is charged with making organizational encounters with risk formal, manageable, and routine, that is, governable. Among the tasks is mobilizing and accounting for the facts of risk, near-misses, contingencies, and cost–benefit tradeoffs. As Power (2005b: 142) states, "[T]his is the re-institutionalization of certainty from uncertainty and the fashioning of risk management into a new moral technology."

In this respect CROs are perhaps better conceived as "chief uncertainty officers." "They are part of the ways organizations manage uncertainties in their environments, specifically those created by legislative, regulatory and market pressures" (ibid.: 137). Indeed, CROs are to somehow orchestrate a new regime of corporate security in the context of all of the dimensions of the politics of uncertainty discussed in this chapter. The position came into being and continues to expand in the context of volatility in financial markets, corporate financial scandals, credit downturns, growing appreciation of scientific uncertainty, growing appreciation of limited knowledge to deal with operational risks in complex systems, anti-corporate activism, increasingly adversarial legal environments, and new demands for corporate social responsibility and good governance. As the hub and repository for all of these elements of the politics of uncertainty, CROs are also well positioned to be blamed. They become "chief blame officers," constantly juggling the counter-factuals of risk and the counter-laws of regulation in dramatizations of corporate security (Power 2005b).

Surveillant assemblages within corporate entities vary enormously by the types of risk being addressed and the ways in which employee activities can be effectively monitored. Vaughan (2005) describes how air traffic controllers can be tightly and effectively controlled through a combination of regulations and electronic surveillance devices. Air traffic controllers are provided with a think "bible" of rules, as well as instructions about them, to make the system as standardized and predictable as possible. Ideally, the air traffic controller makes rule-governed decisions without detailed reflection, in the same way that competent drivers make ongoing decisions about vehicular traffic patterns without reflecting in detail on their every move. Just like the driver who hesitates and reflects too much, in the air traffic control context "[t]he timing of decisions is so rapid that having to think or calculate everything is a threat to safety" (ibid.: 48).

Key rules pertain to the degree of separation between aircraft to ensure they do not violate each other's airspace. "[C]ontrollers are not trained to avoid collision per se; they are trained to avoid a violation of the rules of separation, a practice that builds in safety by timing their corrective practices sufficiently prior to a possible collision that accidents are avoided" (ibid.: 56). While much still depends on controller experience and judgment to address mistakes, deviations, and anomalies, the decision-making is effectively rule-governed. There is a punitive sanctioning system aimed at deterrence and greater precaution for any operational errors that result in violation of airspace. The controller responsible for the operational error may be taken off the job for remedial training and be the center of an official inquiry that is highly stigmatizing. If there are three such operational errors in a year, the controller is out of a job. Furthermore, the controller's crew is usually implicated in any breach of safety and there are sanctions against the group; for example, losing rewards such as extra vacation time for long periods without operational errors.

A very different rules assemblage operates in the context of medical liability. Heimer, Coleman Petty, and Culyba (2005) observe that rules pertaining to American medical practice derive from a large number of organizing organizations, often with competing interests in risk-taking and risk management. These sources include legislatures, government regulators, private regulators, insurers, managed care organizations, pharmaceutical entities, medical schools, hospitals, research institutes, and professional associations. Each of these organizing organizations has contributed to the intensification of surveillance and "new legalism" in American medicine in response to the politics of uncertainty. The politics of uncertainty in this field relates to the growth in medical knowledge and experimentation that pose new risks; operational risks faced by healthcare providers and resultant malpractice and other medical liability lawsuits; and efforts by insurers and managed care organizations to control costs through rule-governed surveillance of clinical practice. In this complex environment, the surveillant assemblage does not uniformly or unidirectionally benefit a single group or security concern. Each part conducts intensive surveillance on the other parts at enormous administrative cost, as well as the costs reflected in human suffering (ibid; see also the discussion in chapter 3; McClusky 2002; Baker 2005).

Electronic technologies are integral to corporate surveillant assemblages, providing behavioral indicators of whatever is imagined to be risky. CCTV and smart-card entry systems record all movement within the physical spaces controlled by the corporate entity; computer-software devices monitor every use of computers by employees; and computer-software devices data match and data mine to detect anomalous activities (Haggerty and Ericson 2006). For example, in the healthcare field there is sophisticated monitoring of billing practices aimed at detecting excessive or fraudulent claims by both health service users and providers. In the field of financial transactions, new computer software allows instantaneous detection of trading practices that indicate illegal manipulation. Such technology has been a key factor in the US Security and Exchange Commission's crackdown on insider trading in financial institutions, and in its ability to export its "zero tolerance" model in this field to other countries (Braithwaite 2003). Computer technology is also used to address the catastrophic potential of computer technology itself. The Y2K computer problem exemplified how, when the catastrophic imagination is exercised on low-probability, high-impact events, extreme precautionary logic takes hold and excessive risk management of everything results. With images of financial institution collapse and aircraft beyond the control of air-traffic controllers, billions of dollars were invested to allay fears of system failures.

In the contemporary politics of uncertainty over corporate liability for harm, there is incessant elaboration and refinement of rules and surveillance infrastructures within corporate entities. In an environment of adversarial legalism, organizations are bound to define the risks they face in relation to imagined criminalization or other legal liability, and to take defensive action in the form of more regulatory mechanisms that suggest things are under control. As Heimer observes in her analysis of the legalization of medicine, medical professionals and organizations have been forced to elaborate their own legal system, complete with surveillance and punishment functions, as a way of defensively drawing the boundaries of self-regulation and control. This internal legal system is in part a response to

> risks faced by healthcare providers and organizations. With the heightened consumer activism and legal scrutiny of informed consent statutes, malpractice suits and push for a patients' bill of

rights, physicians and medical organizations have protected their turf by developing their own rules. Although the individual rules are important in themselves for establishing the standard of care in an area or establishing routines for informed consent, as a body these medical protocols also make a claim about self-regulation. For instance, they create a boundary between what is properly within the purview of the courts and what is not. Without clear protocols, courts are much more likely to question the appropriateness of medical practice . . . Within the medical world, medical protocols serve many of the functions of any other legal system (as described, for example, by Lempert and Sanders 1986). Medical protocols make authoritative statements about what people may do, must do and must not do; they categorize actors and assign rights and obligations depending on which category people fall into; they arrange for punishment of those who break the rule. (Heimer, Coleman Petty, and Culyba 2005: 95, 97)

This tireless elaboration of internal control systems is a way of showing that decisions are technical and thus defensible when things go wrong. It is a kind of counter-law of "defensive legalism" which can compromise the interests of other parties, including the clients the organization is supposed to be serving, in the interest of reducing the risk of criminalization against members of the organization. This defensive legalism is deeply precautionary, as its norms become "embedded into organizational routines not because the real risks of litigation are well understood, but because the mere possibility creates a defensive orientation towards the need to justify decisions in retrospect. Accordingly, records are maintained in a particular form both for possible legal consumption, but also for related defensive purposes" (Power 2004: 47).

The diligent corporation is indeed rewarded for fully developed internal control systems when things go wrong and prosecutions are contemplated or pursued. In the USA, for example, a fully developed internal control system is not an affirmative defense, but it does ameliorate prosecution and sentencing policies and practices. "Counter indicators for corporate prosecution include the existence of a generally effective compliance programme; where the offence is committed by a 'rogue' employee; the corporation's past history; co-operation; and voluntary disclosure [*Federal Principles of Prosecution of Corporations*, U.S. Department of Justice, 1999]. Prosecution discretion thus fits with the philosophy of the federal sentencing guidelines for corporate offenders in rewarding prevention and compliance. Sentencing credit is given for effective compliance and for self-reporting" (Wells and Elias 2005: 158–9).

The surveillant assemblages of corporate security hard-wire precaution into the procedures and routines of the organization. This hard-wiring provides connectivity to a culture of defensiveness and blame. Instead of focusing on the real risks to the organization and organizational responsibility to absorb these risks on behalf of others, organizational actors focus on risks to themselves – possible litigation, loss of reputation, or dismissal for failing to take precautions – and how to displace responsibility to others. Here risk is a forensic resource, a rhetoric for pinning responsibility on someone else.

These processes are analyzed by Power (2004) and Hutter and Power (2005: chap. 1). First, the elaboration of rules and procedures and intensification of surveillance create a culture of "defendable compliance" and "responsibility aversity" as organizational members are rewarded for demonstrating that they followed procedures when things go wrong and thereby avoid blame. Second, the internal risk management system is designed to collect data on everything possible. A lot of the data collected are irrelevant to operations and consume resources unnecessarily. However, data collection continues because it is what risk managers need to demonstrate that they are indeed managing some risk, even if it is not risks that actually pose the greatest sources of harm to the organization. Third, since anything can be a possible source of operational risk, stakeholders external to the organization are also understood and managed as risks. This includes customers of the organization, who are treated as risks on two levels: their capacity to contribute to the profits of the organization (market segmentation), and whether they are likely to be litigious about product safety and quality. Fourth, the organization engages in reputational risk management, for example through corporate social responsibility measures that suggest it is concerned about the public good as well as the bottom line. However, unless these measures are accompanied by substantive evidence of better performance they will backfire. The greater the need for reputational risk management the less successful it is likely to be. Fifth, all of the above processes displace expert judgment in favor of defendable compliance and reputation. Organizational actors think, act, and communicate within the four square corners of risk classification schemes and internal procedures, and avoid taking hard decisions and expressing opinions that are more honest. "This trend is resulting in a dangerous flight from judgment and a culture of defensiveness that create their own risks for organizations in preparing for, and responding to, a future they cannot know" (Power 2004: 14–15). Sixth, without such judgment there will be more normal accidents. There is the real operational risk of "incubation" whereby relevant risk information about real threats is available but not accessed or acted upon because actors are operating within the narrow grooves of internal risk management and regulation. "[C]rises and catastrophes do not just happen suddenly, they are in an important sense 'organized' and have their origins in failures of management and intelligence processes over a long period of time" (ibid.: 44).

Incubation can be conceptualized as the risks of risk management through surveillant assemblages. Operating within surveillant assemblages, organizational actors may actually become less reflexive about the real risks to the organization and act with "tunnel vision." Tunnel vision is a taken-for-granted framework for selecting and de-selecting information that closes off important information about risks that lead to catastrophe. Of course, all decision-makers operate with a particular framework to produce knowledge and act upon it, and this framework necessarily includes ways of de-selecting, ignoring, and forgetting information. Not every risk can be attended to, and there is an "atrophy of vigilance" (Freudenberg 2003: 115) with respect to some risks. In the specific case of tunnel vision, it is the important risks and sources of risk that are atrophied, resulting in man-made disasters.

One source of tunnel vision is organizational models that are followed too closely, closing off knowledge about emerging or reactive risks. Adherence to models generates normalities around them, and they become ways of not knowing. In highly complex environments of risk and uncertainty, such as those associated with global financial markets, the problem is not simply one of blind following of what the model indicates, but rather how its imitation by many organizational players can lead to disaster when certain unanticipated interventions occur in the marketplace. The model may be widely accepted as best practice in the marketplace, but the model itself becomes a source of risk when an anomaly arises that requires a response outside the framework. Mackenzie (2005) describes this process in detail in accounting for the financial crisis associated with Long-Term Capital Management, the highly sophisticated hedge-fund whose model was based on the work of two of its partners, Robert C. Merton and Myron Scholes, who won the 1997 Nobel Prize in Economics for their contributions to finance theory.

Another source of tunnel vision is legal proceduralism. The rules assemblage that is entwined with the surveillant assemblage can foster rule-following as an end rather than a means. A legalistic logic of best practice takes over, which tends to "close organizations around assemblies of codified risk management knowledge" (Hutter and Power 2005: 29). The result can be new risks to the organization, for example something important is not attended to, or profitable forms of risk-taking and innovation are curtailed because of precautionary procedures.

Tunnel vision can also result from risk technology proceduralism. Organizational actors follow the inspections, audit check lists, and precise reading of warning devices to the tee, but fail to look for emerging and reactive risks outside of these formats of control. Ironically, this technical proceduralization can greatly reduce full disclosure of risk information. The organizational actor does not go beyond the "boilerplate" descriptions required of her job for fear of legal or other repercussions. As Power (2004: 54) observes in the context of auditors' opinions to shareholders about whether a company's accounts give a "true and fair" assessment, "[t]he opinion only means as much as the art through which it is expressed," and this opinion is "cautious and coded because of exposure to unlimited legal liability."

A related but different aspect of risk technology proceduralism is the way in which technologies of control are trusted and otherwise desensitize organizational actors to the risks of failure or mistake. Vaughan (1996, 1999, 2005) documents this form of tunnel vision in the case of NASA space mission disasters. The Three Mile Island nuclear disaster is another case in point, as operatives "refused to believe indicators showing the reactor was close to meltdown and revealed a misplaced faith in the efficiency of safety back-up systems" (Hutter and Power 2005: 17).

Tunnel vision is also a product of occupational cultures. Decision-makers collectively develop their own peculiar ways of getting the job done while at the same time appearing to fit the models, rules, and technologies of their organization. The occupational culture is vital for creating some autonomy in decision-making, and openness to emerging and reactive risks. However, it also closes off how the decision-maker thinks and acts upon risk and uncertainty. It constitutes a working ideology that is a procedure not to know, leading to significant risks being ignored or responded to in ways that also incubate disaster.

Research on occupational cultures in various organizational settings indicates that decision-makers typically normalize unanticipated or deviant risky occurrences into their daily routines. Early warning indicators of risk appear frequently and are routinely ignored or explained away. Near misses are taken for granted as "routine non-conformity" in the operational system (Vaughan 2005), and absorbed into the "rational normality" of the organization, incubating disaster (Turner and Pidgeon 1997). Exceptions to safety rules and procedures are also normalized. Even some practices that are criminally negligent may be accepted as routine (Bensman and Gerver 1963; Beamish 2002). Ironically, rules may actually normalize deviant practices that incubate disaster. For example, in her analysis of the Challenger space shuttle disaster, Vaughan (1996) found that NASA rules and procedures were used to convert scientific uncertainty into a veneer of facts and certainty. This process occurred in an occupational culture characterized by production efficiency, innovation, and secrecy; and in a wider political culture that pressed the NASA space program for dramatic displays of modern scientific progress. The rules normalized deviance as they effected closure over the contradictory evidence, ambiguous results, and endless controversies that characterize NASA space science and technology.

When disaster strikes, the typical response is further refinement of the surveillant assemblage through more early warning devices, regulations, inspections, audits, and private policing. Always there is a belief that more will work where less has not. Without a fundamental rethinking of how the organization addresses corporate security and can be more responsive to emerging and reactive risks, an intensification of the surveillant assemblage is likely to incubate risks of its own in an amplifying spiral. The surveillant assemblage becomes part of the problem rather than the solution, and political pressure mounts to expand innovative forms of counter-law I, laws against law that criminalize corporate entities for security failures.

The Two Leviathans

Harms caused by the "manufactured uncertainties" of corporations pose many of the most significant threats of the 21st century. Corporate security efforts to address these threats produce myths. These myths in turn constitute new realities of crime, risk, and uncertainty.

The over-arching myth in most efforts to criminalize corporate liability for harm is that rogue employees are responsible for disasters. This myth articulates with a number of institutional features of contemporary society. First, it is obviously functional for the corporate entity to scapegoat the individual bad apple to avoid the view that it is a rotting barrel. Second, the myth fits with the view in popular culture, perpetuated in the mass media, that crime results more from bad people than bad institutions, and that these people must be criminalized. Third, the myth also fits with the emphasis in criminal law on individual culpability for harm. Fourth, the myth resonates with the explanatory frameworks of some academic experts and their political constituencies. In addressing the causes of ordinary crime in domestic security contexts, these experts use structural explanations that emphasize the need for greater socio-economic equality. At the same time they eschew explanations that attribute criminal conduct to moral weakness or individual pathology. However, when the focus is shifted to harms caused by corporate entities, explanations of moral weakness and pathology come to the fore in efforts to criminalize, and structural explanations are moved to the side. As Zimring and Hawkins (1993: 288) comment in the case of catastrophic losses to all American taxpayers that resulted from the Savings and Loans industry crisis, "To address the problem as if bad men and Swiss bank accounts were the heart of the matter will divert our attention and resources away from society and government that can better protect us from loss."

Rogue employees thus become the suitable enemies, the Leviathan as sea monster leaving death and destruction in its wake. Corporate liability for harm is treated as a problem of white collar crime, of employees acting against the corporation, rather than as corporate crime, the corporation acting against a range of social interests and the public good. This treatment helps reproduce myths of corporate security – of control and accountability – when the real problems lie in the structure, organization, and regulation of corporate entities.

This treatment can result in unjust criminalization of scapegoated individuals. The individuals may have been conducting business as usual in a corporate culture accepting of the activity that ultimately proved harmful. He or she may have been following the "notional normality" or "routine non-conformity" of the risk management system in accordance with expectations in the corporate culture, not knowing that disaster was incubating. He or she may have been following the rules, procedures, and technological requirements to a tee, but that proceduralism led him or her to miss signs of an impending disaster that incubated it. He or she may not have directly participated in, or even had direct knowledge of, the hazardous practices that culminated in a harmful outcome.

In many cases, scapegoating extends to individuals in regulatory agencies and to political authorities deemed criminally responsible for errors and omissions at great distance from their knowledge and control. They too are sometimes charged and punished for actions that emerge as criminal only in retrospect. Swept up in the zero tolerance crime waves of the politics of uncertainty, they also experience demonization and ruin in the wake of the authoritative certainty of criminal punishment.

An emerging trend in the politics of uncertainty is to view the corporate entity itself as responsible for the harmful results of its activities. The focus shifts away from individual members of the corporate entity to its structure, culture, and organization. This focus requires the myth of anthropomorphization, treating the corporate entity as if it is human-like and rational and can therefore be held responsible for its collective knowledge and actions. Anthropomorphization in turn feeds the legal myth that the corporate entity is a legal person.

These myths are taken further by activists concerned about corporate greed and power. They create myths of the corporation as pathological in ways parallel to individual criminal psychopaths. Legal scholar Joel Bakan (2004) takes this approach, strategically using the documentary film and popular book media formats to advance the view that corporations reduce to self-aggrandizement and greedy profit-making without any regard for the disastrous consequences to other human beings.

> The corporation itself may not so easily escape the psychopath diagnosis, however. Unlike the human beings who inhabit it, the corporation is *singularly* self-interested and unable to feel genuine concern for others in any context . . . [There are] characteristics common to all corporations: obsession with profits and share prices, greed, lack of concern for others, and a penchant for breaking legal rules. These traits are, in turn, rooted in an institutional culture, the corporation's, that valorizes self-interest and invalidates moral concern . . . As a psychopathic creature, the corporation can neither recognize nor act upon moral reasons to refrain from harming others. Nothing in its legal makeup inhibits what it can do to others in pursuit of its selfish ends, and it is compelled to cause harm when the benefits of doing so outweigh the costs. Only pragmatic concern for its own interests and the laws of the land constrain the corporation's predatory instincts, and often that is not enough to stop it from destroying lives, damaging communities, and endangering the planet as a whole. (ibid.: 56, 58, 60)

It follows that, like the individual criminal psychopath, corporations must be criminalized and subject to dangerous offender legal provisions to halt the devastation in their wake. They are the Leviathan as biblical sea monster, the Moby Dicks that Melville captured in his famous novel on corporate power and its devastating effects (Ruggiero 2002).

Myths enact legal realities. As we have seen, there have been political struggles in English law to develop the offense of corporate manslaughter in ways that criminalize the corporate entity beyond the scapegoating of rogue employees. The most recent effort is a draft bill to make corporate manslaughter a statutory criminal offense with the sanction of unlimited fines levied against the corporate entity. As *The Times* commented, this proposed legislation is part of a politics of uncertainty in which politicians are playing to constituencies that have an emotive, retributive urge to label corporations as "intrinsically bad." It is also an effort to underpin a precautionary logic in corporate entities that will instantiate more warning devices, regulations, inspections, audits, and private policing.

This last consideration points to the fact that the myths of corporate criminality help constitute the realities of counter-law surveillance. These realities undermine the Leviathan of the liberal social imaginary and its promises of security and prosperity. In the everyday world of the risk management of everything within corporate entities, employees work in heavily surveilled environments where their every movement is monitored, regulated, inspected, and audited. These are criminalized environments of suspicion, limited rights, little or no privacy, and punishment for failures in risk management that may be no fault of the employee's own.

The regulatory state plays a significant role in this regime of counter-law. Playing to the catastrophic imagination in the politics of uncertainty, the state uses law to institutionalize precautionary regimes in corporate entities in the name of corporate security. In doing so it creates an increasingly public role for the state in the affairs of private corporate entities. Ironically, the neo-liberal state has meant more regulation, and this regulation is having effects that rest uneasily with its social imaginaries. Enormous state and private corporate resources are expended on the risk management of everything. The risk management of everything can incubate harmful activity and become part of the problem rather than the solution. Corporate entities are sometimes destroyed, and along with them the lives and livelihoods of employees and communities. The neo-liberal state begins to resemble the biblical social imaginary of Leviathan as sea monster leaving death and destruction in its wake.

5

Domestic Security

Crime, Disorder and the Politics of Uncertainty

In an age of uncertainty over global sources of catastrophic risk they cannot do much about, communities and individuals turn to local crime and disorder as risks they can address more directly. The catastrophic imagination breeds malicious demons in the domestic environment, for example sexual predators, dispossessed underclasses, unruly youth, and disruptive neighbors. Fear escalates, and with it, intolerance. Precautionary logic sets in, and the focus shifts to threats more than the actual occurrence of harm.

Freedom from fear and threat has become the new focus of domestic security policy and practice. This imaginary of freedom is symbolized in official statements of police organizations. For example, the mission statement of the New York Police Department includes "reduce fear" as a key objective, and the motto of the Thames Valley Police in the United Kingdom is "To reduce crime, disorder and fear."

The focus on fear and threat has arisen at a time when, in most Western nations, official rates of ordinary domestic crime involving interpersonal violence and property loss have been declining (Zimring 2006). Furthermore, the constituents for the policing of threats are typically better-off communities and individuals who actually face relatively little threat of ordinary domestic crime. Exercising their catastrophic imaginations, these constituencies press for extraordinary "pre-crime" (Zedner 2005) measures of prevention that exclude, incapacitate, and further marginalize populations they construe as threatening. As Dubber (2001: 848) observes, they "face not crime, but the threat of crime . . . [P]erhaps driven by a bourgeois obsession with the wonderous and hyperanalyzed complexities of their inner lives, [they] seek not freedom from crime, but freedom from the *fear* of crime, or as Richard Nixon put it in 1968, 'freedom from fear,' period."

This focus on fear and threats has led to innovative forms of counter-law. There are new laws against law – for example, anti-social behavior orders, laws of criminal possession, laws against transience, and laws that facilitate private policing and surveillance – in the search for more certainty. There are also new surveillant assemblages – involving innovative forms of private policing and electronic technologies – that provide practical expressions of certainty. These new forms of counter-law reflect expanding definitions of criminal deviance, less tolerance of deviance so defined, an emphasis on security more than justice, and the use of criminalization as a governing principle in social policy, community planning, and individual lifestyle choices.

Counter-law I: Laws Against Law

The dream of using law to preempt threatening signs of harm is not new. The late 19th-century social defense movement sought to identify and deal with "dangerous offenders" before they cause harm, and this effort continues today (Wooton 1959; Garland 1985; Brown and Pratt 2000). The field of criminology originated in this imaginary of identifying human disasters before they happen, and invoking whatever measures – rehabilitative treatment, incapacitation, elimination, sterilization – would reduce the threats they pose.

Roscoe Pound, the distinguished American legal theorist, viewed the emerging "penal treatment" regimes of the 1920s as "interference to prevent disobedience" against "well recognized types of anti-social individuals and anti-social conduct" (Pound 1927; see also Green 1995). Various preemptive legal regimes were developed in the name of controlling the dangerous, often with disastrous consequences for those subject to the "treatment" of these regimes (Burtch and Ericson 1979). At the same time excesses were often checked by appreciation of the limits of criminological science, especially the problem of false positives: selecting people for extra penal treatment as dangerous offenders when they turn out not to be dangerous at all (Visher 2000). Excesses were also checked by criminal law principles, standards, and procedures regarding just punishment: power should not be taken over a person's life that is greater than what is in just proportion to the offense proven.

The recent approaches to counter-law in the field of domestic security go well beyond such efforts to identify and preempt dangerous offenders. There is a declining emphasis on "actuarial justice" – statistically based standards for identifying the dangerous and taking extra power over their lives in the name of science – because such knowledge is regarded as too equivocal and surrounded by uncertainties. In its place is the precautionary logic of uncertainty. Threats are identified and criminalized according to political and pragmatic criteria. The new laws of criminal threat assign criminal status on the basis of imaginary extrapolation to unknown futures. The language of risk is still used, but not as part of an actuarial science approach to threats. Rather, risk is a forensic resource of stigma and taboo against whomever is judged threatening in local contexts of domestic security (Hudson 2003: 63–7). Threats are not identifiable acts causing direct harm to others, therefore the foundational criminal law principle of *actus reus* is rendered irrelevant. Threats cannot be guilty, therefore *mens rea* also becomes irrelevant. As we saw in the case of terrorism and national security, the operating principle is *finus reus*: if preempting threats serves local interests of domestic security, then the principles, standards, and procedures of criminal law are preempted, finished.

In what follows I analyze four types of laws against law that have emerged to address uncertainty, fears, and threats in domestic security contexts. The first type is anti-social behavior laws. These laws criminalize a potentially unlimited range of imagined sources of harm, for example any "behavior that causes alarm and fear" and "behaving in a manner capable of causing nuisance or annoyance to others." Civil law procedures and contractual mechanisms are used to govern future behavior, backed up by strict liability criminal proceedings and punishment for breach of the behavioral contract. The civil law route is explicitly designed as a way of circumventing the higher principles, standards, and procedures of criminal law, including those relating to fundamental human rights.

The second type is laws of criminal possession variously aimed at regulating, excluding, and incapacitating marginal populations. The police focus is increasingly on proactive efforts to find these populations in possession of contraband: illegal drugs, unregistered weapons, stolen property, and so on. Evidence of the seized contraband is usually all that is necessary to secure a conviction without trial, thereby preempting many requirements of criminal procedure and due process of law that might otherwise be invoked. Changes in sentencing law and practice related to criminal possession facilitate severe punishments that guarantee the targeted populations a permanent place in the underclass.

The third type is law aimed at the policing of transience. New laws against law are devised to ensure that homeless populations are excluded from domestic spaces where they appear as a threat or mere annoyance. These laws target any signs that the person may be taking up subsistence activities that threaten the smooth flow of commerce in everyday domestic life.

The fourth type is laws related to private policing. These laws are structured in ways that are enabling for private policing entities to act on behalf of their clients' interests, and to undertake a wide variety of enforcement actions that would be illegal for the public police to engage in. Counter-laws of private policing ensure that much domestic security is based on the imagined sources of threat and precautionary logic of each client.

These four types of law against law cohere with each other, and with the surveillant assemblages analyzed later in the chapter. The particular individual or population seen as a source of threat can be targeted through any one or a combination of types of counter-law. For example, the homeless person may be criminalized through the enabling laws of private policing that ban her from particular private spaces; laws preventing her from setting up a home and making a subsistence living in specified public spaces; laws of possession of contraband she regards as crucial for her psychological survival and self-defense on the streets; and anti-social behavior orders that define her everyday habits as a source of harassment, intimidation, or fear. This person is also routinely captured in the surveillant assemblages of domestic security that reveal her movements through space and time.

Laws of anti-social behavior

In the past decade, anti-social behavior legislation has emerged as a politically popular form of counter-law in the field of domestic security. While this type of legislation appears in various jurisdictions (Hornqvist 2004), it has proliferated in England and Wales and I will focus on developments in that jurisdiction.

Anti-social behavior laws became imaginable in the context of debates about how to curb troublesome conduct in local housing estates and communities. The issues were articulated in a number of policy documents, for example a 1995 Labour Party publication, *A Quiet Life: Tough Action on Criminal Neighbours*. The task was to design laws articulating "the legitimate bounds of dealing with behaviour which can terrorize communities" (Manning, Manning, and Osler 2004: 2). With local "terrorists" as the target, an opening was created for sweeping new forms of counter-law that would criminalize without the formalities of criminal law principles, standards, and procedures.

Anti-social behavior legislation was introduced in section 1 of the Crime and Disorder Act 1998, and elaborated upon in the Anti-Social Behaviour Act 2003. Anti-social behavior has never been given a proper legal definition. Rather, it is left extremely vague, providing scope for whatever may be defined locally as terrorism by neighbors or other undesirables. The only statutory definition is section 1 of the Crime and Disorder Act 1998: conduct "causing or likely to cause harassment, alarm or distress" to a person who is not a member of the same household as the accused. A source of "harassment, alarm and distress" is identified, for example noise, high hedges, trespass, intimidation, littering, graffiti, being truant or excluded from school, vandalism, drunken or abusive behavior, attending raves, public demonstrations, theft, and burglary. The person identified as the source is subject to an anti-social behavior order (ASBO) made in civil proceedings that obligates him or her to desist from the harmful activity and, in many cases, to agree to conditions such as curfews, supervision, remedial training, and compensating loss. Applications for an ASBO can be made by the police, a local government authority, a social housing authority, and county courts in specified circumstances. Breach of an ASBO is a criminal offense triable either by summary procedure (maximum penalty on conviction is six months' imprisonment and/or a fine up to the statutory maximum), or by way of indictment in a Crown Court (maximum penalty is five years' imprisonment and/or a fine).

Many anti-social behavior initiatives arose in housing contexts, for example where local housing authorities sought to reclaim and regenerate housing estates that were experiencing extensive property damage and other forms of conduct that made the properties unattractive to tenants. Hence, housing-related legislation is a key component of anti-social behavior initiatives. For example, the Housing Act 1996 provided for an "introductory tenancy" whereby the social housing tenant is on a probationary form of tenancy for the first year. The Anti-Social Behaviour Act 2003 provides for a "demoted tenancy" under which security of tenancy can be suspended by the court in the case of anti-social behavior. That Act also creates wider scope for injunctions against tenants available to a wider range of social landlords, and more enabling conditions to evict tenants and take possession of the property in case of anti-social behavior. Obviously, being threatened with the loss of one's home, or actually losing it, is a potent sanction. This sanction may be accompanied by others, for example being "blacklisted" from other housing following eviction, and being without a permanent address and subject to the policing of transience.

Obligations are also placed on social landlords that make them liable for the security of their tenants and require them to evict problem tenants. The Anti-Social Behaviour Act 2003 requires social landlords to publish policies on anti-social behavior. A proposal by the Law Commission would impose a public law duty on social landlords to police anti-social behavior, including "a term in all tenancy agreements that the landlord should take all reasonable steps to ensure that the tenant is free from the effects of anti-social behaviour by other tenants of the same landlord" (Ashworth 2004: 269). In the private market housing context, a draft housing Bill includes provision for licensing landlords in certain circumstances as a means of regulating their failure to control anti-social behavior of tenants and of turning them into front-line policing agents (ibid.).

ASBOs exemplify how legal forms are being reconfigured to address domestic crime and disorder. They are part of a "continuing trend towards the application of civil remedies to control breaches of criminal law, primarily due to difficulties of proof which lie at the heart of the criminal justice system. By this route, it may be said that certain aspects of criminal law are becoming 'civilized' even if criminals themselves are not" (Manning, Manning, and Osler 2004: 11).

The civil law route creates more enabling conditions for the authorities regarding procedure and evidence. Pragmatic problems of evidence that would pertain in criminal procedure can be sidestepped. For example, hearsay evidence is normally admissible in civil but not criminal proceedings. The admissibility of hearsay evidence allows authorities to make claims about the scope and persistence of behavior complained of without having to rely upon myriad direct witnesses who may be reluctant to come forward, unavailable, or sources of conflicting accounts.

In developing ASBO legislation, Parliament clearly intended that evidence would be assessed according to civil standards of proof (Ashworth 2004). However, in *R (McCann) v Manchester Crown Court* [2002, UK H339], the House of Lords decided that "while such orders were civil in nature, the civil standard of proof (balance of probabilities) was a flexible standard, requiring a higher or lower level of proof depending on the severity of the allegations made and the remedy sought. In anti-social behaviour cases the court would therefore require proof to a civil standard indistinguishable from the criminal standard, i.e. beyond a reasonable doubt" (Manning, Manning, and Osler 2004: 34).

The ASBO is a civil order whose terms and conditions go well beyond desistance from the behavior established by the court. A broad range of requirements can be attributed to the order, for example restrictions of time, place, and association (e.g., curfew orders, ban orders); compulsory activities for personal betterment and behavioral change (e.g.. counseling, schooling); and compensation to victims and the community (e.g., restitution, community service). In this respect the ASBO functions much like a criminal probation order. Also like a criminal probation order, it is backed up by criminal proceedings for breach, with a substantial maximum penalty.

An additional feature of the ASBO as law against law is that sentencing for breach of the order takes account of previous behavior not proven or admitted in a criminal court. This feature circumvents fairness standards in criminal court sentencing, for example that punishment should not be retrospective and should be proportionate to a specified proven or admitted offense. Such standards have been argued to be inapplicable to preventive orders of this type because they are future-oriented for public protection (Ashworth 2004).

The first anti-social behavior legislation was passed in 1998, the same year as the first Human Rights Act in England and Wales. Several features of the ASBO provisions outlined above were explicitly constructed to limit the scope and application of the rights stipulated in the Human Rights Act and its cousin, the European Convention on Human Rights. As Ashworth (2004: 265) remarks, "there comes a point when the legislative devices being used or proposed are so disrespectful of fundamental principles that questions have to be asked about their legitimacy in a country committed to the protection of human rights." Again the counter-law of security is designed to trump law that seeks to protect citizens from excesses of security.

The ASBO is consistent with the trend toward contract-based governance in all spheres of social and institutional life (Ericson, Barry, and Doyle 2003; Crawford 2003). As we have seen in our analysis of national, social, and corporate security environments, contractual governance is a means of governing the future through a precautionary logic and counter-law regime that facilitates local policing, especially self-policing. It constitutes surveillant assemblages of monitoring, audit, and inspection that control the minutiae of behavior deemed conducive to preventing harm and identifying those responsible for harm. In the sphere of domestic security, "Contracts are the social equivalent of crime prevention through environmental design. They seek to 'design out crime' through a complex array of instruments that inscribe incentives and disincentives into the physical environment and social relations" (Crawford 2003: 500).

Anti-social behavior laws also exemplify the new emphasis on freedom from fear in domestic security. They are "laws of fear" (Sunstein 2005) that respond to and fuel imaginaries of malicious demons and precautionary logic. As such, they focus much more on the potential for harm – the signs of possible harm – than on actual harms caused.

For example, The Anti-Social Behaviour Act includes a large number of new provisions that reflect a fear of the madness of crowds (Mackay 1980; Chaplin 1959). The Act

greatly extends police powers to preempt people from congregating in groups of any size, especially young people. It
gives the police new powers to disperse "public assembly"
groups of *two* or more people of any age, whereas the previous limit was 20 people. It also gives them powers to appre-
hend and return home youths under 16 who are unsupervised
by adults in public places between 9 p.m. and 6 a.m. Police
powers to preempt congregation extend to private premises
in various contexts, for example premises where drugs are
being used unlawfully, noise is deemed excessive, or people
are assembling for good times (e.g., raves) or because of hard
times (e.g., political mobilization). All of these new police
powers "seem to be premised on the belief that anti-social
conduct would be less prevalent if people could be prevented
from congregating together" (Manning, Manning, and Osler
2004: 101).

The preemption of raves is illustrative. A rave is legally
described in the Criminal Justice and Public Order Act 1994
as a crowd that enjoys a particular music format in a particular place and time.

> . . . [A rave is] a gathering on land in the open air of 100 or more
> persons (whether or not trespassers) at which amplified music is
> played during the night (with or without intermissions) and is
> such as, by reason of its loudness and duration and the time at
> which it is played, likely to cause serious distress to the inhabitants
> of the locality; and for this purpose (a) such a gathering continues
> during intermissions in the music and, where the gathering
> extends over several days, throughout the period during which
> amplified music is played at night (with or without intermissions);
> and (b) "music" includes sound wholly or predominantly charac-
> terized by the emission of a succession of repetitive beats.

Section 63 of this Act provides:

> If a police officer, of at least the rank of superintendent, reason-
> ably believes that two or more people are making preparations
> on land in the open air for the holding there of a rave, and/or that

ten or more persons are waiting there for a rave to begin, and/or that ten or more persons are attending a rave there which is in progress, he may give directions to these people and any other people who attend there for the same purposes that they are to leave the land and remove any vehicles or other property which they have with them on the land. It is a criminal offence to fail to leave the land in accordance with a direction or to enter the land again within seven days of the direction. (cited by Manning, Manning, and Osler 2004: 135).

The Anti-Social Behaviour Act 2003 increases these police powers in several areas. The power to direct people to leave the land with their personal property now applies to gatherings of 20 or more rather than 100 or more. The power to police raves on land in the open air is extended to raves in buildings where there are 20 or more people trespassing on the land. A new, broader criminal offense is also created whereby not only people who fail to follow the direction to leave while on the land, but also those who know about the direction and still prepare to attend the gathering, are subject to prosecution.

The criminalization of raves illustrates that anti-social behavior laws also express a fear of "pollution" of one's neighborhood by sights and sounds of disorder. As Mary Douglas (1990, 1992; see also Hacking 2003) has taught us, people produce order and community through ritualistic efforts to clean up their immediate environment. This theory articulates with social policy, for example "broken windows policing" (Kelling and Coles 2001), and with strategies to attract business investment. The UK government's Sustainable Development Strategy document (2002), *Living Places, Cleaner, Safer, Greener*, provides a clear statement of the theory and practice:

> Dirty and dangerous places encourage graffiti, vandalism and anti-social behaviour, which in turn undermine public confidence in them and leads people to avoid them . . . A high quality local environment is a big influence in making people visit a

place, spend money and invest in it. Conversely, a low quality environment can lead to places becoming stigmatized and drive people, businesses and investment away.

Parts 6 and 8 of the Anti-Social Behaviour Act 2003 enact these cleansing rituals in fine-grain detail, criminalizing everything from noise, litter, graffiti, and fly-posting to high hedges. Much of this legislation is preemptive, for example, prohibiting the sale of aerosol paint containers to persons under 16 for fear they might be graffiti artists; and compelling victims of graffiti to remove it from their property. Regarding high hedges, the Minister for Regeneration declared:

> High hedges can block out the light from neighbours' homes and gardens and make their lives a misery. This is anti-social behaviour, just as much as graffiti and noisy neighbours, and it isn't fair on those who have to suffer as a result. That is why we want to take action through the Anti-Social Behaviour Bill so that local authorities will have the power to sort out high hedge disputes and where necessary to chop those hedges back. (cited by Manning, Manning, and Osler 2004: 145)

While individuals can do little to preempt the real harms of environmental pollution that emanate from manufactured uncertainties (see chapter 4), they can clean up their local community and give it the veneer of domestic security.

Anti-social behavior laws against law provide a means of governing through vague terms (Cradock 2004). These laws are not circumscribed by any coherent definitions or conceptual limitations. Rather, they are open to the incorporation of all manner of troublesome behavior, defined through the politics of uncertainty and interpreted in each local context of political interest. In the opinion of barristers Manning, Manning, and Osler (2004: 2–3):

> Without any definitions of what can and should legitimately be regarded as genuinely anti-social, we risk entering a world of legal relativism where any conduct is a legitimate target of

government action . . . [This risk is evident in] the platitudinous and generalistic assertions emanating from White Papers and consultation documents that it is conduct which makes other people's lives "a misery." That sort of definition could certainly encompass a whole range of human behaviour, much of it entirely legal. Taking the implications of the [Anti-Social Behaviour] Act to their logical conclusion, moreover, everything which constitutes any kind of criminal offence or breach of civil obligation (or even which is wholly lawful but may be disruptive or inconvenient or simply upset someone) could amount to anti-social behaviour. The breadth with which the legislative net is cast certainly gives the impression that the government's starting point was to make a list of things people do in any sphere of activity which may be considered (whether by individuals or indeed by government) socially undesirable, and then legislate to prohibit or restrict it in the Act.

Ashworth (2004: 287) shares this opinion, emphasizing that it "may be dangerous or misleading" to use the term "anti-social behaviour" in law and policy because it is so vague and may have quite different meanings to different parties and political interests. However, vagueness is precisely the feature that is crucial to the success of anti-social behavior legislation as counter-law. It simultaneously provides the means for targeting signs of threat, taking action against the targeted population, and mobilizing the support of political con-stituencies in the process.

At the same time, as we have learned from other efforts to use counter-law against "terrorists" in our midst, governing through vague terms creates a regime of fear and uncertainty among those targeted. Ironically, to the extent that it targets unfairly and promotes injustice, anti-social behavior legisla-tion can itself be a source of "harassment, alarm and distress."

Laws of possession

The laws of criminal possession provide another means of criminalizing troublesome populations in the field of domestic security. These laws generally make possession of contraband a criminal offense in and of itself. Contraband includes scores of items in various arenas of everyday life, for example proscribed drugs and drug paraphernalia; weapons including imitations and ammunition; anti-security devices; stolen property; instruments of crime such as burglary tools and graffiti instruments; counterfeit money and instruments; other forgery instruments and devices; gambling devices; specified computer-related material; obscene material; unauthorized recordings of performances; fireworks; noxious materials; specified fishing equipment; and premises used for identified illegal purposes. In the State of New York in the mid-1990s, there were 153 possession offenses, of which 115 were felonies carrying a *minimum* penalty of one year's imprisonment (Dubber 2001: 835, 859).

It is likely that on any given day, most people are in possession of some contraband that could be criminalized. For example, it is estimated that 2.5 million Canadians use cannabis sometime during a given year. At the same time, less than one percent of these people are criminally charged with possession of cannabis (Rodopoulos 2005). The obvious question is: who is targeted for criminalization and why?

The answer to this question is that many possession offenses are also a convenient way to deal with troublesome populations and the signs of threat and disorder they give off. Just like the laws of anti-social behavior, the laws of possession are first and foremost used as laws of fear based on a precautionary logic. They criminalize possession as a preemptive measure in the hope that other imagined sources of harm will not eventuate. As we have seen in other contexts of counter-law and security, when crime as a serious harm inflicted upon others actually occurs, it is taken as a sign of system failure with serious repercussions for the system. The new criminalization focuses on identifying threats of harm and eliminating them. Indeed imagined threats and fearful emotions resulting from them are defined as criminal harms worthy of counter-law measures.

Eager to eradicate threats, this regime will always feel the pressure to intervene at the earliest possible moment, without awaiting the manifestation of the threat in the form of a criminal act. And the pressure will increase with every failure to incapacitate, with every "false negative" . . . The goal of nipping every potential threat in the bud, combined with the impossibility of its achievement, sets in motion a continuing expansion of preventive measures, an infinite regress along the causal chain toward the origins of threats, the heart of darkness. (Dubber 2001: 841–2)

The targeted populations are those diffusely defined as "dangerous," which typically means the underclass also targeted by the laws of anti-social behavior, transience, and private policing. Possession offenses allow sweeps of troubled areas and people on the basis of early warning signs about the threats they pose. The contraband seized has several functions. It is used as a key sign of threat in the police clinical diagnosis of dangerousness. It provides grounds for further investigation of the person as a threat. It also provides grounds for prosecution and severe sanctions aimed at eliminating the threat. As Dubber (2001: 864) observes, "Modern possession liability transfers the danger from an object to its possessor and holds him liable as a source of danger, without the object's danger ever having manifested itself."

In many contexts possession is combined with other statuses – such as being a young person, a convicted criminal, or non-resident of a country – to constitute a double status offense: for example, a youth in possession of graffiti equipment, a convicted criminal in possession of a weapon, a non-resident in possession of forged documents. In the USA, non-residents are officially categorized as "aliens" which itself signifies threat. Aliens as a category "have not been found to be 'person[s] of good character, attracted to the principles of the Constitution of the United States, and well disposed to the good order and happiness of the United States' " (Dubber 2001: 923, citing 8 U.S.C. 1427 (a) (3) (1994 and supp. 1999)).

Laws of possession have many of the characteristics of laws against law with which we are by now familiar. They join in the farewell to *actus reus* and *mens rea* as fundamental principles of criminal law. Being in possession of drugs, for example, does not involve an affirmative act or failure to act, a traditional requirement of *actus reus*. Making the possession of contraband statutory is the simple way to eliminate *mens rea*. In many states in the USA, *mens rea* or knowledge of the criminal nature of one's actions in possessing drugs is deemed irrelevant. There is also an evolving counter-law of "constructive possession" in which people in the vicinity of discovered contraband can be deemed liable. For example, all people in a vehicle stopped by the police in which drugs and/or weapons are found may be held liable for possession.

> [It] is the very fact that possession ignores so many of the basic rules, even bedrock principles, of traditional criminal law, which turns it into such an attractive weapon in the war on crime. This is so because every substantive principle has its procedural analogue. Without actus reus, no act needs to be proved. Without mens rea, no evidence of intent is required. Without omission, there's no need to establish a duty. Without inchoacy, the prosecutor can do without proving intent. Possession is unclassifiable, it is everything and nothing, an unspecifiable offence for a task best left unspecified: the control of undesirables. (Dubber 2001: 918)

In the USA, the regime of policing possession is consistently underpinned by the decisions and jurisprudence of the US Supreme Court. The US Supreme Court has constructed a framework of criminal procedure that facilitates the dangerous diagnostic work of the police to identify and eliminate threats. Most fundamentally, the decision in *Terry v. Ohio* [392 US 1 (1968)] allows the police to stop people on the basis of "reasonable suspicion" rather than the higher standard of "probable cause," and to undertake a variety of searches for contraband such as frisks of the person, car sweeps to stops for traffic violations, and sweeps of buildings in which an arrest has just occurred. Since the *Terry* decision, there have been about 150 US Supreme Court case decisions involving possession, most of which are enabling for the police on the view that, as McBarnet (1981) puts it, due process of law is *for* crime control.

This enabling law of criminal procedure combines with the strict liability nature of many possession offenses to ease the task of criminal prosecution. The evidence is at hand, and there is usually no need to deal with troublesome matters such as the perceptions and desires of victims, witnesses, and informants. Criminal justice in Anglo-American jurisdictions is based on guilty plea settlements, and in the case of possession offenses, such settlements are routine (Ericson and Baranek 1982; Ericson 1993). Dubber (2001: 859) reports that in the State of New York in 1998, there were 106,565 arrests for possession offenses, constituting 17.9 percent of all arrests. Only 295 (.27 percent) of these arrests for possession resulted in a verdict after trial, and only 129 (.12 percent) resulted in an acquittal.

While the substantive and procedural laws of possession enable routine guilty plea settlement, sentencing law and policy facilitate the elimination of threats. As mentioned previously, there are 115 felony offences for possession in the State of New York carrying a minimum sentence of one year's imprisonment; eleven of these offenses carry a maximum term of life imprisonment. Many other types of offenses carry sentence enhancements if the person is found to be in possession of contraband, for example a restricted weapon. In the USA, special policies are also used to up the sentencing ante in particular circumstances. For example, "Project Exile" made use of punitive federal weapons possession laws to sentence offenders to penitentiary for several years. Offenders were thereby literally "exiled" from their local communities as a means of eliminating the threat posed by the fact that they were found in illegal possession of restricted weapons.

The courts have also demonstrated their willingness to exercise their discretion in the interest of threat elimination. Dubber (2001: 858–9) cites the New York case of *People v. Young* [94 N.E. 2d 171 (NY 1999)], in which the accused was acquitted of burglary charges on a "technicality," but convicted of possession of stolen property. Calling the possessor a "scourge to the community," the judge sentenced him to a prison term of 25 years to life. The US Supreme Court has also supported threat elimination through incapacitation. For example, regarding a case of simple drug possession (*Harmelin v. Michigan* 501 U.S. 957 (1991)) the Court upheld a mandatory sentence of life imprisonment without the possibility of parole.

The policy of taking possession of selected populations in possession of contraband accounts for a substantial proportion of the US prison population. In New York State in 1998, 20 percent of all sentences of incarceration were imposed for possession offenses (Dubber 2001: 835). Among the 106,565 arrests for possession that year, 33,219 or 31 percent resulted in incarceration (ibid.: 859). There has been a sevenfold increase in the US standing prison population since 1970, to a total of about two million. A substantial proportion of this increase is for drug-related offenses, including possession. In 1993 there were 350,000 drug offenders in US prisons, which is double the *total* number of prisoners in the early 1960s (ibid.: 854). Between 1970 and the early 1990s, drug offenders in federal prisons increased eighteenfold, from 3,000 to 50,000 (ibid.), and constituted about 60 percent of the federal prison population (O'Malley 2004: 156). Over the 1990s, the average sentence for these offenders has doubled (ibid.). This program of threat elimination has been focused on specific populations, especially Blacks. In 1994 there were 678,000 Blacks in US prisons, which exceeded their number in institutions of higher education (Braithwaite 2000: 53). In this context, the malleability of criminal law to the politics of uncertainty and precautionary logic has resulted in the mass internment of "enemy minorities" as if they are "unlawful enemy combatants."

Laws of transience

Laws against law have also been enacted to deal with perceived threats posed by transient populations, especially in urban centers (Waldron 1991; Huey, Ericson, and Haggerty

2005; Mopas 2005; Hermer et al. 2005; Huey 2005). As
Hermer et al. (2005: 59–60) observe, "Homeless people are
inherently subversive in communal space because their permanent transience is fundamentally different from the temporary transience of most others, who are moving through
communal space toward a particular destination." If the
person is not using the space for the good of commerce, or to
move between private spaces such as a permanent home and
work, he or she is signified as a threat and treated as such
through laws of transience. Permanent transients must treat
communal spaces as if they are home – places to relax, be
entertained, sleep, and so on – and counter-law measures are
taken to ensure that they do not become too comfortable.

The laws of transience are said to be necessary to prevent
general threats to public safety. This formulation is evident in
the title of the Ontario, Canada, Safe Streets Act (S.O. 1999,
c. 8), which seeks to displace transient street people as signs
of threat. This Act has been used to effect sweeps of urban
areas, in particular retail and urban entertainment destinations where suburbanites and tourists desire a "risk-less" environment. It includes anti-solicitation provisions that exclude
people from earning their living by begging or selling goods
and services in specified locations, with punishment of a fine
up to $500 on first conviction, and a fine up to $1,000 and/or
imprisonment up to six months on any subsequent conviction. Hermer et al. (2005: 63) observe that "the definition of
'soliciting' is sufficiently broad that it could conceivably
capture the mere presence of needy and visibly indigent
people who, by simply being in particular places in communal space, are viewed as requesting donations."

It is arguable that such laws of transience have been developed as part of a broader package of counter-law that targets
threatening populations most negatively affected by neo-
liberal policies. As we saw in chapter 3, the cutbacks in social
welfare and disability provision have left large numbers in
desperate straits, some of whom become permanently transient and as such an imagined source of threat. Being literally
at the margins, these people are also likely to be possessors

and distributors of contraband, either as a means of seeking a little pleasure in their lives, or as a means of trade that allows them to eke out an existence. As such, they remain prime targets for a precautionary regime of threat control that is constantly scanning for imagined sources of disasters waiting to happen.

At the same time, laws of transience such as the Ontario Safe Streets Act are a limited part of counter-law efforts against transience. The policing of transience is also effected through laws of private policing, and the surveillant assemblages that hard-wire control into both public and private spaces.

Laws of private policing

Private policing is increasingly salient in the provision of domestic security. As discussed in chapter 2, there has been a rapid expansion of private policing organizations and personnel in recent decades. Private police not only provide security on mass private property sites such as commercial complexes and government buildings, but also police streets and other public spaces on behalf of business owners and residential communities (Rigakos 2002; Huey, Ericson, and Haggerty 2005). Domestic security has become a private commodity more than a public good (Loader 1999; Loader and Walker 2001).

This development has many roots, and I will mention only the most salient. First, the public police are often *unwilling* to deal with crimes they see as the responsibility of commercial enterprises, local communities, and individual property owners. Second, the public police are often *unable* to effectively prevent and solve crimes that affect these entities. Third, the private police are subject to direct control by, and accountability to, their paying customers in contrast to the public police who function in a structure of political and legal accountability. Fourth, private policing can be less costly than public policing because of lower wage and employment standards and competitive markets. Fifth, private policing has arisen in the neo-liberal context of the "cult of efficiency" (Stein 2001). The state has abandoned responsibility for some forms of security it previously offered, on the grounds that security provision should be left to market choices. In fields of security it still wishes to participate in, the state frequently "contracts out the work that it expects can be done more efficiently by others, whether that work is maintaining military bases, providing policing, delivering development assistance, supplying military training, managing prisons, running schools, providing security at airports, or delivering healthcare" (ibid.: 66). This development has in turn opened the door for the marketing of security products, including private policing services, as a consumer need (Loader 1999). This marketing of (in)security plays on uncertainty and precautionary logic in everyday life (Haggerty 2003; Hunt 2003). Sixth, private policing is relatively unencumbered by criminal law and procedure. Indeed, private policing is greatly facilitated by the state through counter-laws that ensure private police organizations and operatives are not burdened by the principles, standards, and procedures of criminal law, or even by meddlesome regulation through administrative law. Private police are extraordinarily free to operate beyond criminal law, even though much of what they do, including the coercive powers they exercise, is parallel to the public police.

The legal division of labor between public and private policing assigns criminal law enforcement powers to public police, and the powers of property owners and ordinary citizens to private police. When they are acting as agents of private property owners to control behavior on the property, private police are relatively unconstrained by law. Indeed they become legally authorized "to 'defend' the property from unauthorized access, predation, or damage, and in some circumstances to employ physical force and/or pervasive and continuous random surveillance in doing so" (Hermer et al. 2005: 34). This right to control what transpires in relation to real and personal property is entwined with the right to privacy which, in English law, normally trumps all other interests, including those of the sovereign: "Our law holds the property of every man so sacred, that no man can set his foot upon his neighbour's close without his leave; if he does he is a trespasser though he does no damage at all; if he will tread upon his neighbour's grounds he must justify it by law" (*Entick v. Carrington* (1765) 19 St. Tr. 1029, at 1029, cited by Hermer et al. 2005: 35).

Of course, there are many incursions on the rights of property owners, many of which are enacted through municipal government regulations regarding different types of property (e.g., commercial, residential, educational, religious) and how they are zoned, planned, constructed, maintained, used, and policed. Increasingly, domestic security considerations regarding crime and disorder are embedded in local authority regulation of property. In England and Wales, for example, the Crime and Disorder Act 1998 places a legal duty on local authorities to include crime and disorder considerations in all planning exercises and functions, "and to do all that they reasonably can to prevent crime and disorder in the area. In essence, this requires local authorities to anticipate the potential crime consequences of all of their policies" (Crawford 2003: 486). This requirement articulates with the anti-social behavior measures outlined previously, including many which allow state intervention into homes and commercial property to improve security, as well as foster expansion of private policing.

Laws pertaining to freedom of commerce and contract are also foundational to the powers of private policing. As Hermer et al. (2005: 35) point out, these laws allow property owners to make submission to private police procedures – for example, detention, interrogation, searches of personal property, searches of the person, and giving personal information – a condition of access to the property, facilities, and services in question. "The fact that the contracting parties often do not actually have equal bargaining power (e.g. an individual contracting with a bank for credit facilities) means that powerful institutions are often able to effectively impose such arrangements on their customers as a condition of access to the services they control. The law typically supports such arrangements" (ibid.).

Laws of criminal procedure governing public police behavior (Dixon 1997) are largely irrelevant to private policing (Slansky 1999). This fact is evident in law school courses and textbooks on criminal law and procedure which usually ignore private policing altogether, or mention it only in passing. For example, the American text by Allen et al. (2001), *Comprehensive Criminal Procedure*, is over 1,500 pages in length but includes only two pages on private policing (Joh 2004: 50). While there are recent isolated efforts to write texts on law pertaining to private policing (e.g., Sarre and Prenzler 2005), this task entails cobbling together various statutory and common law provisions directed at a motley range of non-state policing activity by for-profit policing agencies, voluntary associations, and individual citizens.

Statutory regulation of private policing occurs in the fields of property rights and civil law rights. In federated states such as the USA, Canada, and Australia, these laws are a matter of state or provincial jurisdiction. They address, for example, the licensing and standards of contract security agencies and personnel; the policing jurisdiction and activities of businesses and other property owners; and the enforcement of property laws such as trespass. Statutory regulation of private policing varies greatly across jurisdiction, from minimal to non-existent. For example, in the USA eight states have no regulation at all. Other states have very minimal requirements, for example that an applicant must be of a certain height or undertake a brief training course (Joh 2004: 108; Hazelkorn 2003). Training requirements never extend beyond a few days.

Constitutional law protections for those subject to police action are generally held to apply only to police action that is attributable to the state. In Canada, the Charter of Rights and Freedoms applies only to the activities of government. Therefore, it is not generally held applicable to non-state policing activities unless they can be construed as transpiring on behalf of the state. As a consequence, courts have been reluctant to apply Charter standards to the policing of quasi-public spaces such as mass private property sites. As Hermer et al. (2005: 31) observe, "the legal environment generally provides much greater latitude for coercive and intrusive policing activities of non-state authorities than for those of state authorities."

The legal environment is similar in the USA. Constitutional due process constraints placed on the public police – for example, regarding search and seizure of persons and property, and interrogation and confession – are consistently held by the US Supreme Court and lower courts to be inapplicable to private police. This is the case even though what the private police do is often identical to what the public police do, and would be subject to constitutional due process protections if conducted by the public police (Joh 2004: 93ff; Slansky 1999). Joh (2004: 102) describes the representative case of *United States v. Lima* [424 A.2d 113 (D.C. Ct. App. 1980]:

> Lynn Johnson, a plain-clothes store detective for a Lord and Taylor department store, watched through the slots of a fitting room door and observed Adelaide Lima remove the tags from a blouse and place it in her purse. When Lima left the store, Johnson approached her, physically restrained her, and escorted her to the store's security office. Johnson searched Lima and recovered the stolen blouse from her purse. Although the trial court suppressed evidence of the stolen blouse in Lima's prosecution for petit larceny, the District of Columbia Court of Appeals held the Fourth Amendment inapplicable to "mere employees performing security duties" and reversed. Rejecting Lima's argument that private police who "go around 'walking, talking, acting and getting paid like policemen'" should be treated as state actors, the Lima court noted in support of its conclusion that "the fact that the private sector may do for its own benefit what the state may also do for the public benefit does not implicate the state in private activity." The essence of Johnson's duties rested in the right of Lord and Taylor "to protect [its] property from damage and loss." Such businesses, unlike public police, "enjoy no special public trust."

Rules of criminal procedure are likely to have some effect only when prosecution is desired. Even then, such rules can be blunted by counter-law policies and police practices that ensure due process of law is for crime control. In many spheres of private policing, crimes are handled internally with no intention of calling the public police or of otherwise invoking the criminal process. The laws of criminal procedure are typically irrelevant in such cases. Private police operate within the procedural logic of their own private justice system. Indeed, this is a key reason why many entities prefer to pay for private police rather than involve the public police. The greater the legal constraints on the public police, the more private police will be turned to for "dirty work" (Joh 2004: 115; Ericson, Doyle, and Barry 2003: chap. 9), sometimes by the public police themselves (Hermer et al. 2005: 48).

All of these legal forms of escape from the principles, standards, and procedures of criminal law allow the private police to effect summary justice. The private police can simply ban culprits they identify from further involvement with the organization concerned. "Central to the private property right is the ability to exclude, which the Supreme Court has described as 'one of the most essential sticks in the bundle of rights that are commonly characterized as property'" (Joh 2004: 75–6, citing *Kaiser Aetna v. United States*, 447 US 164, 176 (1979)). The trespasser is kicked out, the shoplifter is subject to a permanent ban order from the store, the credit card or insurance contract of the alleged fraudster is cancelled, access to future flights by unruly passengers is cut off, and so on. Contraband such as drugs may also be seized and confiscated during various private security search and interrogation processes.

In the case of employees captured by private security operatives working for the same company, the punishment is typically summary dismissal. Although there may be recourse to labor relations law, this avenue is rarely pursued. Joh (2004: 118–20) describes the case of Cumberland Farms, a chain of 1,100 convenience stores in the USA whose private police operatives were each assigned a monthly quota of 30 confessions to employee theft and a demand for restitution. The investigators became full-time interrogators, forcing confessions and/or resignations and restitution on threat of criminal prosecution as the alternative. Between 1976 and 1989 over 30,000 employees were interrogated and most were fired. In one six-month period in 1986, there were 2,600 interrogations and 1,492 confessions involving almost one-third of the workforce!

In recent years, businesses have turned to civil law remedies regarding property crime committed by employees and customers. For example, many large retail firms in the UK use civil law remedies to seek restitution from employees who pilfer. The civil law route is more expedient than recourse through the criminal justice system, and this expediency in turn is believed to have a much greater deterrent effect on employees who are inclined to pilfer. Civil restitution and recovery laws have developed in the USA over the past 20 years to deal with shoplifters. In some states the recovery includes not only the cost of the item stolen, but also legal, administrative, and security expenses related to the case. If the accused does not respond to the civil demand letter, she may be subject to an additional civil order for damages. In contrast to the formality and delays of the criminal justice system, this civil demand route is expeditious and, in some contexts, even profitable for retailers (Joh 2004: 121–2).

These myriad laws of private policing constitute a powerful counter-law regime aimed at preempting harms and effecting summary justice as defined by private clients. As Hermer et al. (2005: 66) conclude:

> [T]he law's attempt to draw a relatively clear demarcation between "public policing" and "private policing" constitutes an entirely inadequate response to the complex and fluid networks of policing institutions and the variety of policing contexts and practices that have been evolving in recent decades, and that will continue to evolve. Similarly, the law has failed to respond adequately to changing patterns of property relations and uses and to the social and political implications of modern policing

arrangements for these emerging spaces. The result, as we have shown, is that all too often the law recognizes and supports policing arrangements that do not reflect or promote core democratic values such as fairness, equity, inclusiveness, transparency, justice, and the protection of fundamental human rights and civil liberties, and that often benefit the few at the expense of the many.

Counter-law II: Surveillant Assemblages

Counter-laws of anti-social behavior, possession, transience, and private policing combine to provide powerful legal resources to target threats and preempt imagined sources of harm. However, as we have seen in other fields of security, the most powerful resources derive from hard-wiring surveillant assemblages into the routines of domestic life. The objective is to prevent crime and disorder from festering by monitoring every imaginable sore point. Ideally, through mobilization of private policing, surveillance technologies, and self-policing, there is no need to mobilize law. As articulated in the American dream of total information awareness (see chapter 2), everyone is to function simultaneously as watchers as well as watched and the bearers of their own control (Shearing and Stenning 1984).

Private policing is embedded in local webs of surveillance serving the interests of those who own and control the spaces concerned. For example, in retail and entertainment environments such as suburban shopping malls and downtown shopping precincts, private security operatives use both their own direct observations and various electronic surveillance technologies to order consumption. City center shopping precincts in the UK are highly developed in this regard. Typical is the city of Oxford as I observed in 1999 (Ericson and Haggerty 2002). All downtown stores have full-time security officers. The security officers in each store are linked to their counterparts in other stores through a radio communication system that is also connected to the local police station. These security officers spend a substantial part of each day watching customers on surveillance cameras, and they use the video evidence from these cameras to proceed against shoplifters. In many cases the store goods are electronically tagged to trigger an alarm at the store entrance should a shoplifter proceed that far. The private security operatives and their surveillance cameras extend to the public streets outside their stores, so that they also police the downtown public space during the hours of store opening. They do all of the work of preventive security, public order policing, detection, apprehension, arrest, rights cautioning, production of evidence, and statement-taking. The public police only enter the picture when called upon, and then only to refine the information on the offender and offense for prosecution or brokerage to other institutions.

In many North American jurisdictions, downtown business improvement associations organize private policing, paid for through a levy of their membership. In some cases funding is also provided by the city government which, instead of giving the money to its own public police organization, sees the advantage of private police capacities for surveillance and summary justice. Such an arrangement developed in Vancouver in 2000 (Huey, Ericson, and Haggerty 2005). The Downtown Vancouver Business Association paid for uniformed private police to patrol the public streets for signs of threat to consumption order, and to assist with calls regarding trouble in retail and entertainment establishments. There were also two-person undercover teams with remit to proactively look for threats and conduct surveillance on "hot spots", such as locations where thefts of and from vehicles were frequent. Anything perceived as a threat to the consumption order of this environment was dealt with by confronting the culprits and threatening invocation of the available arsenal of anti-social behavior, possession, transience, and private policing mechanisms. When the criminal process was invoked, these private security operatives prepared the case documents for prosecution. In these cases the public police only came in after the fact to further process the accused for custody or release, and eventual plea settlements in court.

Downtown corporate office complexes also have private police as the hub and repository of their surveillant assemblage. Joh (2004) describes the "control center" of a private police operation in a Manhattan corporate office and retail complex that spans six blocks and includes 19 high-rise buildings and an outdoor plaza.

Enclosed within glass walls, the control center resembles a space launch command center in miniature, with multiple monitors, computers, and communications equipment. From here, two Protection officers watch the cameras monitoring the property: sixteen in the outdoor spaces, and nearly three hundred within the building. To demonstrate how well they worked, one officer operated a surveillance camera so that he, from several stories up, could read the headlines of a newspaper held by a person sitting in the outdoor plaza . . . Not only do officers monitor the cameras, they maintain logbooks for people who enter the buildings at night, collect and monitor work authorizations for hundreds of service employees who enter the property, and maintain electronic records on all employees who use computer identification cards to enter the building . . . [T]hey may ask, as a condition of access, for all kinds of personal information, and implicitly receive consent to monitor personal movement. (ibid.: 78)

Similar control centers function in high-rise apartment complexes, while less elaborate variations are built into gated communities. Crawford (2003: 494) reports that in the USA, there are approximately 231,000 community associations compared to 500 forty years ago, and that 20 percent of these pertain to communities that are gated and walled. One-half of new housing developments in major cities include such associations and the contractual forms of regulation they entail.

It is estimated that 40 million Americans are domiciled in these regimes of private government. Moreover, when these inhabitants go to work, shop, or be entertained, they are also subject to the surveillant assemblages of private policing. The border is everywhere: people pass from one private policing jurisdiction to another, and have their behavior constantly monitored by private police operatives, CCTV cameras, electronic access cards, and the like. Indeed, in some areas the same private security company surveils conduct through all of the spaces of everyday life. For example, in Florida it is possible to live in a gated community policed by the multinational private security company Wackenhut, go to work on a commuter train policed by Wackenhut, and work in a corporate building also policed by Wackenhut. If one breaches security in any of these environments and a sentence of imprisonment results, the prison may be staffed and operated by Wackenhut. If one exhibits further disturbing signs of disorder in the prison, there may be civil commitment to a mental health facility also staffed and operated by Wackenhut (Canadian Broadcasting Corporation 1998). In this scenario, one is no longer just passing through private security "bubbles of governance" (Shearing 1998; Rigakos and Greener 2000), but rather caught up in *streams* of governance effectively managed by a multinational private security company.

The commodification and marketing of domestic security has been expanding over several decades. However, it was given unprecedented impetus and crystallized in the aftermath of 9/11, especially through the development of "homeland security" in the USA (see chapter 2). Department of Homeland Security materials give particular emphasis to individual responsibility for domestic security. For example, its 204-page document, *Are You Ready? An In-depth Guide to Citizen Preparedness*, locates individual citizens at the foundational base of a pyramid of responsibility for domestic security (figure 5.1). This document repeatedly emphasizes that the individual must take personal responsibility as the front-line of defense against all manner of imagined threats to domestic security. For example, the reader is asked, "Are You Ready?" then told he or she better be ready: "We live in a different world than we did before September 11, 2001. We are more aware of our vulnerabilities, more appreciative of our freedoms, and more understanding that we have a

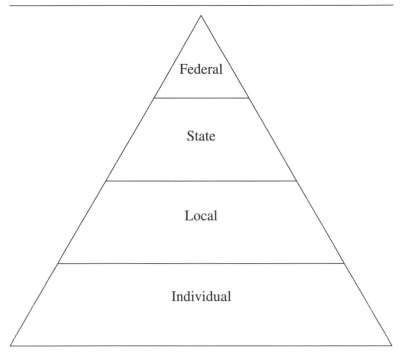

Figure 5.1 *Pyramid of responsibility for domestic security*
Source: Adapted from Department of Homeland Security (2004: 9)

personal responsibility for the safety of our families, our neighbors and the nation." There is a specific admonition of *"Personal Responsibility.* Developing a household prepared-ness plan and disaster supplies kits, observing home health and safety practices, implementing disaster mitigation mea-sures, and participating in crime prevention and reporting."

The individual is urged to step up the pyramid to the local level and get involved in volunteer programs through Citizen Corps, or at least enroll in educational programs on vigilance and risk monitoring. Citizens Corps asserts a mandate to deal with a very broad range of threats, eliding crime and disorder with everything from public health issues to major sources of disaster, including terrorism. "The mission of Citizens Corps is to harness the power of every individual through educa-tion, training and volunteer service to make communities safer, stronger and better prepared to respond to the threats of terrorism, crime, public health issues, and disasters of all kinds."

Realizing that a 204-page document may not prove popular reading, the Homeland Security/America Prepared Campaign has mobilized the entertainment industry to market domestic (in)security and individual responsibility for surveillance. The America Prepared Campaign is sponsored by the NBC television network. Stars of NBC security-related programs, for example *Law and Order* and *Emergency Response*, endorse the need for individual responsibility. Individual responsibility is exhibited by taking security precautions such as purchasing an emergency preparedness kit from America Prepared Campaign's retail partners Wal-Mart, Costco, Home Depot, Sam's Club, and Gracious Home.

As Haggerty (2003) documents, individuals were already attuned to their responsibility to preempt crime and disorder, and bought into the marketing of domestic security products, long before 9/11. He provides a partial list of security products marketed in the USA:

> Personal alarms, access controls, steering wheel locks, pepper spray, gated communities, guard dogs, bullet proof vests, cellular telephones, instruction in martial arts, car alarms, surveillance cameras, handguns, motion-sensitive lighting, vehicle geographic positioning systems, home alarms (infrared, ultrasonic, photo-electric, and audio sensor), personal electronic monitors, motion detectors, missing child kits, private security services, light timers, window bars, fencing, safes . . . tasers . . . "anti-pedophile" internet software, personal geographic positioning systems, encryption programs, and home-based drug tests. (ibid.: 194)

These security products are marketed on the basis of fear, desire, and identity (Slater 1997), much the same as health-care, fitness, and beauty products. Security is portrayed as a desirable, objective end-state. The security product is not only a way of obtaining this end-state but also of relieving fear. Typically fear is generated by advertisements for the product, inviting the audience to use their catastrophic imaginations regarding all manner of malicious demons in order to feel the need for the product. Fear is simultaneously valorized as an early warning device for the precautionary individual who must always be on the lookout for threats in a world full of uncertainties (De Becker 1997).

A typical marketing format is to include ads for security products during television shows that feature crime, disorder, and policing. This format allows the ads to be reinforced by the fear of crime and disorder generated by the shows. For example, Doyle (2003: 54) describes how the FOX television network ran successive half-hour episodes of shows such as *COPS* and *America's Most Wanted* in prime-time. These shows were interspersed with advertisements for security products, such as one that featured pepper spray as a "great stocking-stuffer" to give to a loved one at Christmas time. Many advertisements leave nothing to the catastrophic imagination, but rather provide it. A car magazine featured an ad for a remote ignition system which "allows you to start your car remotely to first see if anyone accidentally planted a bomb in your car before you get in. Pretty clever" (cited by Haggerty 2003: 202–3). An advertisement for a woman's self-defense book, *Kick the Rapist Where it Hurts*, emphasizes that violence can happen to any woman, anywhere, at any time:

> I've seen it all in the movies and read it in the papers. But those things happen to others and not to me – *or so I thought* . . . Just think about the world we live in today. I don't want to scare you. I just want you to realize the fact – No one is immune to violence. Doesn't it make sense to know how to be AWARE and also be PREPARED before it's too late? (cited by Haggerty 2003: 205)

There were also government programs to mobilize citizens as vigilant agents of surveillance well before 9/11. A prime example is the development of state sex offender registries in the USA following the requirements of the Wetterling Act (Pub. L. 104–145, 110 Stat 1345), as amended by Megan's Law, and the Pam Lyncher Act (Pub. L. 104–236, 100 Stat.

3093). As of February 2001, almost 400,000 convicted sex offenders were registered in these systems (Bureau of Justice Statistics 2002).

As part of the community notification requirements of these systems, each state maintains a website. A general website (www.sexualpredators.com) provides links to all of the state websites, and to the FBI and National Center for Missing and Exploited Children. It also features a home page of "Wanted Sexual Predators and Sex Offenders," complete with names, mug shots, and an invitation to click for more information. At the head of this page is an announcement of two "TV series coming soon": *Sexual Predator Alert* and *Missing in the USA*.

Taking the example of the Washington State website (www.ml.waspc.com), instructions are provided on how to search for maps pinpointing where convicted sex offenders reside, and for mug shots and names of these malicious demons. For example, the user can enter his or her own address and select a radius of between one and fifteen miles to ascertain where the nearest sex offenders reside. He or she can also sort by whether the looming threat is classified as a level II or level III risk.

In the frequently asked questions section, there is considerable detail about the "actuarial risk prediction" that places offenders in category I (low risk and not identified), category II (medium risk), and category III (high risk). An analogy is drawn to how insurers use driving records to assess levels of risk and therefore premiums and contract conditions, emphasizing that while poorer driving records signify higher risks this does not mean the higher risks will actually have an accident. This commentary sets up the central message that such actuarial knowledge is limited and surrounded by uncertainty: "There is no way that anyone can accurately predict the future behavior of another person." Precautionary logic inevitably follows:

> Q: Now that I know a sex offender lives in my neighborhood, what should I do differently to protect myself and my family?

A: . . . In general terms, tell your children that this person has hurt someone before. Explain to them that they should stay away from this individual. Review safety tips, and be aware of common lures. Remember that the purpose behind community notification is to reduce the chances of future victimization of persons by this offender. The information gained by this notification should assist you and your family in avoiding situations that allow for easy access to victims. Don't harass your neighbor. An offender put in a stressful state is more likely to relapse. Let's help them succeed; we all win with fewer victims.. . .

Q: Are you going to tell us if the offender moves out of this neighborhood, so we don't have to worry anymore?

A: No. The information shared about sex offenders is basic safety information that we should all be aware of. There are many sex offenders in Washington, as well as in every other state. It would serve no purpose to have people relax, or not follow safety measures because the sex offender they knew about moved from the neighborhood. Sex offenders, like anyone else, establish friendships and business relationships in the area where they are living. These is no reason to believe they would give up these relationships just because they moved to another part of town or county.

Stating that "It would serve no purpose to have people relax, or not follow safety measures because the sex offender they knew about moved from the neighborhood" negates the rationale for community notification. If malicious demons are always looming, no one can ever relax and eternal vigilance is required.

Instructions on vigilance pervade the website. For example, a sidebar entitled "Safety and Protection" instructs on home security: "Leave porch lights on at night or when you expect to return after dark. Leave an interior light on in a room or two with the shades drawn. Leave a radio on." An extensive section offering "Warning Signs and Safety Tips" regarding sexual predators includes a general warning in bold letters of the need for eternal vigilance: "ABOVE ALL BE OBSER-VANT AND AWARE OF YOUR SURROUNDINGS AT

ALL TIMES." There is a subsection on "Characteristics and Behavioral Indicators of Adults who Molest Children," but again with the rider that risk indicators are of limited value: "CAUTION: Some people who have molested children or plan to molest children exhibit no observable behavior pattern that would be a clue to their future actions." There is fine-grain detail on "general personal safety options" at home, in the car, and on the street, "safety tips for caregivers with children," "safety tips for children," and "acquaintance rape: can I reduce my risk?"

This website also includes various threats and disclosures to users that exemplify the urge to "legalize" everything in organizations caught up in the politics of uncertainty (Power 2004; Hutter and Power 2005). For example, a policy statement on acceptable use of the website threatens criminal prosecution of anyone who uses information provided to harm a registrant. This threat of criminalization is backed up by surveillance on the surveillance activities of those who use the website: "Due to the sensitive nature of this information, activity on this site is monitored." At the same time, disclaimers are made regarding the registry's responsibility for the accuracy of the information, completeness of the information, and "errors or omissions produced by secondary dissemination of this information."

Child abduction by strangers is extremely rare. For example, in Canada, with a population of 32 million, there are under 100 reported cases annually. The vast majority of these cases involve culprits who are close relatives or friends of the child and do not have legal custody, rather than complete strangers (Ericson and Haggerty 2002: 265–7). While recognizing its own evidence in this regard, the *Annual Report of Canada's Missing Children* (1991) nevertheless stresses the need for eternal vigilance about the risk of stranger abduction:

> [B]ecause such high profile is given to any stranger abduction, the public's perception is that this phenomenon is common in Canada. This in fact is not the case. However, it is still prudent for parents to teach their children to be "street smart" and to be

aware of the dangers of our society. Street proofing of children is essential to preventing such tragedies. Many of Canada's police are actively involved in preventative policing and are able to provide tips on preventative safety. It is important to remember that the legal definition of "stranger" is anyone who does not have custody of the child. Therefore, children who are taken by a grandparent, aunt, uncle, or friend of the family would be entered into CPIC [Canadian Police Information Center] under the category of stranger abduction. (Royal Canadian Mounted Police, Ottawa 1991)

This statement is testimony to the fact that the abduction of a child is a risk that has no price, and therefore any statistical argument about low frequency of occurrence is beside the point. Precautionary logic dictates that surveillant assemblages must be intensified to monitor every movement and activity of the child. It also dictates extensive education in self-policing to ward off malicious demons.

Parents are mobilized as the hub and repository of surveillant assemblages pertaining to child safety. They are admonished to accompany their children through public spaces. Adams (1995) reports that in Britain in 1971, 80 percent of seven- and eight-year-old children went to school on their own, but in 1990 only 9 percent did so. Parents are also strongly urged to regulate their children's travels in virtual spaces. Mopas (2006) describes the parental responsibility program of the Media Awareness Network organization in Canada. This organization fosters surveillance of children using the Internet by having parents ensure that the computer is in a part of the home where children using it can be watched; develop lists of approved websites; participate in an "Internet Savvy" program equivalent to "street proofing" programs; and purchase computer filtering and blockage software.

A wide range of surveillance technologies are marketed to parents as aids in the surveillance of children. As Haggerty (2003: 200) notes, advertisers for these technologies play on the prospect of child abduction, often misusing statistics about missing children (Best 1989). One such technology is the "nanny cam," a miniature camera that can be embedded in household items and accessed by Internet. The nanny cam provides visual governance-at-a-distance of how a child is being treated by a minder other than parents. One model is sold with a camera embedded in a teddy bear, "a move that hardwires the technology of insecurity into *the* icon of childhood security" (Haggerty 2003: 205). One nanny-cam advertisement reinforces the view that precautionary surveillance technologies are the only recourse regarding precious lives that have no price. "Two angelic children stare at the viewer from a surveillance camera photograph. Above them a caption reads, 'My Mommy and Daddy say that I'm the most important and precious thing in their lives. ' " (ibid.).

Parents are also enjoined in child safety partnerships with other institutions and their uses of electronic surveillance technologies. The fear of child abduction begins in the cradle. An electronic ankle bracelet for infants, trademarked "Hugs," is marketed to hospitals as

> A fully supervised and tamper-resistant protection system that automatically activates once secured around an infant's ankle or wrist. Staff is immediately alerted at a computer console of the newly activated tag, and can enter pertinent information such as names and medical conditions. Password authorization is needed to move infants out of the designated protection area and – if an infant is not readmitted within a predetermined time limit – an alarm will sound. An alarm also sounds if an infant with a Hugs tag is brought near an open door at the perimeter of the protected area without a password being entered. The display console will then show the identification of the infant and the exit door on a facility map. Alternatively, doors may also be fitted with magnetic locks that are automatically activated. As well, Hugs can be configured to monitor the progress and direction of the abduction within the hospital. Weighing just 1/3 ounce, each ergonomically designed infant tag offers a number of other innovative features, including low-battery warning, the ability to easily interface with other devices such as CCTV cameras and

paging systems and time and date stamping. (*Canadian Security* 1998)

As children reach school age, other electronic technologies provide discipline of time and place. In Japan and the USA, elementary schools have borrowed an electronic tag system first developed for inventory control by commercial entities. For example, these tags have been used in Japanese restaurants to monitor the freshness of sushi revolving on conveyor belts in front of diners; and, in the USA, by suppliers to monitor the shipment of goods to Wal-Mart stores. In the school context, the tags record the child's entry and exit, with confirmation emailed to parents' mobile telephones. Tagless trespassers on school property trigger an alarm. In the USA, "Each student is required to wear identification cards around their necks with their picture, name and grade and a wireless transmitter that beams their ID number to a teacher's handheld computer when the child passes under an antenna posted above a classroom door" (Leff 2005).

In Japan, this surveillance technology is part of an expanding surveillant assemblage for child inventory control. This expansion was precipitated by catastrophic incidents. In particular, in 2001 a man entered a school and stabbed 21 victims, eight of whom died.

Most Japanese schools now lock their gates and dispatch teachers on campus-wide security checks. Many show films and display posters reminding children to be wary of strangers, or teach students basic self-defense. Some post private security guards at gates or wire closed-circuit cameras to keep tabs on students and visitors. A few have gone a step further, buying mobile phones with embedded Global Positioning System technology so parents can track their children all the time. (Hall 2004)

Parents are also asked to partner with schools and the police to provide complete documentation of their child's identity (Ericson and Haggerty 1997). The documentation typically includes an extensive form asking for identifying details, photographs, and a DNA sample, all to be kept as a package at home in case a need arises. In 2002, the West Vancouver school district cooperated with police in encouraging parents to participate in such a program. There was a very high sign-up rate among parents, in spite of the fact that, as a police spokesperson admitted, there had never been a case of stranger abduction of a child in the district.

Child identification kits are also marketed to parents on an individual basis. For example, a company called Kinderprint markets a DNA sample kit to parents, claiming that "Every year more than 800,000 children are reported missing. The kiDNA kit can provide you with the way to identify your child in these difficult circumstances" (www.kinda.com). As discussed previously, this type of claim is typical of advertisements for child surveillance products. In this case, the figure of 800,000 missing children seems grossly exaggerated (Best 1989, 1990). In any case, a method of identification such as DNA would only be needed in the very few instances in which the missing child faces tragedy. Again, precautionary logic is assumed to take hold and make the product sell itself. In marketing the wonders of the product to retailers, Kinderprint stresses, "The KiDNA kit is very easy to sell. Parents and grandparents like the secure feeling from having a DNA sample of their children for potential identification for those situations that it is required." The company also points out that the product is an obvious marketing centerpiece for a retail operation, attracting customers who will in turn buy other products.

> This DNA kit will provide the boost in sales you are looking for. Since most loving parents want to feel secure with their child, these DNA kits sell themselves. When they take them home and see how easy they are to use, they will likely tell their friends and family about these DNA kits and where to buy them. What does this mean to you? Increased store traffic, which translates into increased sales and profits. The kiDNAkit is an easy cross-sell with baby cards, baby shower gifts, birthday cards, etc.

The promotion of child safety through cross-selling is a standard marketing practice. There is no better way to mobilize community consensus than initiatives which protect innocent children, and commercial sponsors are eager to associate their products with these initiatives.

This promotional strategy is encapsulated in the children's safety village concept that has developed in various North American jurisdictions in recent years. In 1997, I visited a typical children's safety village in Ontario, Canada. The village is a theme park on a rural highway accessible from three medium-sized cities. It includes an entrance building with offices, and two classrooms dedicated to instruction about traffic, fire, and crime safety. Beyond the entrance building is the village itself, with a roadway in which children drive miniature electric cars and thereby experience signs and situations of traffic safety. There are also miniature buildings that represent what is typical in contemporary Canadian villages.

School buses full of children, their teachers, and parents approach an entrance that is dominated by signs of two insurance companies, the largest sponsors of the village. Signs of the insurers also adorn the classrooms, with one captioned, "Educating Today for a Safe Tomorrow." The insurers' logos and signs penetrate every experience in the safety theme park. For example, they appear on the toy cars, including the caption, "Helping Children Play Safe"; on certificates given to children to recognize their "graduation" from this academy of safety; and on insurance preventative safety brochures placed for the parents attending, and for children to take home to parents who could not attend.

The "Wall of Honor" in the foyer of the entrance building indicates that corporate sponsorships flow when an educational enterprise is conducted in the name of children and safety. The Wall of Honor lists dozens of private corporate, community, and government sponsors, from private security companies to McDonald's restaurants. The safety village itself neatly mimics the commercial reality of contemporary Canadian village life. Miniature buildings, standing on lots that cost their sponsors $10,000 each, represent large fast-food corporations, clothes retailers, and drugstores, as well as the local homebuilders' association, the Royal Canadian Legion, the Humane Society, and so on. A telephone company provides a telephone booth, where children can practice "911" emergency calls prompted by a voice mail script. The local newspaper is represented by a newspaper box. A railway company offers a railway crossing to be experienced on the toy-car drive through town. A street is named after one of the models produced in the local car manufacturing plant.

Back in the classroom, children are given instructional material sponsored by Canadian Tire Corporation. The police and firefighters who provide the classroom instruction are not supposed to endorse particular businesses directly. However, a firefighter does mention that the safety ladders he uses in a demonstration can be purchased at a large chain hardware store, informing me later that he always "drops" the name of this corporation because it donated $90,000 to the enterprise. On their break from this implosion of commercialized knowledge of risk, children are treated to doughnuts provided by the large doughnut chain that also sponsors a building in the safety village. When they receive their graduation certificate endorsed by the insurance company sponsors, children are further rewarded with a local mini-golf center pass and a McDonald's restaurant voucher.

Community volunteer organizations, public police, and firefighting agencies are also involved. The mega-organizations of community safety are represented by signs in the village theme park: Crime Stoppers, Neighborhood Watch, and Block Parents. Local police and firefighters staff the classrooms to provide safety lessons they used to offer through visits to schools. They are clearly the state's partners, albeit surrounded by dozens of private corporate sponsors who signify what an employee of one of the sponsoring insurance companies said to me: "it is very much the buzz word in governance now . . . the whole concept of partnerships, which has been used as a euphemism for offloading [responsibility for security] . . . It's a new way of business."

The de-centering of public police officers in this context is best symbolized by "Officer Broker." Officer Broker is a robot who patrols the safety village, complete with a mini-television screen that shows safety videos. This Robocop is also sent on the road to shopping malls, where it further blends lessons on preventive security with risk-less mass consumption. At a construction cost of $30,000 to its insurance industry association sponsor, Officer Broker exemplifies the ways in which private insurance entities configure themselves at the fulcrum of domestic security initiatives and market their products accordingly.

Insurance companies are able to broker with a large number of other corporate sponsors who sell security products that make people into agents of surveillance and self-policing. They are also able to broker with business enterprises that sell hamburgers, doughnuts, and clothes because they too derive promotional benefit from marketing domestic security, especially as it involves children and their families. As a school teacher mentioned to me during my visit to the safety village, the children return home imbued with this division of labor in risk and responsibility. They are keen to instruct their parents and siblings on precautionary strategies that would not have been attended to or even thought about otherwise. They are equally keen to instruct on the best places to buy hamburgers, safety devices, and insurance.

In the age of television and the Internet, it is possible to visit other virtual realities of child safety without ever leaving the home. As discussed previously, the US Department of Homeland Security/America Prepared Campaign maintains a website that addresses all manner of threats to domestic security. While this initiative originated in the aftermath of 9/11, it rapidly expanded into every conceivable source of terrorism in everyday life. A great deal of the website material pertains to children, either as little terrors themselves (bullying, drug use, alcohol use, drinking and driving, risks of sexual activity and pregnancy), or as victims of these terrors. Detailed safety tips are offered regarding each of these sources of terror, supported by endorsements from commercial sponsors of the website and America Prepared Campaign, and by television celebrities from security-related drama programs.

> Peer pressure, bullying, drugs, dating . . . Your kids are going to talk with someone about them. Shouldn't it be you?
>
> Mekhi Phifer, *Emergency Response*

> One wrong click of the mouse is all it takes. Know when and where your child is online.
>
> Linda Cardellini, *Emergency Response*

Parents who fail to become enmeshed in surveillant assemblages that effectively protect their children, and other children from their children, face the prospect of criminalization. For example, under anti-social behavior legislation in England and Wales (Manning, Manning, and Osler 2004: 85–100), parents who fall down in their responsibilities can be made subject to parenting contracts or parenting orders.

When a child is deemed likely to engage in, or actually engages in, anti-social behavior or other criminal conduct, a parental contract can be requested. There is also provision for parental contracts where children are truant from school, or excluded by school authorities. One type of parenting contract involves the parent and school authorities. The parent agrees to a number of measures to control the child and/or attend counseling programs on how to be a better parent, and the school agrees to support the parent in these endeavors. Another type of parental contract is between a Youth Offending Team (YOT) and the parent. Again the parent agrees to the terms of the contract regarding child control and lessons in better parenting, and the YOT agrees to facilitate the process.

The actual terms of the contracts are left completely open in the statutes, similar to criminal court bail or probation order conditions. Although the contract does not create a binding obligation on either party, the parent is in effect sanctioned for non-performance because the court can take into account failure to enter into or comply with a contract in deciding whether to make a parenting order.

The initiation of a child parenting order is based on similar criteria and procedures as parenting contracts, although there are some differences. For a parenting order, the young person must have actually engaged in some anti-social behavior or other criminal conduct. Furthermore, it is a legally binding anti-social behavior order, breach of which is a summary conviction offence that can result in a fine.

It is perhaps a little ironic that preventing offending by children and young people (rather than supporting others to prevent it) is already supposed to be the role of the YOT and indeed the principal statutory aim of the youth justice system. It would be more ironic still if the consequence of the wholesale adoption of parenting contracts was to shift the focus of responsibility for any failure to prevent offending or re-offending on to the parent rather than criminal justice system (whether in the form of the YOT or otherwise) (Manning, Manning, and Osler 2004: 91)

The Two Leviathans

Crime and disorder are real threats. Domestic security efforts to address these threats produce myths. These myths in turn constitute new realities of crime, risk, and uncertainty.

The Leviathan as sea monster raises its fiery head in the political uses of crime and disorder to address uncertainty. Precautionary logic takes hold, and there is a search for signs of threat everywhere. The signs themselves are feared, and they are eventually transformed into real threats subject to further criminalization. War is declared on domestic terror in the ever-elusive quest for freedom from fear.

Chief among the domestic terrorists are dangerous offenders, especially child sexual predators. Entire dangerous populations are also conjured up as malicious demons, especially the dispossessed underclass. Youths pursuing distinctive identities and pleasures are also targeted for any signs that they are little terrors. At the extreme, troublesome neighbors and anyone else who terrorizes tranquility is deemed in need of preemptive strikes.

These myths of terror in the war on crime and disorder constitute new realities of crime, risk, and uncertainty. There is the reality of counter-law I, laws against law. Anti-social behavior legislation is developed to enable preemption of every imaginable source of disruption to domestic security. This legislation also preempts the established principles, standards, and procedures of criminal law, mainly by substituting civil law and procedure and its contractual forms. The anti-social behavior order is a future-oriented contract that compels the offensive individual to meet its terms on threat of exclusion from membership in a valued community and commodity, for example housing, school, leisure activity, or lifestyle. Exclusion for breach of contract can be augmented by criminal prosecution and imprisonment. This form of criminalizing through contract is even more powerful and punitive than the criminal justice system because it places total responsibility on the individual who has failed to live up to the obligations that they themselves have agreed to. Such failure makes escalating punitive interventions into their lives seem obvious, necessary, and legitimate.

The laws of possession provide another expanding area of counter-law, in this case still within criminal law and its administration. Laws of possession of drugs, weapons, stolen property, and other contraband provide the means of policing signs of threat posed by the underclass. In this arena of criminal law, due process standards are eased, evidence problems are simplified, and discretion is available for steep prison sentences that incapacitate threatening people for long periods. In the USA in particular, laws of possession are the preferred police method to target signs of threat and sweep the streets clean of those they diagnose as dangerous. These laws allow selective incapacitation of "unlawful enemy minorities" as the domestic security equivalent of the "unlawful enemy combatants" of national security. The prisons have swelled with hundreds of thousands of people found in possession, especially drug possession. The remaining fragments of traditional criminal law – the formal requirements of due process, the occasional trial – serve primarily as a veil of administrative decency over an otherwise efficient and silent system of preemptive counter-law.

Laws of transience allow the police to pick up the truly dispossessed. Laws such as the Ontario Safe Streets Act displace transient street people who are deemed subversive of urban order. Similar to laws of possession, and sometimes used in conjunction with them, laws of transience also allow sweeps of undesirable people in urban retail and entertainment destinations where consumers desire an unthreatening ambience.

The most efficient policing of transience, especially in commercial space that is privately owned but publicly used, is through private policing. In this regard, laws pertaining to private policing must be considered as a cornerstone of the counter-law regime in domestic security. The laws of criminal procedure that govern public police are generally inapplicable to private police activity. Enabling conditions for private policing are also created by the nonexistent or minimal regulation of their activities through administrative law. Private police operate primarily through the rights available to private property owners who employ them, which allow defense of the property through intrusive surveillance and coercive powers of investigation and exclusion. The result is private orders of domestic security constituted through a counter-law regime that benefits some and totally excludes others, and violates human rights and civil liberties when viewed from the traditional principles, standards and procedures of criminal law.

The laws against law of anti-social behavior, possession, transience, and private policing are underpinned by the surveillant assemblages of domestic security. Organizations, communities, and individuals have bought into the neoliberal program of local responsibility for domestic security by purchasing an enormous range of private policing services and surveillance technologies that promise to preempt sources of threat. They have also engaged educational programs and informational campaigns that instruct on how to act as agents of surveillance and self-policing. These developments are especially evident in surveillant assemblages organized around the safety of children. The obsession with child safety has assured a whole new generation of precautionary citizens who will respond to uncertainty by criminalizing all signs of threat.

These new forms of counter-law signify the transformation of the state as Leviathan. The Hobbesian Leviathan as a state that expresses the liberal social imaginary of physical security and prosperity begins to break down. The biblical Leviathan as sea monster rears its ugly head, sweeping up populations of suitable enemies and leaving devastation in its wake.

Of course, strong liberal elements remain in some of the counter-law measures. For example, the new ways of criminalizing anti-social behavior through civil law and contract are explicitly based on models of freely choosing rational individuals who are utilitarian, calculative, and seek freedom and autonomy. But this is a form of fragmented contractual governance that operates within a neo-liberal dynamic of social segmentation and exclusion. It contrasts sharply with a form of social contract that operates within a dynamic of citizenship rights and inclusion.

Ironically, as it is transformed into a sea monster reflecting the biblical social imaginary, the state becomes a source of terror. Individuals swept up in its crime and disorder control waves are terrorized, sometimes for life. More generally, terror looms for those whose housing, education, leisure, and lifestyles are threatened by the ways in which significant fields of state policy are becoming criminalized. Most generally, everyone is terrorized by the growing intolerance of deviance, criminalization of new areas of deviance, and emphasis on preemptive security measures rather than procedural justice.

Ironically, an amplification of anti-social behavior is the inevitable result. Neighbor is pitted against neighbor in the perpetual search for signs of anti-social behavior, and in the use of private policing services and surveillance technologies aimed at displacing troublesome people onto someone else's territory. While not a war of all against all, this anti-social security environment generates "terror . . . [that] arises from a pervasive sense of disestablishment, that things are in the unmaking" (King 1981). And that is the real cost of criminalization as a response to uncertainty. Uncertainty proves itself.

6
Insecurity

Governance through Uncertainty

Western societies are now governed through the problem of uncertainty. The problem of uncertainty subsumes and replaces the problem of order as envisaged by Hobbes and a whole generation of sociologists who followed his lead. It is not simply order through physical security that is of concern, but a broader intolerance for any activity suggestive of refractory outcomes. The problem of uncertainty also subsumes and replaces the problem of risk as envisaged by risk society theorists of the late 20th century. It is not simply risk assessment and management through science and technology that is of concern, but limitations of knowledge as a capacity to act and how they magnify uncertainty.

Scientific knowledge is used less as a source of greater certainty for taking risk, and more as a source of greater uncertainty for preempting risk. As an object and instrument of suspicion, and a principle of challenge, science constantly sows the seeds of uncertainty. In this role, science uses risk as a forensic resource to magnify the problem of uncertainty. It demonstrates how risk serves as a political rhetoric to select some harms for regulation and not others, to blame some parties for harmful consequences of risky activity and not others, and to provide reassurances about the manageability of threats that are refractory and not others.

Surveillance technologies as products of science are another means of addressing uncertainty. They have expanded exponentially on the view that they provide early warning signs and direct behavioral accounts of harm. The "house of certainty" is constructed through architectures of observation: environmental designs and electronic technologies that enable vigilance. However, the problem of uncertainty does not go away. The very power of surveillance technologies to produce grounds for suspicion leads to the invention of new forms of intolerable behavior in an amplifying spiral of uncertainty. At the same time, as part of intensified risk management regimes, some forms of surveillance incubate risks, contribute to tunnel vision, participate in normal accidents, and manufacture new uncertainties.

The problem of uncertainty is also manifest in law as an institution and technology of risk assessment. Scientific risk assessment or "actuarial justice" is used across legal forms to engage in cost–benefit analyses as a basis for decision. However, law confronts the fact that scientific risk assessments are only probability statements surrounded by uncertainty. It also confronts the fact that cost–benefit analyses are inevitably based on both scientific assessment of risk and political values. Law must take into account local public perceptions of harm and fear; how individuals and corporate entities in civil society wish to conduct their affairs and the limits the state should place on this; what risk-taking should be allowed; and what risk-taking should be curtailed or eliminated. There is no meta-rationality or consensus for settling these matters. Forced to make hard decisions and express authoritative certainty in doing so, law necessarily privileges one perspective on risk costs and benefits at the expense of others. This power of assigning privilege in each case decision inevitably serves some interests and not others. For the unprivileged, it is a power that hurts, causes resentment, provokes a sense of injustice, produces insecurity, and poses again the problem of uncertainty. Thus law is the inevitable battleground of the politics of uncertainty. In making risks visible, articulating cost–benefit tradeoffs, establishing standards, allocating discretion and responsibility for risk, and holding parties responsible for failures in risk management, law makes its own role in the reproduction of uncertainty starkly evident.

Law as an institution and technology of risk management is also a contributor to the problem of uncertainty. Parallel to what can occur with surveillance technologies used in risk management, legal technologies can incubate risks, contribute to tunnel vision, participate in normal accidents, and manufacture new uncertainties.

Law also contributes to the problem of uncertainty when it is used as intended in liberal democracies: to sustain high standards of rights and due process. Indeed, the higher the enforced standards of due process, evidence, and culpability in law, the greater the uncertainty in the capacity of the legal system to prevent, discover, build a case against, and successfully prosecute offenders. Justice is surrounded by uncertainty, and thus viewed as a problem to be overcome.

At the beginning of the 21st century, the problem of uncertainty is increasingly addressed through new forms of criminalization. Criminalization occurs in relation to an expanding array of harms that are viewed as involuntarily imposed and as having severe consequences. It engulfs not only those judged responsible for harm, but also those deemed responsible for preventing it.

Suitable enemies are demonized in public culture. This demonization trickles down and has real effects on the institutional practices and social relations of everyday life. Terrorists are depicted in such broad terms of population characteristics and behavior that prejudice, discrimination, torture, and exclusion become widespread. People on disability and welfare benefits are characterized as fraudsters requiring constant suspicion and vigilance to the point where many are confirmed in marginal identities and condemned to poverty. Corporate actors are rewarded for creative risk-taking until there is a catastrophic loss, at which point they and the corporate entity are pathologized and demonized in ways that destroy lives and livelihoods. Those who disturb domestic security – youth, the dispossessed, the diffusely dangerous – are excluded and punished for mere signs of threat and the uncertainties they arouse.

This new wave of criminalization is enacted through counter-law. Counter-law I entails the creative development of laws that counter the traditional principles, standards, and procedures of criminal law. Through new forms of criminal law, as well as new uses of civil and administrative law, counter-law seeks to reduce or eliminate due process protections that create uncertainty in investigations. It also increases the discretionary capacity for preemptive strikes against the suspicious, including incapacitation and severe punishment. Counter-law II involves broader and deeper surveillant assemblages that cast widely for signs of threat in the hope of preempting disasters waiting to happen. Enabled by counter-law I, counter-law II seeks to make legal process unnecessary. It does so either by making suitable enemies uncomfortable to the point that they go elsewhere, or by making their suspicious signs and harmful behavior visible in ways that make exclusion and punishment seem obvious and necessary.

Criminalization through counter-law has become *the* way of expressing authoritative certainty. For political authorities, it is the strongest expression of state authority in face of a lack of trust in public institutions and an increasing sense of ungovernability. While other approaches to government seem to yield more uncertainty, governing through crime sends a strong signal of certainty. When there is a persistent threat that is said to affect the quality of life, or a catastrophic failure in a risk management system for which the government is held responsible, criminalization through counter-law provides an ending to the political narrative of uncertainty in the short term, and perpetuates the myth of governability in the long term.

For private authorities the task is much simpler. Criminalization is less an expression of authoritative certainty than an act of sheer power. Through the counter-laws of private policing and surveillant assemblages, private authorities can decide who and what is undesirable and engage in preemptive action accordingly. At the whim of their catastrophic imaginations, they can declare, "You are not a member of the population of our private entity. We are not even concerned about governing you because you have no business with us. If nevertheless you cross our path – step on our territory, appear in our data systems – due process is irrelevant because you are not a member, and we will exclude you." For members the situation is different, although there is also a perpetual search for malicious demons among the membership. When malicious demons are identified among members, the declaration is somewhat different. "Since you are a member there will be some due process but only within the logic of our private justice system. We will use our surveillant assemblages to monitor, inspect, audit, and regulate your membership and associated privileges, and downgrade or exclude you as an undesirable when we deem it necessary."

The forms and practices of criminalization through counter-law vary not only between public and private entities, but also across different political jurisdictions and social institutions. Criminalization as a response to the problem of uncertainty is politically contingent, determined by situational opportunism and power, linked to the prevailing culture, and a product of the dominant ideologies of that culture. Indeed, much counter-law, such as anti-social behavior legislation, is written to be used differentially in each local context of the politics of uncertainty. Of course, the subtleties of this variation are not captured in my analysis. I have selected illustrations that best exemplify the trends I am identifying. This is inevitably a partial enterprise – choosing poignant examples across different jurisdictions to advance my argument – and cannot possibly take into account subtleties of local difference. Appreciation of this limitation will hopefully spur comparative research to extend and modify my analysis.

The Undermining of Law

Efforts to address every imaginable source of harm through criminalization result in the undermining of law as a democratic institution. Ironically, when law and other democratic institutions are most threatened, the response is to devise new legal measures that further threaten these institutions. Law is transformed into an instrument of suspicion, discriminatory practices, invasion of privacy, denial of rights, and exclusion.

The undermining of law is starkly evident in counter-law responses to terrorism. The USA Patriot Act undermines all existing principles, standards, and procedures of criminal law, and of the US Constitution, by giving unlimited presidential authority to criminalize. The Victim's Claims Fund undermines principles, standards, and procedures of civil law, and of the US Constitution, by preempting the right to sue and taking away the legal jurisdiction of individual states to settle tort claims. The "torture papers" initiative to legitimate torture of detainees subject to interrogation undermines both domestic and international law with respect to the interrogation and treatment of detainees. The US regime of counter-law in this field proposes governance without law as conventionally conceived. The government seeks to cast the net of suspicion on everyone, identify suitable enemies, not worry about false positives, dispense with *actus reus* and *mens rea* elements of criminal offenses, dispose of due process, and effect summary justice through incapacitation, torture, and elimination.

The undermining of law is equally evident in efforts by governments to limit the social benefits of those who exhibit an inability to become fully responsible, enterprising, neo-liberal citizens. All applicants for disability and welfare benefits are treated as suspected fraudsters in need of perpetual surveillance and sanction. Welfare law such as the Ontario Works Act is blended with criminal code provisions for fraud to the point where the two are inseparable. Administrative law is used to legitimate investigative procedures against disability claimants that would be judged blatantly unacceptable if held up to the principles, standards, and procedures of criminal law. Again the regime of counter-law proposes to govern without law as conventionally understood. All members of the designated population are suspects, subject to intrusive surveillance and preemptive measures of summary justice without effective legal recourse.

The undermining of law is also evident in upperworld contexts of corporate security. As the risk management of everything in corporate life intensifies, employees find that their every move becomes part of surveillant assemblages. They exist in criminalized environments of suspicion, minimal privacy, limited rights, and punishment for failures in risk management. When things go badly wrong, "rogue employees" are singled out for punishment, although they may not have directly participated in, or even had direct knowledge of, harmful practices. If they were parties to the harmful practices, they may nevertheless have been conducting business in a corporate culture that valorized what they were doing, whether it was entrepreneurial risk-taking at the edge, or exceptional proceduralism that incubated disaster. Regardless, they face demonization and ruin as the "criminal" other no less than their counterparts in other fields of security.

The individual pathology model applied to rogue employees is extended in some contexts to the corporate entity. Corporations are depicted as aggrandizing monsters seeking only profits and leaving destruction in their wake. They are said to be worse than individual criminal psychopaths because they are even more self-centered and recalcitrant, and affect a greater number of victims. This anthropomorphization of the corporation as pathological is used to construct a very different "legal person" than has traditionally been the case. Instead of granting the corporation traditional "legal person" rights, the pathological view creates a new fiction that paves the way for criminalization of the corporate entity itself. The consequences can be disastrous for the entire corporation. Again "heads roll," only this time in the thousands, as the employees of Arthur Andersen can testify following the Enron debacle.

The undermining of law in the field of domestic security is even more multifaceted, although similar patterns are evident. The Anti-Social Behaviour Act 2003 in England and

Wales undermines criminal law principles, standards, and procedures in the extreme. There is no proper definition of anti-social behavior, creating the capacity to criminalize whatever may be defined locally as sources of "harassment, alarm and distress" caused by neighbors who terrorize. This form of governance through vague terms allows the net to be cast widely for signs of suspicion that are criminalized.

The key counter-law measure is to make anti-social behavior subject to civil procedure. The civil law route is taken to circumvent the higher standards in criminal law of what constitutes a criminal offense, evidence, due process, and suspects' rights. A civil order is used to obligate the offender to conduct himself or herself in specified ways and to become part of surveillant assemblages that record conformity. It is backed up by punishment through criminal law in the event of a breach of agreement, with strict liability elements in procedure and a maximum of five years' imprisonment as punishment.

Anti-social behavior legislation of this type is intended to help people deal with the uncertainties of everyday life. Ironically, it is also a source of uncertainty. Open to the incorporation of any troublesome behavior as defined by the local politics of uncertainty, and explicitly designed to preempt the human rights requirements of other legislation, the Anti-Social Behaviour Act 2003 creates an environment of arbitrary and capricious criminalization. To the extent that it targets unfairly and is experienced as unjust by those accused of being little terrorists, anti-social behavior law is itself a source of "harassment, alarm and distress" that is deeply anti-social and divisive. Such an extreme form of legal relativism can only produce problems of uncertainty.

Laws of criminal possession of drugs, weapons, and other contraband also undermine law to the extent that they are used to target the underclass. Laws of criminal possession are routinely used as a preemptive measure to disrupt the activities of the diffusely dangerous and criminalize them on the basis of extrapolation to unknown futures. Similar to anti-social behavior laws, they allow governance through vague terms that is arbitrary and capricious and creates uncertainty for the populations subject to them. Criminal possession is a catch-all residual or "kicker" charge used by police to control undesirables who cannot be controlled in other ways. These laws are enabling for police sweeps because *actus reus* and *mens rea* elements of an offense are usually not required; evidence requirements are limited to the facts of possession, which are loosely interpreted to the point where guilty plea settlements are routine; and sentencing structures allow incapacitation through long periods of incarceration. The laws of criminal possession allow the state to take possession of significant segments of the population through penal orders, in particular the poor and racial minorities, in effect treating "unlawful enemy minorities" as if they are "unlawful enemy combatants."

Laws of transience undermine law by targeting the same class of little terrorists. Formulated as laws that provide safe streets and greater certainty, they are mainly for the good of commerce in urban areas where prosperous consumers wish to shop and be entertained without signs of risk. As such, they function as laws of threat that target specific behavior likely to cause harassment, fear, or distress to consumers. In this capacity, they are a first cousin of anti-social behavior laws and the laws of criminal possession, helping to keep the streets clean of undesirables. They are also related to the counter-laws of the disability and welfare benefits systems because most of the transients targeted are on the streets as a result of having been rejected by, or kept well below the poverty line through, these systems.

Laws of private policing undermine law in different ways. These laws ensure that private policing organizations and their operatives are not burdened by the principles, standards, and procedures of criminal law, or even by the lesser requirements of administrative law. Private police operate efficiently at the margins of the law or beyond the law. They are taking over many functions of the public police, including their coercive powers, without due process of law. Indeed laws of criminal procedure are simply not applicable in many contexts of private policing. Moreover, even when they are potentially applicable, they remain irrelevant in most cases because private police effect punishment through the private justice system of the corporate entity that hires them with no intention of using the criminal justice system. Their most common sanction against undesirables is simply exclusion from further involvement with the corporate entity, occasionally backed up by civil orders. Civil orders are far more efficient than criminal prosecution because they are based on lesser standards and procedures than criminal law and they facilitate direct recovery of loss by the private entity.

Law is further undermined by surveillant assemblages that alternatively facilitate private justice without recourse to law, or, if law is invoked, effect trial by surveillance media in ways that preempt due process of law. Surveillant assemblages combine with laws against law to effectively make criminal law a lost cause. While some requirements of *actus reus*, *mens rea*, and due process remain formally in place in some areas of criminal law, they function primarily as a veil of administrative decency over preemptive counter-laws that effectively take justice out of criminalization processes and fundamentally undermine law as *the* democratic institution of liberal social imaginaries. We are witnessing the end of criminal law.

The Unraveling of Civil Society

The Leviathan of the liberal social imaginary transforms into the Leviathan of the biblical social imaginary. Myriad suspect populations are demonized and criminalized as if they are sea monsters who threaten to leave death and destruction in their wake. In this process the state takes on the character of the biblical Leviathan and liberal civil society unravels. The state is a source of terror, injustice, insecurity, and diminished prosperity for the suspect populations it engulfs.

The state as Leviathan of the biblical social imaginary appears in various mythologies across Western nation-states.

However, it is most fiery in the USA where a "war on" everything is institutionalized as the political expression of precautionary logic. "War on" figurative language spells coercive, preemptive measures aimed at a final solution in a zero-sum game. It was in extensive use well before 9/11 in all fields of security, helping to create the realities of extraordinary criminalization that characterize American society more than any other Western nation-state. However, 9/11 fueled catastrophic imaginations to new heights and a "war on" everything is now a permanent feature of everyday political and practical life.

In this new world of catastrophic imagination and uncertainty, there is a shift from the "culture of control" to a culture of suspicion. We are all suspects now, at once suspected of never doing enough for homeland security and of being a possible source of terror, big or little. As such we are all watchers as well as watched and the bearers of our own control. The inevitable result is not just a chilly climate, but a new cold war of suspicion and fear. There is the well-documented increase in distrust of people and institutions, discriminatory practices, and fragmentation into population segments of aliens and the alienated.

When everything is read for its criminal potential, then we have indeed reached a state of being governed through crime. Crime becomes the governing principle in social policy, community planning, individual lifestyle choices, and everyday practical decisions.

Life is lived under the threat of penal sanction for the most trifling thing. For example, anti-social behavior laws function as laws of risk and dirt, aimed at cleaning up the minutiae of everyday pollution – noise, litter, graffiti, fly-posting, high hedges – to give local communities the veneer of domestic security. Apparently one can no longer rely on good citizenship, nor even community discipline and pressure to conform, for this domestic work of social vacuuming. Rather, it now requires the coercive threat of the state's most serious sanction – up to five years' imprisonment for breach of an anti-social behavior order – to do the dirty work.

Efforts at sociability are also criminalized. Anti-social behavior laws are deeply anti-social, for example prohibiting assembly of two or more people in various contexts, and placing curfews on those under 16 between 9 p.m. and 6 a.m. Such measures seem to be based on the belief that anti-social conduct will be less prevalent if people are prevented from interacting. Sociability is itself posed as a threat out of fear that something anti-social might eventuate. Of course, the target of such provisions is socially undesirable segments of the population – the young, the dispossessed, those with something to protest – who signify threat continuously. Here counter-law acts, as always, to reinforce divisions in society and foster regimes of fear.

Life is lived in webs of surveillance in which everyone is simultaneously a suspect and a police agent. Homeland security demands perpetual policing of others and oneself. People are to be on the lookout for any signs of terrorism, big or little, and institutionalize a "better safe than sorry" precautionary logic in their everyday lives. The websites for community notification of sex offenders exemplify this precautionary logic. Visitors to the sites are told to shun identified sex offenders; that risk indicators regarding sexual predators are crude and not to be relied upon; that people who look innocent may not be; and that even when identified sex offenders move away from the community one's guard should not be let down. Furthermore, visitors to these websites are told that they themselves are under surveillance, and that any misuse of the information can result in criminalization.

Neighbor is also pitted against neighbor in the very act of obtaining the means of security. The purchase of private security services and technologies creates an escalating environment of private protection in which the have-nots are left more vulnerable. Their vulnerability derives not only from the lack of private security provision, but also the fact that they see signs of security everywhere and therefore become more fearful and desirous of security commodities. Ironically, incivility among neighbors results not only from incessant policing for signs of anti-social behavior, but also from signs of private security protection that invite invidious comparisons. The sense of incivility is further aroused when those subject to criminalization through counter-law realize that their ordinary behaviors are condemned while similar behaviors by others are condoned. In the context of national security, ethnic and racial minorities can be detained and deported for behaviors and associations that are normal for others. In the context of social security, welfare claimants who are kept below the poverty line are forced to be enterprising to make ends meet. However, their enterprising efforts – receiving gifts, free meals, income supplements, and support by partners – are subject to criminalization, even while such conduct is the very lubricant of social life for full citizens. In the context of corporate security, behavior that is widely lauded as entrepreneurial and at the leading edge of "creative compliance" can suddenly be criminalized as "rogue" and pathological when things go wrong. In the context of domestic security, counter-laws of anti-social behavior, possession, transience, and private policing are used to determine when one person's version of a good night out is another person's version of what is most threatening and must be criminalized.

More Risk, Uncertainty and Crime

The liberal social imaginary promises security as freedom from harm to life and its potential. Security is safety, something that guarantees and guards a secure condition and thus provides freedom from danger. Security contributes to certainty: freedom from doubt, fear, and anxiety about danger. Certainty is a question of knowledge, of knowing for sure. Certainty as knowledge combines with security as safety to provide reliability – something that can be relied upon to happen – and thus confidence in taking action.

Security has two connected paradoxes that can undermine the Leviathan of the liberal social imaginary and transform it into the Leviathan of the biblical social imaginary. The first paradox is based in the problem of uncertainty. Uncertainty is the basic condition of human knowledge. Efforts to convert uncertainty into risk expose the limits of knowledge and extent of uncertainty. As a result, security is never an end-state but always a fragile process. It is more within us as a yearning than outside us as a fact.

The problem of uncertainty creates the urge to hunker down, avoid risk, and limit the freedom of others in the name of security. These measures limit the entrepreneurial risk-taking that liberalism needs for prosperity. Ironically, the neo-liberal subject becomes a risk-avoider rather than a risk-taker and thus not so neo-liberal after all.

Ironically, liberalism requires a degree of uncertainty as a positive dimension of freedom. A degree of uncertainty, and associated insecurity, is an engine of the competitive market relations, entrepreneurial risk-taking, creative enterprise, self-governance, prosperity, and well-being of the liberal social imaginary. The question for liberal regimes is how much uncertainty and insecurity to leave in play to foster the prosperity of individuals and corporate entities. At what point do "houses of certainty" become counterproductive to liberal social imaginaries of prosperity and well-being?

This question raises the second, connected paradox of liberal social imaginaries. Liberal subjects and corporate entities must curtail freedom through security measures in order to promote conditions in which freedom can flourish. There is a need for guaranteeing secure conditions to provide reliable conditions for action. There is a need for law, scientific risk assessment, and surveillance infrastructures to provide knowledge as a capacity to act in predictable ways. Meeting these needs restricts some freedoms to facilitate other freedoms. It also restricts freedoms of some to facilitate freedoms of others.

As documented throughout this book, neo-liberal subjects are at least being enterprising in their creative development and use of laws, sciences, and technologies that promise more security and greater certainty. But in the process of doing so they are buying into a program of security that is highly restrictive at both the level of the catastrophic imagination of doubt, fear, and need for precaution, and at the level of everyday behavior. They have gone too far, reaching the point where the regimes in which they operate look less and less liberal. Law as the institution and technology of liberal governance undermines itself through laws against law. Surveillant assemblages become the constitutive mechanism of governance. Civil society unravels. There is more risk and uncertainty.

There is also more crime. While a decrease in "index" crime has been widely touted in recent years, the index does not capture the new forms of criminalization as a response to uncertainty documented in this book. It does not include the hundreds who have been detained indefinitely as "unlawful enemy combatants," the tens of thousands who have been detained temporarily and profoundly stigmatized because they were suspected of being terrorist suspects, and whole populations who live in national security webs of surveillance and categorical suspicion. It does not include benefits system claimants who are deemed presumptively fraudulent, and who must somehow survive in a structure of benefits suppression that leaves them well below the poverty line and compels behavior that the system then treats as fraudulent. It does not include new forms of white collar and corporate criminalization aimed at scapegoating the visible few to save the face of the many who engage in similar actions as a normal way of doing business and exhibiting creative compliance with regulations. It does not include the kaleidoscope of deviance that is now criminalized through the laws of antisocial behavior, criminal possession, transience, and private policing in combination with the surveillant assemblages of everyday domestic security. These new ways of making crime prove once again that crime is an artifact of institutional processes for defining, discovering, and responding to it, and that there are many institutions involved in making crime in addition to criminal justice.

Criminalization through counter-law preys upon what it condemns. It terrorizes innocent populations as terrorists. It stigmatizes vulnerable populations as fraudsters. It eliminates populations of political and corporate leaders for failing to eliminate uncertainty. It punishes merely offensive populations as criminal neighbors.

While counter-law offers the promise of certainty and security, this is an impossible mandate because catastrophic harms are inevitable, and each loss reveals the failure of the counter-law regime. Indeed counter-law regimes organize their own disasters by creating new harms and incubating risks. Similar to the myth of the full enforcement of the criminal law that was prevalent until the 1960s, and even entrenched in statutes of some US states, the myth of certainty and security through counter-law becomes transparent in actual processes of law enforcement.

Allowing for some uncertainty, including failures in risk management without punitive blame, creates zones of freedom for positive innovation and change. It also provides conditions of trust in which people are allowed to be themselves, experiment with the boundaries of acceptable behavior, take risks, and make mistakes, without fear of exclusion as the criminal other when things go wrong. As English dramatist William Congreve wrote in *Love for Love* three centuries ago, "Security is an insipid thing, and the overtaking and possessing of a wish reveals the folly of the chase."

References

Adams, J. (1995) *Risk*. UCL Press, London.

Adams, J. (2003) Risk and morality: three framing devices. In: Ericson, R. and Doyle, A. (eds.) *Risk and Morality*. University of Toronto Press, Toronto, pp. 87–103.

Agamben, G. (2005) *State of Exception*. University of Chicago Press, Chicago.

Altheide, D. (2006) *Terrorism and the Politics of Fear*. Altamira Press, Blue Ridge Summit, PA.

Amoore, L. and De Goede, M. (2005) Government, risk and dataveillance in the war on terror. *Crime, Law and Social Change* 43, 149–73.

Anderson, D. (1999) The aggregate burden of crime. *Journal of Law and Economics* 42, 611–42.

Andrew, D. (1989) *Philanthropy and Police: London Charity in the Eighteenth Century*. Princeton University Press, Princeton, NJ.

Angell, M. (2004) *The Truth About Drug Companies: How They Deceive Us and What to Do About It*. Random House, New York.

Ashworth, A. (2000) Is the criminal law a lost cause? *Law Quarterly Review* 116, 225–56.

Ashworth, A. (2003) *Principles of Criminal Law*. Oxford University Press, Oxford.

Ashworth, A. (2004) Social control and "anti-social behaviour": the subversion of human rights? *Law Quarterly Review* 120, 263–91.

Atiyah, P. (1997) *The Damages Lottery*. Hart Publishing, Oxford.

Awerbuch, M. (1992) Whiplash in Australia: illness or injury? *Medical Journal of Australia* 157, 193–6.

Ayres, I. and Braithwaite, J. (1992) *Responsive Regulation: Transcending the Deregulation Debate*. Oxford University Press, New York.

Bakan, J. (2004) *The Corporation: The Pathological Pursuit of Profit and Power*. Constable, London.

Baker, T. (1996) On the genealogy of moral hazard. *Texas Law Review* 75, 237–92.

Baker, T. (2005) *The Medical Malpractice Myth*. University of Chicago Press, Chicago.

Baker, T. and Simon, J. (eds.) (2002) *Embracing Risk: The Changing Culture of Insurance and Responsibility*. University of Chicago Press, Chicago.

Barak, G. (2005) A reciprocal approach to peacemaking criminology: between adversarialism and mutualism. *Theoretical Criminology* 9, 131 52.

Baudrillard, J. (2003) *The Spirit of Terrorism and other Essays*. Verso, London.

Bayatrizi, Z. (2005) *Death Sentences: The Modern Ordering of Mortality*. Ph.D. thesis, Department of Anthropology and Sociology, University of British Columbia.

Beamish, T. (2002) *Silent Spill: The Organization of Industrial Crisis*. MIT Press, Cambridge, MA.

Beck, U. (1992) *Risk Society: Toward a New Modernity*. Sage, London.

Beck, U. (1999) *World Risk Society*. Polity, Cambridge.

Bell, P. and O'Connell, J. (1997) *Accidental Justice: The Dilemmas of Tort Law*. Yale University Press, New Haven.

Bennett, C. (2005) What happens when you book an airline ticket? The collecting and processing of passenger data post-9/11. In: Zureik, E. and Salter, M. (eds.) *Global Surveillance and Policing: Borders, Security, Identity*. Cullompton, Willan, pp. 113–38.

Bensman, J. and Gerver, I. (1963) Crime and punishment in the factory: the function of deviancy in maintaining the social system. *American Sociological Review* 28, 588–98.

Berlin, I. (1969) Two concepts of liberty. In: I. Berlin (ed.) *Four Essays on Liberty*. Oxford University Press, Oxford, pp. 118–72.

Bernstein, P. (1998) *Against the Gods: The Remarkable Story of Risk*. Wiley, New York.

Best, J. (1989) Dark figures and child victims: statistical claims about missing children. In: *Images of Issues: Typifying Contemporary Social Problems*. Aldine de Gruyter, New York, pp. 21–37.

Best, J. (1990) *Threatened Children: Rhetoric and Concern about Child Victims*. University of Chicago Press, Chicago.

Bok, S. (1979) *Lying: Moral Choice in Public and Private Life*. Vintage, New York.

Bok, S. (1982) *Secrets: On the Ethics of Concealment and Revelation*. Pantheon, New York.

Braithwaite, J. (1985) *To Punish or Persuade: Enforcement of Coal Mine Safety*. State University of New York Press, Albany, NY.

Braithwaite, J. (2000) The new regulatory state and the transformation of criminology. In: Garland, D. and Sparks, R. (eds.) *Criminology and Social Theory*. Oxford University Press, Oxford, pp. 47–69.

Braithwaite, J. (2003) What's wrong with the sociology of punishment? *Theoretical Criminology* 7, 5–28.

Braithwaite, J. and Drahos, P. (2000) *Global Business Regulation*. Cambridge University Press, Cambridge.

British Columbia Whiplash Initiative (1997) *Whiplash-Associated Disorders: A Comprehensive Syllabus*. Physical Medicine Research Foundation, Vancouver.

Brodeur, J.-P. (1981) Legitimizing police deviance. In: Shearing, C. (ed.) *Organizational Police Deviance*. Butterworths, Toronto, pp. 127–60.

Brodeur, J.-P. and Leman-Langlois, S. (2006) Surveillance fiction or high policing. In: Haggerty, K. and Ericson, R. (eds.) *The New Politics of Surveillance and Visibility*. University of Toronto Press, Toronto, pp. 171–98.

Brown, M. and Pratt, J. (eds.) (2000) *Dangerous Offenders: Punishment and Social Order*. Routledge, London.

Brunsson, N. and Jacobsson, B. (2000) *A World of Standards*. Oxford University Press, Oxford.

BSE Inquiry Oral Transcript, December 17, 1999: 4–5.

Bureau of Justice Statistics (2002) *Summary of State Sex Offender Registries, 2001*. US Department of Justice, Washington.

Burke, J. (2004) *Al-Qaeda: Casting a Shadow of Terror*. I.B. Tauris, London.

Burtch, B. and Ericson, R. (1979) The control of treatment: issues in the use of prison clinical services. *University of Toronto Law Journal* 29, 51–73.

Campbell, R. (2002) America acts: the swift legislative response to the September 11th attack on America. Paper to the conference,

Liability and Insurance after September 11th, Insurance Law Center, University of Connecticut School of Law, 21–22 March.

Canadian Broadcasting Corporation (1998) *In Security*. Witness Program Video, CBC, Toronto.

Canadian Broadcasting Corporation (2004) *In Search of Security*. CBC Ideas Transcripts, Toronto.

Canadian Security (1998) The importance of hugs. November/December.

Carson, W. (1979) The conventionalization of early factory crime. *International Journal of the Sociology of Law* 7, 37–60.

Chaplin, J. (1959) *Rumor, Fear and the Madness of Crowds*. Ballantine Books, New York.

Cheaney, R. (2004) The sleeper scenario: terrorism-support laws and the demands of prevention. *Harvard Review on Legislation* 42, 1–90.

Chunn, D. and Gavigan, S. (2004) Welfare law, welfare fraud, and the moral regulation of the "never deserving" poor. *Social and Legal Studies* 13, 219–43.

Clarke, R. (2004) *Against All Enemies: Inside America's War on Terror*. Free Press, New York.

Cole, S. (2001) *Suspect Identities: A History of Fingerprinting and Criminal Identification*. Harvard University Press, Cambridge, MA.

Committee of the Sponsoring Organizations of the Treadway Commission (2004) *Framework for Enterprise Risk Management*. COSO, Jersey City, NJ.

Conference Board of Canada (2001) *A Composite Sketch of a Chief Risk Officer*. Conference Board of Canada, Ottawa.

Cradock, G. (2004) *Governing Through Vague Terms: Child Abuse, Community and Government*. Ph.D. Thesis, Interdisciplinary Studies, University of British Columbia.

Crawford, A. (2003) "Contractual governance" of deviant behavior. *Journal of Law and Society* 30, 479–505.

Dandeker, C. (1990) *Surveillance, Power and Modernity: Bureaucracy and Discipline from 1700 to the Present Day*. St. Martin's Press, New York.

De Becker, G. (1997) *The Gift of Fear: Survival Signals that Protect Us from Violence*. Little Brown, Boston.

Department of Homeland Security (2004) *Are You Ready? An In-depth Guide to Citizen Preparedness*. Federal Emergency Management Agency, Jessup, MD.

Dershowitz, A. (2002) *Why Terrorism Works: Understanding the Threat, Responding to the Challenge*. Yale University Press, New Haven, CT.

Dixon, D. (1997) *Law in Policing*. The Clarendon Press, Oxford.

Dornstein, K. (1996) *Accidentally on Purpose: The Making of a Personal Injury Underworld in America*. St Martin's Press, New York.

Douglas, M. (1985) *Risk Acceptability According to the Social Sciences*. Russell Sage Foundation, New York.

Douglas, M. (1990) Risk as a forensic resource. *Daedalus* 119, 1–16.

Douglas, M. (1992) *Risk and Blame: Essays in Cultural Theory*. Routledge, London.

Douglas, M. and Wildavsky, A. (1983) *Risk and Culture*. University of California Press, Berkeley, CA.

Doyle, A. (2003) *Arresting Images: Crime and Policing in Front of the Television Camera*. University of Toronto Press, Toronto.

Dratel, J. (2005) The legal narrative. In: Greenberg, K. and Dratel, J. (eds.) *The Torture Papers: The Road to Abu Ghraib*. Cambridge University Press, Cambridge, pp. xxi–xxiii.

Dubber, M. (2001) Policing possession: the war on crime and the end of criminal law. *The Journal of Criminal Law and Criminology* 91, 829–996.

Duncan, G. (2003) Workers' compensation and the governance of pain. *Economy and Society* 32, 449–77.

Durr, E. (1994) With whiplash, the future comes from behind. *Sygeplejersken* 94, 34–6.

Eakin, J., Clarke, J. and MacEachen, E. (2002) *Return to Work in Small Workplaces: Sociological Perspectives on Workplace Experience with Ontario's "Early and Safe" Strategy*. Report to the Research Advisory Council of the Ontario Workplace Safety and Insurance Board.

Edgerton, R. (1985) *Rules, Exceptions, and Social Order*. University of California Press, Berkeley, CA.

Ellenberger, J. (2000) The battle over workers' compensation. *New Solutions* 10, 217–36.

Ericson, R. (1975) *Criminal Reactions: The Labelling Perspective*. Saxon House (D.C. Heath), Westmead, Hants.

Ericson, R. (1993) *Making Crime: A Study of Detective Work*. 2nd edn. University of Toronto Press, Toronto.

Ericson, R. (1994) The decline of innocence. *University of British Columbia Law Review* 28, 367–383.

Ericson, R. and Baranek, P. (1982) *The Ordering of Justice: A Study of Accused Persons as Dependants in the Criminal Process.* University of Toronto Press, Toronto.

Ericson, R. and Doyle, A. (2003) The moral risks of private justice: the case of insurance fraud. In: Ericson, R. and Doyle, A. (eds.) *Risk and Morality.* University of Toronto Press, Toronto, pp. 317–63.

Ericson, R. and Doyle, A. (2004a) *Uncertain Business: Risk, Insurance and the Limits of Knowledge.* University of Toronto Press, Toronto.

Ericson, R. and Doyle, A. (2004b) Catastrophe risk, insurance and terrorism. *Economy and Society* 33, 135–173.

Ericson, R. and Doyle, A. (2004c) Criminalization in private: the case of insurance fraud. In: Law Commission of Canada (ed.) *What is Crime? Defining Criminal Conduct in Contemporary Society.* University of British Columbia Press, Vancouver, pp. 99–124.

Ericson, R. and Doyle, A. (2006, forthcoming) The institutionalization of deceptive sales in life insurance: five sources of moral risk. *British Journal of Criminology* 46.

Ericson, R., Barry, D., and Doyle, A. (2000) The moral hazards of neo-liberalism: lessons from the private insurance industry. *Economy and Society* 29, 532–58.

Ericson, R., Doyle, A., and Barry, D. (2003) *Insurance as Governance.* University of Toronto Press, Toronto.

Ericson, R. and Haggerty, K. (1997) *Policing the Risk Society.* University of Toronto Press, Toronto; The Clarendon Press, Oxford.

Ericson, R. and Haggerty, K. (2002) The policing of risk. In: Baker, T. and Simon, J. (eds.) *Embracing Risk: The Changing Culture of Insurance and Responsibility.* University of Chicago Press, Chicago, pp. 238–72.

Evans, R. et al. (1994) *Why are Some People Healthy and Others Not? The Determinants of Health of Populations.* Aldine de Gruyter, New York.

Ewald, F. (2000) Risk in contemporary society. *Connecticut Insurance Law Journal* 6, 365–79.

Ewald, F. (2002) The return of Descartes's malicious demon: an outline of a philosophy of precaution. In: Baker, T. and Simon, J. (eds.) *Embracing Risk: The Changing Culture of Insurance and Responsibility.* University of Chicago Press, Chicago, pp. 273–301.

Farneti, R. (2001) The mythical "mythical foundation" of the state: leviathan in the emblematic context. *Pacific Philosophical Quarterly* 82, 362–82.

Ferguson, N. (2005) *Colossus: The Rise and Fall of the American Empire*. Penguin, New York.

Fisher, L. (2000) Drowning by numbers: standard setting in risk regulation and the pursuit of accountable public administration. *Oxford Journal of Legal Studies* 20, 109–30.

Fisher, L. (2001) Is the precautionary principle justiciable? *Journal of Environmental Law* 13, 315–34.

Fisher, L. (2002) Precaution, precaution everywhere: developing a "common understanding" of the precautionary principle in the European community. *Maastricht Journal of European and Comparative Law* 9, 7–28.

Fisher, L. (2003) The rise of the risk commonwealth and the challenge for administrative law. *Public Law* (Autumn), 455–478.

Fisher, L. (2004) *Risk Regulation and Administrative Constitutionalism*. Hart Publishing, Oxford.

Fordyce, W. (ed.) (1995) *Back Pain in the Workplace: Management of Disability in Nonspecific Conditions*. International Association for the Study of Pain Press, Seattle.

Fortun, K. (2001) *Advocacy after Bhopal: Environmentalism, Disaster, New Global Orders*. University of Chicago Press, Chicago.

Foucault, M. (1977) *Discipline and Punish: The Birth of the Prison*. Pantheon, New York.

Foucault, M. (1991) Governmentality. In: Burchell, G., Gordon, C., and Miller, P. (eds.) *The Foucault Effect: Studies in Governmentality*. University of Chicago Press, Chicago, pp. 87–104.

Freudenberg, W. (2003) Institutional failure and organizational amplification of risks: the need for a closer look. In: Pidgeon, N., Kasperson, R., and Slovic, P. (eds.) *The Social Amplification of Risk*. Cambridge University Press, Cambridge, pp. 102–20.

Gandy, O. (2006) Data mining, surveillance and discrimination in the post-9/11 environment. In: Haggerty, K. and Ericson, R. (eds.) *The New Politics of Surveillance and Visibility*. University of Toronto Press, Toronto, pp. 363–84.

Garland, D. (1985) *Punishment and Welfare: A History of Penal Strategies*. Gower, Aldershot.

Garland, D. (2003) *The Culture of Control: Crime and Social Order in Contemporary Society*. University of Chicago Press, Chicago.

Giddens, A. (1985) *A Contemporary Critique of Historical*

Materialism, vol. 2: The Nation-State and Violence. Polity, Cambridge.

Giddens, A. (1990) *The Consequences of Modernity.* Polity, Cambridge.

Giddens, A. (1994) *Beyond Left and Right: The Future of Radical Politics.* Polity, Cambridge.

Giddens, A. (1998) *The Third Way: The Renewal of Social Democracy.* Polity, Cambridge.

Giddens, A. (1999) *The Third Way and its Critics.* Polity, Cambridge.

Graham, J. (1979) *Lavater, Essays on Physiognomy: A Study in the History of Ideas.* Peter Lang, Berne.

Green, M. (2002) Cat models look to predict losses from future attacks. *Best Wire,* 29 August.

Green, T. (1995) Freedom and criminal responsibility in the age of Pound: an essay on criminal justice. *Michigan Law Review* 93, 1915–2053.

Greenberg, K. and Dratel, J. (eds.) (2005) *The Torture Papers: The Road to Abu Ghraib.* Cambridge University Press, Cambridge.

Hacking, I. (1990) *The Taming of Chance.* Cambridge University Press, Cambridge.

Hacking, I. (2003) Risk and dirt. In: Ericson, R. and Doyle, A. (eds.) *Risk and Morality.* University of Toronto Press, Toronto, pp. 22–47.

Haggerty, K. (2003) From risk to precaution: the rationalities of personal crime prevention. In: Ericson, R. and Doyle, A. (eds.) *Risk and Morality.* University of Toronto Press, Toronto, pp. 193–214.

Haggerty, K. and Ericson, R. (2000) The surveillant assemblage. *British Journal of Sociology* 51, 605–22.

Haggerty, K. and Ericson, R. (eds.) (2006) *The New Politics of Surveillance and Visibility.* University of Toronto Press, Toronto.

Hall, K. (2004) Japanese kids get radio ID'd. Associated Press, October 11.

Harvard Law Review (2001a) What we talk about when we talk about persons: the language of a legal fiction. *Harvard Law Review* 114, 1744–68.

Harvard Law Review (2001b) Developments in the law: international criminal law. *Harvard Law Review* 114, 1943–2073.

Hawkins, K. (2002) *Law as a Last Resort: Prosecution Decision-Making in a Regulatory Agency.* Oxford University Press, Oxford.

Hazelkorn, B. (2003) Making crime pay: private security companies are acting like real cops, with virtually no oversight. Where does that lead? *San Francisco Chronicle*, August 17.

Herd, D. and Mitchell, A. (2002) *Discouraged, Diverted and Disentitled: Ontario Works' New Service Delivery Model.* Community Social Planning Council of Toronto and Ontario Social Safety Network, Toronto.

Heimer, C., Coleman Petty, J., and Culyba, R. (2005) Risk and rules: the "legalization" of medicine. In: Hutter, B. and Power, M. (eds.) *Organizational Encounters with Risk.* Cambridge University Press, Cambridge, pp. 92–131.

Hermer, J., Kempa, M., Shearing, C., Stenning, P., and Wood, J. (2005) Policing in Canada in the Twenty-first Century: directions for law reform. In: Cooley, D. (ed.) *Re-imagining Policing in Canada.* University of Toronto Press, Toronto, pp. 22–91.

Hobbes, T. (1985 [1651]) *Leviathan.* Edited by C.B. Macpherson. Penguin, London.

Hornqvist, M. (2004) Risk assessments and public order disturbances: new European guidelines for the use of force? *Journal of Scandinavian Studies in Criminology and Crime Prevention* 5, 4–26.

Hudson, B. (2003) *Justice in the Risk Society.* Sage, London.

Huey, L. (2005) *Negotiating Demands: The Politics of "Skid Row" Policing in Edinburgh, San Francisco and Vancouver.* Ph.D. thesis, Department of Anthropology and Sociology, University of British Columbia.

Huey, L., Ericson, R., and Haggerty, K. (2005) Policing fantasy city. In: Cooley, D. (ed.) *Re-imagining Policing in Canada.* University of Toronto Press, Toronto, pp. 140–208.

Hunt, A. (2003) Risk and moralization in everyday life. In: Ericson, R. and Doyle, A. (eds.) *Risk and Morality.* University of Toronto Press, Toronto, pp. 165–92.

Hutter, B. (2005) "Ways of seeing": understandings of risk in organizational settings. In: Hutter, B. and Power, M. *Organizational Encounters with Risk.* Cambridge University Press, Cambridge, pp. 67–91.

Hutter, B. and Power, M. (2005) Organizational encounters with risk: an introduction. In: Hutter, B. and Power, M. (eds.) *Organizational Encounters with Risk.* Cambridge University Press, Cambridge, pp. 1–32.

Hyatt, D. and Law, D. (2000) Should work-injury compensation continue to imbibe at the tort bar? In: Gunderson, M. and Hyatt,

D. (eds.) *Workers' Compensation: Foundations for Reform.* University of Toronto Press, Toronto, pp. 261–98.

Ignatieff, M. (2004) *The Lesser Evil: Political Ethics in an Age of Terror.* Princeton University Press, Princeton, NJ.

Insurance Research Council/Insurance Services Organization. (2001) *Fighting Insurance Fraud: Survey of Insurer Anti-Fraud Efforts.* IRC/ISO.

Janus, E. (2004) The preventive state, terrorists and sexual predators: countering the threat of a new outsider jurisprudence. *Criminal Law Bulletin* 40, 576–98.

Joh, E. (2004) The paradox of private policing. *The Journal of Criminal Law and Criminology* 95, 49–131.

Jonas, J. and Pope, H. (1985) The dissimulation disorders: a single diagnostic entity? *Comparative Psychiatry* 26, 58–62.

Kean, T. and Hamilton, L. (2004) *The 9/11Report: The National Commission on Terrorist Attacks Upon the United States.* St. Martin's Press, New York.

Kelling, G. and Coles, C. (2001) *Fixing Broken Windows.* Free Press, New York.

Kemshall, H. (2003) *Understanding Risk in Criminal Justice.* Open University Press, Maidenhead.

King, S. (1981) *Danse Macabre.* Everest House, New York.

Krane, J. (2002) Terrorism worries bring big business: pitch the product the right way and "you'd be amazed at what you sell." *Toronto Star,* 29 August.

Leff, L. (2005) Parents protest as California school requires students to wear computer ID tags. Associated Press, 19 February.

Lempert, R. and Sanders, J. (1986) *An Introduction to Law and Social Science: Desert, Disputes and Distribution.* University of Pennsylvania Press, Philadelphia, PA.

Levi, M. and Wall, D. (2004) Technologies, security and privacy in the post-9/11 European information society. *Journal of Law and Society* 31, 194–220.

Levi-Faur, D. and Gilad, S. (2004) The rise of the British regulatory state – transcending the privatization debate. *Comparative Politics* 37, 105–26.

Lewis, A. (2005) Introduction. In: Greenberg, K. and Dratel, J. (eds.) *The Torture Papers: The Road to Abu Ghraib.* Cambridge University Press, Cambridge, pp. xiii–xvi.

Lind, E. et al. (1989) The changing face of war: into the fourth generation. *Marine Corps Gazette* (October), 22–6.

Lippel, K. (1999) Therapeutic and anti-therapeutic consequences of workers' compensation. *International Journal of Law and Psychiatry* 22, 521–46.

Lippel, K. (2003) The private policing of injured workers in Canada: legitimate management practices or human rights violations? *Policy and Practice in Health and Safety* 1(2), 97–118.

Little, M. (1998) *No Car, No Radio, No Liquor Permit: The Moral Regulation of Single Mothers in Ontario, 1920–1997*. Toronto: Oxford University Press.

Loader, I. (1999) Consumer culture and the commodification of policing and security. *Sociology* 33, 373–92.

Loader, I. and Walker, N. (2001) Policing as a public good: reconstituting the connections between policing and the state. *Theoretical Criminology* 5, 9–35.

Lofquist, W., Cohen, M., and Rabe, M. (eds.) (1997) *Debating Corporate Crime*. Academy of Criminal Justice Sciences, Northern Kentucky University, Highland Heights, KY.

Lowther, B. (1996) Maximum coverage. *Monday Magazine* 22 (46), 1, 6–7.

Mackay, C. (1980 [1841]) *Extraordinary Popular Delusions and the Madness of Crowds*. Harmony Books, New York.

Mackenzie, D. (2005) Mathematizing risk: models, arbitrage and crises. In: Hutter, B. and Power, M. (eds.) *Organizational Encounters with Risk*. Cambridge University Press, Cambridge, pp. 167–189.

Malleson, A. (2002) *Whiplash and other Useful Illnesses*. McGill-Queen's University Press, Montreal and Kingston.

Manning, J., Manning, C.-L., and Osler, V. (2004) *Blackstone's Guide to the Anti-Social Behaviour Act 2003*. Oxford University Press, Oxford.

March, J. and Shapiro, Z. (1987) Managerial perspectives on risk and risk taking. *Management Science* 23, 1404–18.

Marx, K. (1967) *Writings of the Young Marx on Philosophy and Society*. Anchor, New York.

Matthews, D. (2004) *Review of Employment Assistance Programs in Ontario Works and Ontario Disability Support Program*. Report to the Ontario Minister of Community and Social Services, Toronto.

Matza, D. (1957) Techniques of neutralization: a theory of delinquency. *American Sociological Review* 22, 664–70.

McBarnet, D. (1981) *Conviction: Law, the State and the Construction of Justice*. Edward Arnold, London.

McBarnet, D. (2006, forthcoming) After Enron, before Enron, beyond Enron. *British Journal of Criminology* 46.

McClusky, M. (1998) Illusion of efficiency in workers' compensation "reform." *Rutgers Law Review* 50, 657–741.

McClusky, M. (2002) Rhetoric of risk and the redistribution of social insurance. In: Baker, T. and Simon, J. (eds.) *Embracing Risk: The Changing Culture of Insurance and Responsibility*. University of Chicago Press, Chicago, pp. 146–70.

McQueen, R. (1996) *Who Killed Confederation Life?* McClelland and Stewart, Toronto.

Melville, H. (2003 [1851]) *Moby Dick*. Penguin Books, New York.

Mills, H. and Horne, G. (1986) Whiplash: manmade disease? *New Zealand Medical Journal* 99, 373–4.

Mopas, M. (2005) Policing in downtown Vancouver's east side: a case study. In: Cooley, D. (ed.) *Re-imagining Policing in Canada*. University of Toronto Press, Toronto, pp. 92–139.

Mopas, M. (2006) *Constructing a Governable Cyberspace*. Ph.D. thesis, Centre of Criminology, University of Toronto.

Mosher, J. and Hermer, J. (2005) *Welfare Fraud: The Constitution of Social Assistance as Crime*. Report to the Law Commission of Canada, Ottawa.

Moyers, B. (2005) Welcome to doomsday. *New York Review of Books* 52(5), 8, 10.

Munglani, R. (1999) The roots of chronicity. *Recovery* 10(2), 14–15.

O'Brien, R. (2001) *Crippled Justice: The History of Modern Disability Policy in the Workplace*. University of Chicago Press, Chicago.

Oestreich, G. (1982) *Neostoicism and the Early Modern State*. Cambridge University Press, Cambridge.

O'Malley, P. (2004) *Risk, Uncertainty and Government*. Glasshouse Press, London.

Organization of Economic Cooperation and Development. (2002) Economic consequences of terrorism. *OECD Economic Outlook* 71, 117–40.

Osborne, D. and Gaebler, T. (1992) *Reinventing Government: How the Entrepreneurial Spirit is Transforming the Public Sector*. Addison-Wesley, Reading, MA.

Pasquino, P. (1991) Theatrum politicum: the genealogy of capital – police and the state of prosperity. In: Burchell, G., Gordon, C., and Miller, P. (eds.) *The Foucault Effect: Studies in Governmentality*. University of Chicago Press, Chicago.

Pauley, L. (1997) *Who Elected the Bankers? Surveillance and Control in the World Economy*. Cornell University Press, Ithaca, NY.

Perrow, C. (1984) *Normal Accidents: Living with High-Risk Technologies*. Basic Books, New York.

Petryna, A. (2002) *Life Exposed: Biological Citizens after Chernobyl*. Princeton University Press, Princeton, NJ.

Physical Medicine Research Foundation (1997) *Our Mission*. PMRF, Vancouver.

Posner, M. (2004) *Catastrophe: Risk and Response*. Oxford University Press, New York.

Pound, R. (1927) Introduction. In: Sayre, F. *A Selection of Cases on Criminal Law*. Lawyers' Co-operative Publishing Company, Rochester, NY.

Power, M. (2004) *The Risk Management of Everything: Rethinking the Politics of Uncertainty*. Demos, London.

Power, M. (2005a) The invention of operational risk. *Review of International Political Economy* 12, 577–99.

Power, M. (2005b) Organizational responses to risk: the rise of the Chief Risk Officer. In: Hutter, B. and Power, M. (eds.) *Organizational Encounters with Risk*. Cambridge University Press, Cambridge, pp. 132–48.

Raban, J. (2005) The truth about terrorism. *New York Review of Books* 52(1), 22–6.

Radzinowicz, L. (1956) *The History of the English Criminal Law and its Administration*, vol. 3. Stevens, London.

Rasmussen, M. (2004) "It sounds like a riddle": security studies, the war on terror and risk. *Millennium: Journal of International Studies* 33, 381–95.

Recovery (1998) Special issue, Truth. *Recovery: A Quarterly Journal on Roadway Causes, Injuries and Healing* 9(4).

Recovery (1999) Special Issue, The Uncertainty Principle. *Recovery: A Quarterly Journal on Roadway Causes, Injuries and Healing* 10(2).

Reiss, A. (1984) Consequences of compliance and deterrence models of law enforcement for the exercise of police discretion. *Law and Contemporary Problems* 47, 83–122.

Reuter, C. (2004) *My Life is a Weapon: A Modern History of Suicide Bombing*. Princeton University Press, Princeton, NJ.

Rigakos, G. (2002) *The New Parapolice: Risk Markets and Commodified Social Control*. University of Toronto Press, Toronto.

Rigakos, G. and Greener, D. (2000) Bubbles of governance: private policing and the law in Canada. *Canadian Journal of Law and Society* 15, 145–85.

Rivers, C. (1994) *Face Value: Physiognomical Thought and the Legible Body in Marivault, Lavater, Balzac, Gautier and Zola*. University of Wisconsin Press, Madison.

Rodopoulos, J. (2005) Policing drug-driving: the science of expertise and the governance of drugs. Unpublished paper, Centre of Criminology, University of Toronto.

Rose, N. (1999) *Powers of Freedom: Reframing Political Thought*. Cambridge University Press, Cambridge.

Roussel, V. (2002) *Affaires de Juges: Les Magistrats dans les Scandales Politiques en France*. La Decouverte, Paris.

Roussel, V. (2003) New moralities of risk and political responsibility. In: Ericson, R. and Doyle, A. (eds.) *Risk and Morality*. University of Toronto Press, Toronto, pp. 117–44.

Royal Canadian Mounted Police (1991) *Annual Report on Canada's Missing Children*. Royal Canadian Mounted Police, Ottawa.

Ruggiero, V. (2002) Moby Dick and the crimes of the economy. *British Journal of Criminology* 42, 96–108.

Sarre, R. and Prenzler, T. (2005) *The Law of Private Security in Australia*. Lawbook Company, Pyrmount, New South Wales.

Scheuer, M. (2004) *Imperial Hubris: Why the West is Losing the War on Terror*. Brassey's, Dulles, VA.

Schiller, R. (2003) *The New Financial Order: Risk in the 21st Century*. Princeton University Press, Princeton, NJ.

Schmidt, R. (2003) U.S. expands clandestine surveillance operations. *Los Angeles Times*, March 5.

Schor, P. (1998) *The Overspent American: Upscaling, Downsizing and the New Consumer*. Basic Books, New York.

Schwartz, M. (2003) *How the Cows Turned Mad: Unlocking the Mysteries of Mad Cow Disease*. University of California Press, Berkeley, CA.

Seery, J. (1996) *Political Theory for Mortals: Shades of Justice, Images of Death*. Cornell University Press, Ithaca, NY.

Shearing, C. (1998) The changing face of the governance of security and justice. Discussion paper, Centre of Criminology, University of Toronto.

Shearing, C. and Stenning, P. (1984) From the panopticon to Disney World: the development of discipline. In: Doob, A. and

Greenspan, E. (eds.) *Perspectives in Criminal Law*. Canada Law Book, Aurora, ON, pp. 335–48.

Shorter, E. (1992) *From Paralysis to Fatigue: A History of Psychosomatic Illness in the Modern Era*. Macmillan, Toronto.

Shorter, E. (1994) *From the Mind into the Body: The Cultural Origins of Psychosomatic Symptoms*. Free Press, New York.

Simon, J. (1997) Governing through crime. In: Fisher, G. and Friedman, L. (eds.) *The Crime Conundrum: Essays on Criminal Justice*. Westview, Boulder, CO, pp. 171–90.

Simon, J. (2006) *Governing through Crime*. Oxford University Press, New York.

Sitkin, S. and Bies, R. (1994) The legalization of organizations: a multi-theoretical perspective. In: Sitkin, S. and Bies, R. (eds.) *The Legalistic Organization*. Sage, Thousand Oaks, CA, pp. 19–49.

Slansky, D. (1999) The private police. *UCLA Law Review* 46, 1165–287.

Slater, D. (1997) *Consumer Culture and Modernity*. Polity, Cambridge.

Smith, A. (1978) *Lectures on Jurisprudence*. Edited by Meek, R., Raphael, D., and Stein, P. Clarendon Press, Oxford.

Somner, H. (1999) Patients in peril. *Recovery* 10(2), 26–7.

Sontag, S. (1979) *Illness as Metaphor*. Allen Lane, London.

Sontag, S. (1989) *AIDS and its Metaphors*. Allen Lane, London.

Spitzer, W. et al. (1995) *Scientific Monograph of the Quebec Task Force on Whiplash-Associated Disorders: Redefining Whiplash and its Management*. *Spine* 20 (Supplement), 2–68.

Stafford Smith, C. (2005) Representing "the enemy": human rights and the war on terror. *Criminal Justice Matters* 58, 44–7.

Standard and Poor's. (2002) Terrorism insurance coverage remains in doubt. *Standard and Poor's Insurance*, 15 April.

Stehr, N. and Ericson, R. (2000) The ungovernability of modern societies. In: Ericson, R. and Stehr, N. (eds.) *Governing Modern Societies*. University of Toronto Press, Toronto, pp. 3–25.

Stehr, N. and von Storch, H. (1999) *Klima-Wetter-Mensh*. C.H. Beck, Munich.

Stein, J. (2001) *The Cult of Efficiency*. Anansi, Toronto.

Stein, M. (2000) The risk taker as shadow: a psychoanalytic view of the collapse of Barings Bank. *Journal of Management Studies* 37, 1215–30.

Sullivan, T. (ed.) (2000) *Injury and the New World of Work*. University of British Columbia Press, Vancouver.

Sullivan, T., Stainblum, E., and Frank, J. (1997) Multicausality and the future of workers' compensation. Paper to the Third International Congress on Medical-Legal Aspects of Work Injury.

Sunstein, C. (2002) *Risk and Reason: Safety, Law and the Environment*. Cambridge University Press, Cambridge.

Sunstein, C. (2005) *Laws of Fear*. Cambridge University Press, Cambridge.

Sustainable Development Strategy (2002) *Living Places, Cleaner, Safer, Greener*. Office of the Deputy Prime Minister, London.

Takei, C. (2003) Building a nation of snoops. *Boston Globe*, May 14.

Taylor, C. (2004) *Modern Social Imaginaries*. Duke University Press, Durham.

Thompson, Jr., W. (2002) *One Year Later: The Fiscal Impact of 9/11 on New York City*. Comptroller of the City of New York, New York.

Tsing, A. (2005) *Friction: An Ethnography of Global Connection*. Princeton University Press, Princeton, NJ.

Turner, B. and Pidgeon, N. (1997) *Man-made Disasters*. Butterworth-Heinemann, Oxford.

Turow, J. (2006) Cracking the code: advertisers, anxiety and surveillance in the digital age. In: Haggerty, K. and Ericson, R. (eds.) *The New Politics of Surveillance and Visibility*. University of Toronto Press, Toronto, pp. 279–307.

Vaughan, D. (1996) *The Challenger Launch Decision: Risky Technology, Culture and Deviance at NASA*. University of Chicago Press, Chicago.

Vaughan, D. (1999) The dark side of organizations: mistake, misconduct and disaster. *Annual Review of Sociology* 25, 271–305.

Vaughan, D. (2005) Organizational rituals of risk and error. In: Hutter, B. and Power, M. (eds.) *Organizational Encounters with Risk*. Cambridge University Press, Cambridge, pp. 33–66.

Visher, C. (2000) Career criminals and crime control. In: Sheley, J. (ed.) *Criminology: A Contemporary Handbook*. 3rd edn. Wadsworth, Belmont, CA.

Waldron, J. (1991) Homelessness and the issue of freedom. *UCLA Law Review* 39, 295–324.

Weait, M. (1993) Icing on the cake? The contribution of the compliance function to effective financial regulation. *Journal of Asset Protection and Financial Crime* 1, 83–90.

Weisberg, H. and Derrig, R. (1991) Fraud and automobile insurance: a report on bodily injury claims in Massachusetts. *Journal of Insurance Regulation* 9, 497–541.

Weisberg, H. and Derrig, R. (1992) Massachusetts bodily injury tort reform. *Journal of Insurance Regulation* 10, 384–440.

Welch, M. (2002) *Detained: Immigration Laws and the Expanding I.N.S. Jail Complex.* Temple University Press, Philadelphia.

Welch, M. (2005) *Ironies of Imprisonment.* Sage, Thousand Oaks, CA.

Welch, M. (2006, forthcoming) Seeking a safer society: America's anxiety in the war on terror. *Security Journal.*

Wells, C. (2001) *Corporations and Criminal Responsibility.* Oxford University Press, Oxford.

Wells, C. and Elias, J. (2005) Catching the conscience of the king: corporate players on the international stage. In: Alston, P. (ed.) *Non-State Actors and Human Rights.* Oxford University Press, Oxford, pp. 141–75.

Whitaker, R. (2006) A Faustian bargain? America and the dream of total information awareness. In: Haggerty, K. and Ericson, R. (eds.) *The New Politics of Surveillance and Visibility.* University of Toronto Press, Toronto, pp. 141–70.

Wilkinson, R. (1996) *Unhealthy Societies.* Routledge, London.

Wooton, B. (1959) *Social Science and Social Pathology.* George Allen and Unwin, London.

Zedner, L. (2005) Pre-crime and post-criminology – inventing an 'ology of security. Plenary address, British Criminology Conference, Leeds, July 11.

Zimring, F. (2006) *The Great American Crime Decline.* Oxford University Press, New York.

Zimring, F. and Hawkins, G. (1993) Crime, justice and the savings and loan crisis. In: Tonry, M. and Reiss, A. (eds.) *Beyond the Law: Crime in Complex Organizations.* University of Chicago Press, Chicago, pp. 247–92.

Index